JAPAN:
The Coming Social Crisis

by Jon Woronoff

YOHAN PUBLICATIONS, INC.
Tokyo, Japan

JAPAN: THE COMING SOCIAL CRISIS

A YOHAN LOTUS BOOK / Published 1980

10th printing May 1990

Cover design by Takashi Suzuki

YOHAN PUBLICATIONS, INC.

14-9 Okubo 3-chome, Shinjuku-ku, Tokyo, Japan

Printed in Japan

Contents

Books by Jon Woronoff

WEST AFRICAN WAGER

ORGANIZING AFRICAN UNITY

HONG KONG: CAPITALIST PARADISE

KOREA'S ECONOMY, MAN-MADE MIRACLE

JAPAN: THE COMING SOCIAL CRISIS

JAPAN: THE COMING ECONOMIC CRISIS

JAPAN'S WASTED WORKERS

INSIDE JAPAN, INC.

WORLD TRADE WAR

JAPAN'S COMMERCIAL EMPIRE

THE JAPAN SYNDROME

Foreword

What, a follow-up to the economic crisis book? Yes, and how could it be otherwise? The basic causes for the rise and fall of any economy are not purely economic matters like monetary and fiscal policy, or even labor costs and utilization of technology, but ability, ingenuity and drive. If people study seriously, work hard, and are willing to accumulate wealth for future growth rather than dissipating it, that growth may well occur. If they plan carefully and implement thoroughly, their projects may become realities. If whatever human virtues they possess hold up over time the economy can probably take off and move into self-sustained growth. If, for any reason, they lose their will or take things for granted, it can just as well sink or come crashing down. The real foundation for Japan's "economic miracle" was a social situation and certain attitudes and virtues that have since been wildly praised. It is thus in society that one must seek the chances of future success or failure.

It is not with particular relish that I publish this "crisis" book, for my findings are quite different from the fluff that one frequently reads. In fact, I have been holding the manuscript back for some time and only submit it now because so many of the unpleasant conclusions I drew have since been confirmed and reconfirmed. The figures for crime, especially juvenile delinquency, drug addiction, teenage runaways and prostitution, have risen steadily. Family conditions could not be terribly settled if the numbers of divorces, youthful suicides and elderly unemployed also keep growing. Opinion polls show that the attitudes of young and old, men and women, are getting no closer together. And the young have not ceased turning in on themselves and forgetting the rest of society. Many economic indicators have been negative, partly due to the oil crisis and recession, but also due to a refusal by young workers to show the old dedication. Factionalism rocked the ruling party after winning an election (what would it have done after a real loss?). New scandals were uncovered in political circles, although no one was punished for the old ones. Even the bureaucracy betrayed its trust by granting itself extra pay and benefits.

Another reason the book must appear is that the established authorities on Japanese affairs are launching a new wave of praise and glorification that seems to overlook so much of this material. How they could have missed these things that so strongly negate many of their conclusions I do not know. It is all carried by the daily newspapers and is further explained in numerous studies, monographs and white papers. Nevertheless, they continue mixing myth into fact, illusion into reality, churning out the most extraordinary visions of a people full of virtue, a nation without problems, and now a model for other countries to follow. Doubtlessly these visions of Japan are more attractive and comforting than mine, and perhaps even seem more "real," since they are updated versions of the *Japan Story* that has circulated for a few decades now.

So, in a land in which people do their very best to hide, dress up, or ignore anything that is not favorable or does not look as it should, and where so many foreign experts have graciously improved on these attempts at embellishment, here *I* go hanging up *their* dirty laundry in public. I certainly do not appreciate the honor. Indeed, this explains my hesitation. But I am not among those who believe that uncritical acceptance, let alone flattery, is the best way of proving friendship or promoting understanding. The only way to help is to show what is wrong and perhaps suggest improvements. But the latter stage cannot even be reached until we have done more to shatter the myths and dissipate the illusions.

It must be admitted that the author is not an "expert" like the others. In fact, he was a blind and naive believer in the mythified visions of Japan when he arrived and it took him years to penetrate the surface. Having been fooled so thoroughly for so long, he could not claim to have attained wisdom. He has just discovered some of his more gross errors. As a "non-expert," he is groping his way toward reality and, given the popular works that abound, has perhaps overemphasized the more obvious blemishes and failings. For this he apologizes, but not for an honest attempt to get at the truth.

The acknowledgements must go, once again, to those who permitted him to realize that what he thought was reality was only illusion and what he could not have conceived of as reality actually was. In short, he wishes to thank those who brought him to understand that Japan is a country like any other and that the Japanese are people like any others, with some major variations on the usual themes. These variations make the Japanese culture and society particularly interesting and intriguing, but they do not raise it to a higher level of being that makes Japan unseizable by ordinary means.

First of all, thanks must go to the few Japanese who were willing to talk openly and objectively, then to those who could express their feelings, positive and negative, after a sufficiently long acquaintance, and finally to those who were able to throw off their inhibitions after a few drinks. Much help also came from the less known authors of more serious studies, surveys, and monographs, which often get missed among the "instant understanding" and "inside story" general works on the bookshelves. Many facts and figures could also be obtained from government sources (MITI, JETRO, Prime Minister's Office, etc.) as well as the Foreign Press Center which was particularly helpful for research and provided most of the charts and photographs.

Finally, I would again like to thank Professor Gentaro Matsumura, author of *The Emperor's Islands*, and Bob Horiguchi, who gives the *gaijin* a glimpse of reality in his "Inside the Weeklies" column in *The Japan Times*. I wish to thank Jack Seward, a foreigner who really does understand Japan, and has written widely on a broad range of subjects, for reading this manuscript as well as his friendly support. Much of my own insight was again mediated through my wife, Maki Hamada, who translated most of the documentation including the material here.

JON WORONOFF

1
Land of Illusions

Japan consists of four major islands, Honshu, Kyushu, Shikoku and Hokkaido, and more than 3,000 smaller ones. It stretches over some 3,000 kilometers, not far off the mainland of Asia, between the 20th and 45th latitudes. Japan's area of 377,582 square kilometers only gives it a mere 0.3% of the world's total land area. About 80% of this is mountainous, although the highest peak, the nearly perfect cone of Mt. Fuji, reaches an altitude of only 3,776 meters. Japan has the sixth largest population in the world, over 115 million, with an average density of 310 inhabitants per square kilometer. This rises well over 2,000 in urban areas such as the massive megalopolis spreading over Tokyo, Yokohama, Nagoya, Osaka, and Kobe, and agglutinating almost 60% of the population in a very small space. There are relatively few readily exploitable raw materials, a dearth of fertile farming land, and untold thousands of small and large factories. The economy, after some initial difficulties arising from the wartime devastation, quickly rose to comparatively high levels, only to slacken considerably in recent years.

It is necessary to specify this so that readers will know which Japan is being dealt with here. It is the Japan located on the planet earth, bathed in the Japan Sea and Pacific, and populated by flesh and blood people. These people are pretty much like people elsewhere in the sense that they eat and drink, work and play, are born, live, and die. Some are good and others bad. The virtues and vices are unevenly spread among them. On the whole, they are not much better or worse than others. However, their behavior has often been sufficiently different to have brought them alternately contempt and honor. But, they were never gods or devils.

Reading about Japan, one sometimes wonders which Japan is meant. We have an old-fashioned view which shows us a nation of people extremely close to one another and bound by an iron code of honor. Due to the obligations of *giri* and *on*, a person had to obey the rules and act in an exemplary fashion, forgetting all selfish interests for the greater good of the community. In tightly-knit family units, the parents lavished affection on their children, brought them up with tender care, but very strictly, so that the children might bear the traits of the nation. The children, bound by filial piety, very naturally looked after their parents in old age. The profound and humane religions of Buddhism and Shinto gave a deeper spirituality to their lives. And an apparently innate sense of beauty moved them to build lovely temples and shrines, gardens and palaces, and practice aesthetic pastimes such as flower arrangement and tea ceremony.

More recent descriptions draw a no less bucolic picture of a society that has modernized rapidly, but without losing its soul. There is a "blend" of old and new. Due to time honored traditions, the factory foreman or company president has become the "father" of his workers and the company itself is just an extension of the family. People are looked after and cared for, and in exchange show the greatest loyalty, discipline and industry in producing finely crafted goods. The modern factories are marvels of technology and Japanese management methods, including lifetime employment and the career escalator, give the employee everything he wants. The bureaucrats are selfless

Japan as some foreigners like to imagine it.
Photo credit: Japan National Tourist Organization

and efficient. Democracy has spread not only on the higher level but also at the grass roots, thanks to the maintenance of the *ringi* system and other methods of consensus making. In the place of classes, there is now a meritocracy based on selection through education, in an educational system left open to all, so that even the humblest can rise to the highest position.

In opposition to these views, each popular with different groups of friends, there is a more diabolic vision. It also has its variations, depending on whether the critics regard Japan from the left or right. Japan is still a feudal society imposing a crushing regimentation on the people and forcing them to remain politically backward and socially passive. The workers are exploited by management, the citizens by conservative political parties. Having lost the war, the reactionary forces are simply gathering strength so that militarism and imperialism may rise again, first through economic policy, then by rearmament. Others merely see the student unrest and demonstrations, the existence of a large (let's say, moderately large) Communist Party, acts of the Red Army, or fear that Japan may now unite with China in some kind of "yellow peril."

Views of Japan, so its seems, have always been a bit larger than life and the islands still lie shrouded in mystery and the source of any number of myths and illusions. The first to weave appealing fiction into reality were the Japanese themselves, or at least their rulers. The islands were created by the tears of Amaterasu, the sun goddess, and were inhabited by spirits and gods. The emperors were divine and the people assumed that they had a glorious role to play. That Japan, first regarded as rather backward by the highly civilized Chinese, should rule over much of China one day was hardly expected. That the country opened up by Perry's ships should ultimately embrace Western learning and defeat great European powers must indeed have seemed miraculous. Soon miracles became the order of the day. However, overplaying its hand, and perhaps believing that the spirit was stronger than the flesh, Japan entered a war against overwhelming odds, was defeated and humbled. The heroes became villains, the model Westernizers, barbarians.

After the war, an army of demythifiers descended on Japan, set about rewriting its history, undermining the moral basis of its institutions, and demanding that the emperor deny his divinity. All too quickly, however, the former enemies were converted by the rapid recovery of the economy and smiling faces of the people. Japan again became a land of miracles, economic and social miracles, technological and political miracles, with the biggest cities and fastest trains, the smartest children and most charming women . . . everything in superlatives. Visiting foreigners lavished more praise on it than they had left over for their own countries. By now the remythification has been going on for several decades and this new mythology has become so convincing and seductive that it blots out reality. It can take a newcomer years to discover that there is any such thing as a real Japan under the stucco and stage props.

It is hard to grasp just why such illusions have been so much more tenacious in Japan than elsewhere. Perhaps one reason is the incredible amount of role playing that goes on: men acting as men should, women as women should, parents as parents should, and so on. They go through the motions, recite the parts (with never an "aside" to let the audience know what they really think). Then, when they go off stage where they can't be seen, they often behave exactly as they like and sometimes very much out of character with the role they should be playing. Another is the tremendous amount of play acting that goes on. The Japanese themselves make a very big distinction between things as they should be and things as they actually are. In Japanese, *tatémaé* refers to what looks good on the outside while *honné* signifies the true feelings or intentions. A superficial observer will never discern the reality, and even the Japanese, who know the difference exists, will often simply regard the external trappings as being somewhat false or for show . . . but without entirely fathoming what goes on underneath. How much easier, then, must it be to fool foreigners, especially those who see the nobility of the play staged in Japan as being so far superior to the reality they know back home.

However, there is no excuse to keep on passing down bits of myths and illusions as consecrated facts or hallowed truths. There are plenty of careful studies and detailed monographs on every aspect of Japanese life. The local and foreign press manage to uncover useful information that can readily invalidate most customary views. In particular, the government, through the Prime Minister's Office and other Ministries, keeps on churning out polls and surveys on men and women, young and old, workers and middle class, economic and social issues, and a wealth of statistics permitting the Japanese to be seized with some clarity. If anything, Japan looks like a nation of hypochondriacs constantly taking its own pulse so that no one can be in doubt as to what is thought about almost any subject. On more intimate matters, one can resort to the popular magazines, which have enquiries, interviews, and especially "letters to the editor" or advice to the lovelorn, or daughter-in-law, or salaryman, or student columns. This provides more than enough ammunition to shatter the toughest of myths and dissipate the thickest smoke screen of illusions.

True, the picture they show may not be particularly attractive. To some, it may be outright unpalatable. And a few will doubtlessly prefer the more comforting views of a nation at peace and a people without problems. But, it does have its advantages for those who have to deal with the Japanese, or live in Japan, and this includes the Japanese themselves. The general impression is of a society undergoing rapid change, not quite certain where it is heading, piecing together what remains of traditional culture with bits and snatches of alien, "modern" models, in what has become not a blend but a clash. If, in the following pages, Japan should show similarities to other nations known to be less perfect than itself, this should not be regarded as absolutely impossible. As was pointed out,

Population Density (1977)

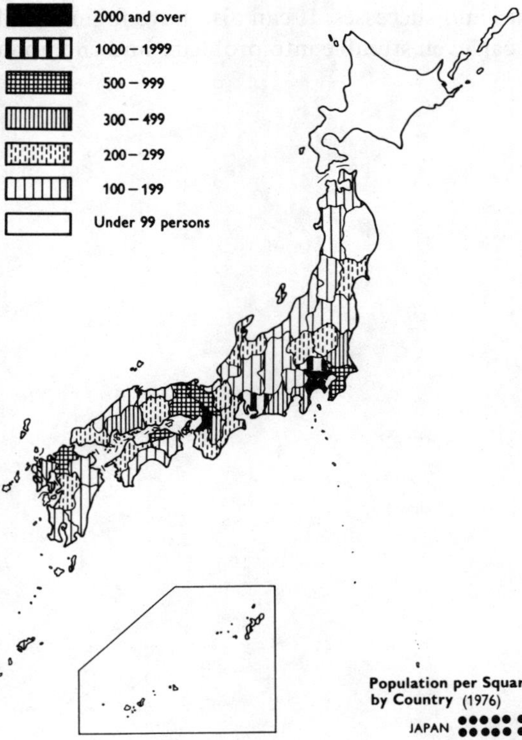

Population per Square Kilometre by Country (1976)

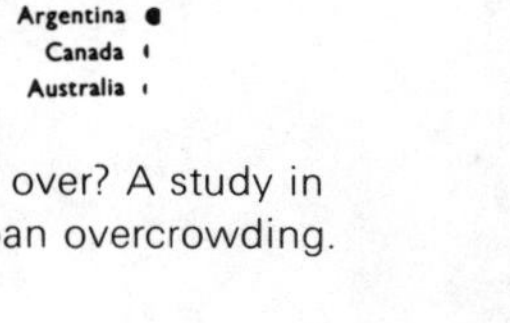

Will Japan sink or just tip over? A study in rural depopulation and urban overcrowding.

Japan is a real country inhabited by real people and not a figment of anyone's imagination. Like other countries, it has its virtues and successes. It can also have failings and setbacks. It can even stumble into problems and end up in a crisis.

2
The Weak Link . . . The Individual

In Japan, one is expected to be exceedingly modest, to put oneself back and the others forward, to be nothing more than a humble servant of the company or state, a modest member of the community, no matter how important one is. As we shall see, the language makes it almost impossible for a person to speak up and society makes it hard for one to stand out. Yet, even in Japan, no matter how humble, self-effacing or insignificant, the individual human being is always the basic building block for any and every higher, or shall we say larger, social unit. This fact may have been ignored in the centuries of relatively stable and fixed social relations, but it can only be neglected with some peril in times of more rapid change.

During the Tokugawa period which lasted almost three centuries, a very comprehensive system was imposed, based on Confucian concepts mixed with some native traditions, to put each individual in his place. There were ranks and classes, starting with the exalted but powerless position of the emperor, the *shogun* as the real power in the land, down to the lords, the *samurai,* peasants, artisans, merchants, and outcastes. Each one of them had definite obligations toward their superiors and expected certain duties from their inferiors. Within each family, the father was the family head, with the oldest son as second-in-command, then the other sons, and the wife, followed by any daughters, under them. The Meiji Restoration was bound to change the ranking somewhat in that the emperor was elevated to a higher position in real terms (although others acted and often decided on his behalf), the *shogun* was removed as such, and all the other classes were lowered—or raised—to the same level. The lords and *samurai* were stripped of their fiefs and authority, although they retained some land or got a stipend, and the merchants were enabled to rise faster than before. Some of these elements were ultimately placed in a small peerage, created as a backstop for the regime. Throughout the nation, the family group or *ié* remained an organized and recognized institution responsible for one another's behavior and welfare. All were, of course, humble servants of the nation and the emperor.

The social structure of the Meiji era, reinforced by many elements of the Tokugawa period which had never been thrown off or quietly returned, placed powerful bonds on all the people. After the heady days of the Restoration and increasingly as the straight-jacket of nationalism was imposed, each person knew his position, his duties and obligations and his rights (as the little ground left over). He knew where he fit into the family and the nation, he knew the role expected of him, he was even fed the words and gestures and the whole machine functioned reasonably smoothly. Of course, the rise of new economic functions, relations, and classes jostled about the rules and people a bit. The introduction of foreign philosophies and ideologies made the framework look a bit old-fashioned to some. And urbanization, in which the younger sons often left the family physically, were freed of its constraints, and developed a new life style in the cities bearing little comparison to the rural one, further weakened it. Still, even well into the twentieth century, the system held.

This system consisted very largely of obligations which there was little chance of shirking or evading. Rights, if any, were seen in relation to obligations as a lack of obligations to someone or an obligation someone else owed you. Even pleasure, in many ways, was nothing more than satisfaction for having met an obligation although the act of doing so may have been quite painful. The examples given of people perishing while saving the emperor's picture from a fire or renouncing marriage with the person they love to satisfy their parents can show that this was anything but an easy life. Yet, try as one might, it was impossible to escape the cycle of receiving and returning *on* (obligation). For, one owed *on* to the emperor, the law, and the nation simply for existing, to one's parents and ancestors for one's birth, and to one's work. These "favors" could not be repaid even partially (to the emperor even for one-ten-thousandth) over any amount of time. *Giri*, or justice and courtesy towards the world, namely to one's lord, family members, and other persons, could at least be repaid and was roughly equivalent to the kindness received. Finally, one also had to observe *giri* to one's own self to protect one's reputation to the extent of avenging an insult or committing suicide. It is no wonder that people often regarded a favor more as an imposition than a kindness since the *on* was an obligation that would have to be paid back later.[1]

With defeat in World War II, there was a revulsion. The system had led the nation into a disaster, many of its elements from the emperor on down to the family system were challenged. Relations between the components, between parents and children, superiors and inferiors, men and women, management and labor, state and citizens, were questioned. More important was that the generation that grew up during the war had only been partly educated in the old ways, and the postwar generations knew exceedingly little of them. On the whole, their feelings were negative, rejecting the old system as feudalistic, backward or old-fashioned. In particular, the old rules were too strict and harsh for a more modern and fast moving society. Thus, referring to the old code, so well described in Ruth Benedict's *The Chrysanthemum and the Sword* and still seen as the key to unlock the mysteries of Japan, was not very helpful and perhaps misleading. The old precepts still applied for some of the older people, especially in rural areas, but it was useless as a means of understanding the young urbanites even if some remnants and similarities appeared on the surface.

Meanwhile, the Japanese were allowed to fish freely in the Pandora's box of Western philosophies to select appealing notions like equality and democracy, individualism, socialism or dictatorship of the proletariat. These alien elements were then mixed with indigenous concepts, bits and snatches of the older code. This rough mixture—very far from any "blend" of East and West—consisted of varying degrees of earlier Japanese customs with an overlay of later Western imports. But, with no authorized or consecrated standard, each person felt reasonably free to make his or her own value system out of such disparate elements, one hardly typified by homogeneity or cohesiveness. Over time, by living with one another, forming groups, and discussing the situations, patterns were formed. But none of them were as strong or pervasive as the older ones had been. Above all, they lacked any central or supreme authority, since the emperor had been desanctified and the nation was still suspect as a guiding concept. This meant that the various parts of society could move about in a rather loose relationship to one another. It made Japan of the latter twentieth century anything but the spontaneously united, purposeful community it was supposed to be.

*   *   *

This atomization is still strong because the old hierarchy, with its sharp differentiation in positions and roles, has not completely disappeared although it has been seriously undermined and largely emptied of meaning. People continue separating into categories and classes along rough lines influenced by the past. There are clear distinctions made between superior and inferior. There are no lords to bow and pay allegience to nowadays, but their role has been taken over to some extent by company officials, high level bureaucrats, heads of faculty, and any number of others. To a greater extent than in most countries that have had a democracy for some considerable time, they are still regarded as superiors, endowed with more than usual prestige, and treated with some of the pomp and circumstance used traditionally. In return, they still bestow their protection and kindness on those beneath them. Fathers, and to a lesser extent, first sons, still do have a definite word to say, even as concerns the situation in the families of their grown up children.

This would not make as much difference if so much of the hierarchy had not been salvaged. But one not only has to deal with the top person as a superior, there is also everyone who comes under him right down to whatever position you are in. These are all the lesser rulers such as department head, section head, foreman, supervisor, etc. As one rises to a higher position, one also becomes a superior to many subordinates. Then there are also the few equals, those in roughly the same situation. Unfortunately, Japan adds another differentiation based on seniority or length of service (*nenko*). So, each category is broken down further by the thin gradations of one year's greater or lesser service. Thus, a person's world consists of three basic categories, *sempai* or seniors, *kohai* or juniors and *doryo* or roughly "colleagues," but largely limited to those of the same Showa entry year. In practice, these age rankings very much coincide with the social or status rankings, elders usually being superior, juniors inferior, and a thin slice of colleagues being one's equals.

There is no reason that Japanese society had to chop itself up into such small chunks that even a year's difference could put someone in a different category. It is also hard to see why age should play that decisive a role in the whole thing. After all, there are plenty of societies, including many Oriental ones, in which the leaders can be younger than the followers with age having little to do with the choice and merit or some other principle a good deal more. A leader, under other circumstances, could be a follower. A master could have disciples who were older, a manager or director would not move into his position because of age alone, and so on. But the Japanese seem to like the principle of ranking as such and have chosen the simplest and most objective basis of all to build it upon: the number of years. In this, they have not followed either the Chinese model, which left considerable room for merit, or the Western models, which gave their citizens more leeway in relations and greater possibilities of mobility through the principles of democracy and equality. As Professor Chie Nakane points out:

"In Japan, in contrast to other societies, the provisions for recognition of merit are weak, and institutionalization of the social order has been effected largely by means of seniority; this is the more obvious criterion, assuming an equal ability in individuals entering the same kind of service. The system of ranking by seniority is a simpler and more stable mechanism than the merit system, since, once it is set, it works automatically without need of any form of regulation or check. But at the same time this system brings with it a high degree of rigidity. There is only one ranking order for a given set of persons, regardless of variety of situations. No individual members of this set (not even the man who ranks highest) can make even a partial change."[2]

In addition to differentiation by status and seniority, there is a further division that cannot be forgotten, namely between the sexes. This also assumes a hierarchical ranking, in that women are not only different but also inferior socially to men. The two are united in the family unit, each with very specific roles and functions, although elsewhere separation or at least a distance prevails. Most of the groups formed among youths of the same age do not include both sexes, although there is obviously more promiscuity when it comes to the period of courtship and early marriage. Soon after, however, the women tend to be relegated to the homes and the men to assume more official positions outside. Even those women who keep on working rarely rise to positions of authority and it is almost as inconceivable for a woman to give orders to men as for a young man to give orders to older men. All legal provisions and principles of equality notwithstanding, one could hardly regard women as integrated as full and equal members of society.

The great pity of Japanese society is thus that one so rarely has to do with equals, namely people of the same status, age and sex. One is almost always being directed by superiors, elders, or men (for the women). There is no end to the parents, grandparents, bosses, bureaucrats, teachers, and so on one has to placate. This requires considerable formality and much bowing and scraping. It is really not much more relaxing to be with inferiors, juniors, or women (for the men). Then, one has to pose as a bit more than one actually is and maintain a very impressive demeanor. It is nice to be flattered and played up to, but boring in the long run. What a relief it must be when one is finally with equals, the few people one knows who are of the same rank, age or seniority, and sex. And this means exclusively such people, for if one superior or inferior is present the group swings back to playing roles. Only with these few can one speak freely, develop much intimacy, express one's hopes and worries. For that reason, Japanese seize every opportunity to join these equals at school reunions, club meetings, lunches or drinking bouts.

Most of the time however, the Japanese are obliged to behave alternately in the three basic status roles (*bun*) of inferior, superior and equal. This can lead to tremendous frustration in the first case, unnecessary ego building in the second, and something approaching equilibrium in the third. But the very fact that one is constantly changing roles has a very unsettling effect and can cause considerable confusion and alienation. A description of the quite common state of mind is given by a very perceptive observer of Japanese society, Jack Seward:

"In their vertical social arrangement, few are equal, and the Japanese spend much of their days calculating how much higher or lower they stand than the next fellow. And these precise distances govern the degree of respect or disrespect, the depth of the bow, the kind of language, the frequency of the smile, the willingness to oblige, and the extent of compliance that one Japanese must extend and show to another. The gauging of these distances and reactions alone is a time-consuming and often frustrating job. The denegation of individuality and the repression of personal choice in which they result would be stultifying to anyone, even people born in such surroundings and aware of no other system. Sometimes individual Japanese can endure it no longer. A trigger will release their pent-up resentment, anger, and frustration, and explosions of varying intensity follow."[3]

* * *

This differentiation is further exacerbated by the language which, rather than building bridges among people, tends to create gulfs and barriers. As it happens, the biggest difficulty in speaking *properly* is something that has largely disappeared from many other languages but remains basic to Japanese, namely the distinctions in the manner of addressing people. Latin and Germanic languages have a way of speaking to intimates (tu, Du, etc.) and to more formal relations (vous, Sie, etc). In Japanese, there is much greater variety not only in grammar or structure but use of completely different words or phrases as well as tone and words for politeness (e.g. the honorific *o*). It would be a social blunder, in Europe, to use the intimate or courteous form improperly. But the price paid would not be as high as in Japan where a person would certainly lose face, be scolded if young, perhaps risk chances of promotion at work, or even make enemies. On the other hand, ability to use the fine points of "polite" language is a professional and social asset out of all proportion.

The hierarchy expressed by language through the use of many, more or less polite forms is unusually comprehensive and complex. First of all. there are strict linguistic patterns conditioned by social status and age. When one is speaking to a superior, an inferior, or an equal, a completely different language is used. This is not just a few special words but a whole elaborate way of expressing oneself in order to demean oneself to a superior, to put an inferior in his place, or to show a degree of intimacy with an equal. This is accompanied by varying degrees of bowing, nodding, physically positioning of oneself to show status. Similarly, one speaks to all seniors as superiors, showing the very greatest deference. A junior gets talked down to. And a person of the same age class is spoken to as an equal. However, before even being able to speak to someone else you must know that person's relative position. Thus, Japanese would not speak to one another during an hour-long plane ride without knowing their relative status or strike up a conversation at a cocktail party without a sufficiently formal introduction to work out the relationship.

Even in the family, there is a way of speaking to one's father and mother or one's children, to an older brother/sister or younger one. Non-family members and their possessions are often referred to as "honorable," while one would never go so far in speaking of one's own relatives or possessions. What is worse, the ranking of words, i.e. whether that word should be honored, demeaned, or neutral, is not fixed. Confusing? Let's take a simple example. In most languages one's father is called "father" just like anyone else's father. Not in Japan. When you are speaking to your own father you have to address him as "*oto-sama*" or "honorable father." But your honorable father is degraded when talking about him to a third party, becoming just "*chichi*" (also meaning father). And the same person can be referred to in many more different ways depending on the relationship to the speaker. Mr. Yamada, who is a section chief (*kacho*), would be referred to as "*kacho*" by his subordinates, "Yamada" by his peers, and "Yamada-*kun*" by his superiors. People outside the company would address him as "*kacho-san*" in his official capacity and "Yamada-*san*" otherwise. You would call him "Yamada-*kun*" if he happened to join the company just one year after you, and as "Yamada-*san*" if he got in a year earlier.

Finally, there is the matter of men's language and women's language. Again, it is not a few words, it is truly pervasive. A man could not speak women's language without appearing ridiculous nor a woman speak men's language without seeming crude and vulgar. Indeed, the very idea is so farfetched that it would hardly occur to anyone. Men's language is harsher, women's softer and more melodious. Men's language is haughty, and sometimes downright rude, when speaking to women, while the women reply in a language full of superfluous words of self-deprecation and frivolity. Moreover, in referring to any number of common objects, the women must precede it with an honorific *o*. Thus a woman refers to *o-saké* while a man just orders *saké*. A mistake here would be most embarrassing. Beyond the language, women are expected to talk only about things within a woman's ken, like home, family, cooking, fashions while a man talks of office, sports, and conceivably public affairs.

Although it is good at conveying distinctions, Japanese is rather poor at transmitting ideas. Often enough no subject is used, so one does not know if it is "me," "you," "us," etc. without fully understanding the context. There are no singulars and plurals, which may not matter that much for everyday conversation when a person can ask but is very unpleasant in science or technology, for example, or in more common cases where a person is likely not to know the context. The language is also vague and ambiguous. It does not have to be, and a person can speak perfectly clear and precise Japanese. Unfortunately, most do not, and many seem to have a preference for maintaining an ambiguity that permits them leeway in later actions. The implication may be as important as the words, yet all too often one does not grasp the implication or, if one does, the reasons behind it may still be unclear. This is not only a problem for foreigners, Japanese also have much difficulty in understanding one another. Thus, Ezra Vogel explains:

"Usually the general meaning, even from subtle clues, is perfectly clear. All that is unclear is the reason underlying the response. When a person complains that he cannot tell exactly what another is feeling, this almost always means that the other did not give a sufficiently positive response, but that one does not know why. Such vague replies often create anxieties greater than a direct explanation would create. Many people who are refused feel there is something wrong with them, and the diffuse nature of the rejection by postponement, avoidance, or vagueness is often felt as an attack on one's entire character. Undifferentiated emotional responses of fear, anger, or self-depreciation are common."[4]

More serious perhaps is that Japanese is not used as a tool of communication in the sense of two-way communication or an attempt to break down linguistic fences created by social barriers. Parents, bosses, and men, when dealing with children, employees, and women tend to communicate downward. They more or less speak in declarations and orders. If the meaning is confused, there may be a request for clarification. More often, there is not, for not to understand is in itself a mark of disrespect. The reply so often heard is "*hai*," which really means I have heard and registered what you said, and "*wakarimashita*," which means I understand. Both these words are often translated by yes, or I shall do so. And, by rights, that is what they should mean. But, if the Japanese inferiors (especially youth and women) are outwardly humble, this does not mean that they will do everything they are told. For there is no safe method of communication upwards; especially in the negative. An inconclusive "*hai*" or "*wakarimashita*" is much easier than a risky attempt at saying no or explaining an alternative solution. Indeed, such language does not exist in Japan. There is no word for telling a boss to go to hell or a father to keep his nose out of your private affairs. The only solution is to say "*wakarimashita*" and do what you want.

But, language cannot be regarded as a cause no matter

how many stumbling blocks it creates for equality, unity or just "communication" in the modern sense. Language is only a result of the existing social barriers and a vehicle of the prevailing philosophy or ideology, although it also tends to reinforce and perpetuate them. It is simply a reflection of society as it exists. If lingustic communication is awkward in Japan then it is because, as we saw, social relations themselves are unnecessarily stiff. For language to be simplified, social relations must first be simplified . . . and not vice versa. On the other hand, no social revolution will ever be complete, as the Chinese eventually realized, without a linguistic reform to convey the new relations.

*　　　*　　　*

In every society, individuals must unite to form larger groups in order to accomplish various tasks. In Japan, the basic relations seem to be vertical links. They trace their origin back to Tokugawa and often far earlier days, and bits of the old system still survive. Hierarchy was extremely important in olden times, and it has maintained much of its strength today. This was clearly pointed out by Chie Nakane in her authoritative book *Japanese Society*. These are strong, personal relations, one-to-one, between leader and follower, protector and protégé, patron and client, lord and retainer, father and child. These links found their epitome in the Emperor system and *ié* regulations of Meiji days. They are, of course, not exclusive to Japan. What is different is that they still continue to pervade its society so greatly and that even in completely new fields or professions where, in theory at least, they would not be necessary, they have been adopted.

The key relationship is between a person with a status assimilated to that of a child (*kobun*) and another acting as a kind of surrogate parent (*oyabun*). Between the two, the links are very strong, and the *oyabun* will do as much as possible to promote the rise of the *kobun*, while the *kobun* in different ways will help support the *oyabun*. But it is often a rather constricting relationship in the sense that an *oyabun* does not have enough time or perhaps nervous strength or wealth to support more than several *kobun*. Having too many *kobun* may also result in quarrelling among them for the greater affection of the *oyabun* and eventually the succession. For a group to grow much further, it is necessary, as in a family, for the *kobun* in turn to become *oyabun* to other persons further below them, thus spreading the network. The relations, in this case, are mediated to the original *oyabun* and not anywhere near as strong. They are indeed so fragile that the disappearance of the originator can send the subsidiary families off into their own orbits as the larger family falls apart. Most people eventually become the *kobun* of someone, since this is a way to rise with the help of a more powerful figure. But, in order to become an *oyabun*, one must possess certain qualities.

This chain linking persons together also places them in specific ranks to one another within the small grouping. The *oyabun* is the superior and all the *kobun* are inferiors, and, although theoretically equals, they do show some further differentiation by closeness to the *oyabun* or length of association, etc. In this relationship, it is obvious that the senior member or *oyabun* is in charge, makes the basic decisions, and is held responsible for mistakes or praised for successes. The system works rather well when it comes to channelling orders downward or rallying those in subordinate position to accomplish specific tasks. However, due to the honor attached to the role of those at the top it is rather difficult to present opposing views let alone offer corrections from below. This can be done, but only by slow and devious methods that permit the people at the top not to lose face. Suggestions from below often seep up; often they are stifled or lost on the way. Indeed, an inferior can act in three ways: forcefully propose a change, which is risky; gently intimate an idea which the superior spontaneously adopts; or let the superior do what he wants and perhaps make a fool of himself.

Although the superior clearly has greater authority and power, he is not without his counter-obligations. First of all, he is to a large extent responsible for any actions his inferiors may take. Thus, the head of the household was, and still somewhat is, implicated in any actions his children may take, an employer for his employees, and a teacher for his students. This applies even if the superior was in no way at fault or completely unaware of the action. Thus, even today, it happens that an official will resign due to the blunder of some underling and it is traditional for the head of the household to be held responsible for the faults of his children or the director to pay off the debts of his company. The superior must also acquit his responsibilities to his inferiors. A husband must care for his wife and children, a foreman look after his workers, and so on. This is not their right, the inferiors being largely without rights, but the counterpart for having fulfilled their obligations. This situation is often referred to as *amaé*, which means dependence or giving their due even to those who are dependent. More recently, however, there has been a trend for inferiors to become aware of the demands of *amaé* and insist they be met while augmenting them some, rather than waiting for them to be discovered.

These situations are of anything but academic interest, for they exert their influence pervasively and throughout all institutions of society. They are not limited to the ranking of *kabuki* actors, *sumo* wrestlers or *geisha* girls. Even a liberal profession like lawyers will refer decisions back to the head of the office, just as is done by teachers of flower arrangement or tea ceremony to the master of their school. Politicians are clearly grouped together in factions, with a faction head and so many followers. The head professors or teachers form *oyabun-kobun* relations with the assistants, which may spread if some former disciples get hired into other schools. This may well happen, for University of Tokyo (and several others) regularly supply teaching personnel to lesser schools and colleges just as the main temple or shrine of a sect has branches under it. The fullest development of this system, moreover, appears in the key institution of modern Japan and one in which it could have been avoided had not the diffuse social pressure and reflex actions turned it in along the same paths . . . the company. There, in addition to the formal ranking from president on down to the freshman employees, ranked both by title and by the Showa year they entered the company, there are a multitude of informal *oyabun-kobun* relations and factions. A larger parent company may also have many subcontractors placed under it and, in the case of conglomerates or *zaibatsu*, a whole family of subsidiaries or independent companies.

* * *

Although the vertical relations have obtained most of the attention, there are also horizontal links which are extremely important and perhaps essential for the present social system. Whereas the vertical links express hierarchy and status, horizontal links are first an expression of group solidarity which can take the form of friendship, cooperation, mutual interest or mutual protection. If extended to cover all of Japan, they could conceivably also form the basis for nationalism, not necessarily in the aggressive sense but of feeling part of one nation. On the other hand, if made too exclusive and pushed too far, they could have a divisive or negative effect.

Groups of equals are often formed spontaneously among children. Being equal would assume that they all came from roughly the same social class, are of roughly the same age (*donen*), and that the boys and girls form their own groups. Each of these little groups plays together, grows up and learns about life together. They would be temporarily weakened during the period of courtship and early marriage, when a person of the opposite sex would claim part of the time. Then, a bit later, the men would start drinking together evenings and the women would meet to gossip. This sort of thing has been going on for centuries in Japan, especially in the traditional villages. For various reasons, it is not as easy in the cities and many young people nowadays find it harder to make friends than their parents or grandparents ever did.

This is partially the fault of city life, since the new neighborhoods are nowhere near as integrated a unit as the villages. More seriously, the people have not done enough to turn the physical units into true social units. They do not go out and introduce themselves to the neighbors, invite one another over to their homes, or form clubs and associations. The children do meet, and play, and go to school. But the stress on "success" in their studies has forced many back into the home to cram rather than play freely and make more friends. *Donen* do form groups, but fewer, smaller and with a greater tendency to splinter later on as members move away from the neighborhood, go into different schools or companies, and lose contact. Nevertheless, these old friendships are treasured, and their value grows with the years.

Nowadays, there are two places where such horizontal groups are formed most readily, at school and at work. This is facilitated by the fact that large numbers of individuals are coming together for the first time and are eager to form links. As equals and beginners such links are easier to establish than entering a group that already exists. But that is still not as easy as might be expected. Students are often kept too busy at primary and secondary school. Then, having just gone through a period of intense and prolonged study to get into college, the students may be rather unsociable and shy. To help them out, the colleges usually provide a whole array of social and sports clubs, to which students have added "radical movements" and other groupings of their own. At work, social relations are also freer among the new recruits. And, to make it even easier, many companies provide clubs and social activities, often at company expense, so that fellow employees can get to know one another and form a tighter unit.

If left on their own apparently many Japanese would be unable to socialize. That, at any rate, is what seems to transpire from some recent studies of the Prime Minister's Office. A Survey on the Social Behavior of Youth, dealing with young men and women between the ages of 15 and 24, showed that only some 36% voluntarily participated in sports, hobby or cultural groups in their school, office or local community. Of the rest, about 8% had participated before but dropped out and fully 56% had not taken part in any group activities. They were too busy with studies or work or simply could not find a suitable group to join. And the 1979 White Paper on Youth, covering the 10-to-15 age group, found the teenagers immersed in exam preparation and admitting that they preferred watching TV to being with friends or playing sports. These are rather astonishing results for a society proverbially known for group-consciousness.

Women often have a harder time than men in entering social groups. Certainly, they are no less eager. But, after leaving school or retiring from work they are relegated to the home, and the home is often just a loose part of any community. They may meet the other women in the neighborhood. However, there the relations are often vertical, the older, more experienced women teaching—or criticizing—the younger. When their children go to school, most women join the PTA and at least can meet women of the same age and with similar problems. But, they still have to fall back on friends they made earlier for any warm social life. Much would be changed if their husbands were also part of home life or they could join together with other couples. Yet, this broader community never really jells.

Beyond the groups based on these close and continuing personal relations, there are any number of other groups such as one finds throughout the world. There are trade unions for workers. There are cooperatives for farmers. There are professional associations of all sorts for doctors, dentists, teachers and so on. Businessmen, through their companies, become members of Chambers of Commerce and trade associations in every possible field. Individual businessmen can join the Lions Club, Rotary or similar groups. There are also sports clubs. All of these units, although often structured internally on hierarchical lines, at the same time permit horizontal relations among members. Yet, even these groups tend to be more restricted than elsewhere. First of all, the member's primary allegience is still to his small group of friends or colleagues, his *oyabun* or *kobun*, and the larger units may just be clusters of groups. More serious is that they do not even include all of the category for which they were ostensibly formed. The most striking example is the trade union, which does not exist on a trade basis (including all steamfitters or brick layers), nor on a sectoral basis (including everyone in the automobile or textile industry), nor even include all workers. Most unions are enterprise unions, including all the "regulars" in a given company, and no one else, and the various labor federations are very loose groupings of such unions.

The horizontal groups are essential for friendship, for emotional ties, for solidarity and mutual aid. They tend to back their members to the hilt. But they often do so to such an extent that many seem closer to cliques and much of Japanese social life is reduced to a cliquism. This occurs in almost every field and the cliques (*batsu*) rival one another for favors or power. Traditionally, there were the *keibatsu* formed through kinship, marriage and extended family, with a broader clannishness in the true sense, due to the clans in different regions. Officers in the army or navy would form *gumbatsu*. In the bureaucracy there are *kambatsu*. Cliques among business leaders are known as *zaikai*, and the grouping of companies into a conglomerate is similar as a *zaibatsu*. Politicians, within the same party, form factions or *habatsu*. There are also regional groupings according to place of origin or often prefecture (*kyodobatsu*). Finally, there is the university clique or *gakubatsu*, which is probably the most pervasive of all. Connections, the fruit of clique formation, known by the Japanized term *koné*, have proven to be Japan's most solid form of interrelations . . . and its bane.

These horizontal links, even when not as strong as the vertical ones, do serve as a counterbalance. First of all, they permit a degree of relaxation of the tension arising out of the hierarchical relationship. They also offer a link from one hierarchical structure to another since the broader bodies may have members living in different areas, involved in different fields, and perhaps working in different companies or branches of activity. They can provide introductions or build the social bridges needed to cross over from one group to another. Finally, they enable the individual to protect his own interests. As a pure act of individualism, this might be disapproved of. However, if the group—which usually consists of very like-minded individuals—were to have a joint interest, or if one member could convince the group that it did, the group would find it much easier and more acceptable socially to do so. A worker cannot simply complain about dangerous machinery, but a group of workers or the trade union could. A student cannot demand better food in the cafeteria, but a group of them might make that its campaign.

These horizontal and vertical groupings form the warp and woof of Japanese society. However, they make a very loose weave since no relationship any longer runs through the whole of the nation and the relations among this multitude of groups are weak. One cause for this is that the vertical or hierarchical relations are so much stronger than the broader horizontal ones, links between small numbers of intimate friends, cohorts or colleagues so much stronger than anything more extensive, that even the broader units are usually just loose groupings of smaller, more compact groups. Then, finally, there is still no one institution that truly includes all Japanese. Government is a loose assembly of political parties, further broken down by internal factions and groups, while the Prime Minister has most often appeared merely as the head of a party, or just a faction in the party, and hardly ever as a national leader or statesman. The emperor, who was at the summit of the old hierarchy, still exists, but his power has faded considerably and the old pyramid on which he was perched, and which supported him with incredible tenacity, has since disappeared.

In its place there is now merely a loosely orbiting system of groups. The groups themselves are relatively solid, but the relations with other groups are so weak that each group tends to develop its own style and sense of values. What is right in one group may be wrong, or simply irrelevant, in another. Deviant groups often have their own code of conduct, such as for gangsters (*yakuza*), which can contravene even the national legislation, yet prevails over it not only with fellow gangsters but also sometimes in the public's eyes as just another value system. Thus, it is extremely hard to decide on the national values or purpose and most people settle down in their own group's system of values, periodically looking around, or watching TV, or reading the newspapers, to check what other groups are doing and then perhaps slightly rectify their own course. This kind of situational ethic may provide the "subtility" and "humanity" often praised in the Japanese; it also leads to a partial or complete disconcern for broader principles or laws.

It is far from certain how often or well these groups will mesh with one another in the interest of the broader community. Worse, it is very possible for them to form barriers instead. By making such strong demands on its members' allegience, a group makes it hard for them to serve as bridges. Thus, in the real family, husband, wife and children will have their own mutually exclusive circles of friends; grandparents, parents, and children may be living according to completely different and perhaps antagonistic values. Within the company "family," the floor workers, the salarymen, the middle management and the directors live very much in their own worlds. A company may follow a policy which is good for its own component groups, that are quite willing to overlook inter-group differences, but which may be very bad for the consumers or the economy as a whole. Or a political party may not hesitate to put the interests of its electorate, or itself, ahead of the general population.

Each individual can also find himself drawn between groups whose demands may not be compatible. Since each person does fulfill several functions and has more than one

Where can the individual hide if not in the crowd?
Photo credit: Foreign Press Center-Japan.

role, conflicts are avoided by dividing life up into self-contained sectors: school, work, home, etc. A man can be a good colleague, a good husband and a good citizen . . . as long as the rules don't clash. When they do, there is considerable anguish and difficulty. Even when they do not clash, the mere fact of being so absorbed or spending so much time with one's colleagues may in fact make the man a bad husband and/or father, not for what he has done but for what he has failed to do, as he may not have enough time and energy to meet all demands. A person must also reconcile his role as a link in the company hierarchy, but also in his group of colleagues. A woman may find it difficult to combine the quality of duty to her mother-in-law and control over her children. And so on.

Another major drawback, although many Japanese may not perceive it as such, is that the group's members are so deeply involved in the group's activities that they have trouble developing their own personality and individualism. Even groups only formed a short time back, for example radical students on campus, will demand that one's whole time, effort and thought be devoted to it (of course, in return for total support). Most groups are also groupings of persons interrelated with one another rather than gathering around a given idea or goal. The relations are built up over time and, by mixing with one another while avoiding outsiders, a similarity of behavior results quite naturally. Should there be any deviation, then subtle—and eventually less subtle—pressure will be used. The person will receive hints, then perhaps a serious talking to. Coercion is almost never necessary, for an individual alone has a hard time getting along and it is very difficult to join a new group. Indeed, the worst threat is simply to withdraw the group's support or to drive a person out of it. Ostracism, in a society where connections mean everything and friendship is hard to find, is usually as devastating a weapon as force.

In practice, the much vaunted unity of Japan is rather hollow. Men and women mix little, high school and college graduates relate poorly, children born a few years apart have different views. There is not much in common between the urbanites and their country cousins. Student concern for worker welfare, if any, is meaningless for students are destined for managerial posts. Workers are concerned about their own wages and conditions in the company but hardly care about what happens to workers in the subcontracting firms. No one but minority members would stand up for minority rights, and few men champion women's rights. Indeed, few enough women help one another. Even the most solid and impressive institutions are only loose groups, a bureaucracy consisting of so many cliques in various departments or a *zaibatsu*, the ultimate in unity, remaining a loose grouping of several companies, subsidiaries and subcontractors revolving around a bank or trading company. Even the state is not a solid entity but a series of groups of politicians, bureaucrats and businessmen, with no one quite certain who runs it or how.

With this lack of unity, many different groups and different codes of behavior and value systems, it is not surprising that friction or rivalry should arise. Anyone with a keen eye to Japanese social relations will recognize this as a no less common occurrence than various forms of cooperation or just coexistence. Overcoming such crises repeatedly puts a strain on the system. Often solutions and compromises are found, but certainly not in every case. Harmony (*wa*) has been Japan's goal for centuries and, in a very stable society with fixed rules, it was reasonably easy (if not always pleasant) to attain. In a more fluid situation, *wa* is just as likely to be a result of self-restraint or a curtain drawn across the scene. Harmony is thus not a positive state but merely a lack of open conflict.

*   *   *

However, in addition to harmony among the many inbred and encapsulated groups, it is still necessary to find a common direction. This raises the problem of decision-making and leadership. Of course, some decisions are quickly-made, routine ones, or where formal guidelines and regulations have been laid down. Indeed, probably the vast majority of decisions come quite naturally as part of the Japanese way of reacting to events or following consecrated patterns.

The number of such is that much larger because of the strong influence of precedent in a relatively conservative society. Rather than take initiatives or innovative actions, they are avoided. Within companies the traditions are followed, families stick to their customs, and the bureaucracy follows well trodden paths. Thus, a man who has doubtlessly sat in on untold thousands of "decisions," Ichiro Kawasaki, comments:

"In a Japanese office or organization, if any decision is required, the first thing for the party concerned to do is to refer to the precedents. Then discussions follow among those concerned on the basis of the precedents without any immediate action being taken. Usually a suggestion as to a possible course of action to take is made and submitted to their superiors, who may approve of the suggested action. Thus the Japanese attitude is to drift with the tide, and nobody really makes a decision. What appears to be a decision is nothing but an anonymous consensus. As a result, the Japanese can be said to be essentially conservative, and seldom lunge into rash action."[5]

In Japan, so we are told, most "new" decisions are reached through the traditional decision-making process of *ringi-sei*. This process, which has intrigued and usually impressed foreign observers, is maintained and indeed promoted as the essence of Japanese society and the means even of running modern companies and bureaucracies. Strictly speaking, the procedure consists of two aspects, *rin* meaning "submitting a proposal to one's superior for approval" and *gi*, "deliberations and decisions." In the simplest terms, this consists of people at a lower level drafting a document called *ringisho* explaining the issues and recommending the measures to be taken. This proposal may be drafted by one or more persons and then slowly channelled upward, passing through each hierarchical level to be read and stamped if approved, if not, returned with suggestions for rewording, and then sent back up again for approval. Slowly but surely all those concerned affix their seals and when this is done by the top person the decision has been taken. It is then sent back to the originator for implementation.

Average time spent on workdays		Average time spent on Sundays
3 hrs 19 min	Watching TV	4 hrs 11 min
35	Listening to the radio	31
20	Reading newspapers	17
36	Associating with others	1 6
4	Sightseeing and appreciation	17

Source: *Nihonjin no seikatsu jikan* (How the Japanese Spend Their Time), Public Opinion Research Institute, NHK, 1975.

Some places the rules of life are taught
and the time devoted to lessons.

Credit: *Facts and Figures of Japan 1980*,
Foreign Press Center-Japan, p. 63.

Another major method is the group meeting, which is liable to take place at almost any time, in any place, and for just about any reason or pretext conceivable. It is part of the *ringisei* or any consultations on any level. These meetings are not unlike African "palavers" in many ways, although this may seem an invidious comparison to the Japanese. Sometimes it is worse, for they do not have any time limits and meetings can very well end with no decision and have to be reconvened later. The classic description of such meetings is given by Richard Halloran:

"A typical decision-making meeting opens with a statement of the problem by the group's senior member. Each member then exposes a slight portion of his thinking, never coming out with a full-blown, thoroughly persuasive presentation. The discussion goes on at great length, each person slowly and carefully presenting his opinion, gradually sensing out the feelings of other people, making a pitch subtly, following it without pressing if he finds it acceptable, quietly backing off and adjusting his views to those of the others if he finds himself not in tune with the evolving consensus. . . . If, by chance, a consensus does not emerge and a deadlock seems likely, the group leader does not press for a decision, does not ask for a vote, does not rule that no consensus seems possible and thus embarrass people. Instead he suggests that perhaps more time is needed to think about the problem, and sets a date for another meeting. . . . By the time the next meeting is called, the differences most likely will have been straightened out and the process can move forward to a final decision."[6]

Herman Kahn regards *ringi* as "a kind of decision-making from below—almost a grass-roots form of participatory democracy—yet placed in a very authoritarian and hierarchical structure." And Vogel refers back to the Japanese term of *nemawashi* or "root binding" whereby, slowly but surely, as many groups as possible are brought into the majority.[7] There definitely is an element of democracy in the process since so many different levels of the hierarchy are consulted. Indeed, the broader the participation, the better the decision is assumed to be and many younger staff are asked to sit in as a learning process of sorts. Yet, one should take all this with a good grain of salt. For, everywhere in Japan, the informal relations are such that a person in a lower position does not tend to disagree with someone higher up. This might endanger his chances of promotion or create serious enmities. If he does feel strongly, he may convince the whole peer group or he may use circuitous routes to feed the idea up to his superior. But there is no reason to assume that such individuals are numerous. Most seem quite happy to let their superiors decide, thus avoiding the risk and responsibility if the decision is wrong. More often what happens is that the superiors hear out the inferiors, incorporate their views to some extent so as not to offend them, and proceed much as they would have anyway.

One thing is certain, as even its proponents admit, namely that the process is very time-consuming. For it tends to draw in not only those directly concerned but any number of people who are just marginally involved, yet must still be listened to. Then, the problem is studied from every possible angle and all eventualities, real or purely imaginary, are taken into consideration. But, the big abuse of time arises because, due to their training, no one wishes to speak up very clearly the first time round and reveal views which may not be acceptable to the majority. If someone disagrees with a view presented, his reply must be couched in the gentlest language possible in order not to offend the person concerned and yet to convey a different opinion. Where there is not much conflict to be feared, especially where personal interests are not much involved—as when deciding where to place a piece of machinery—an objective and straightforward approach can be adopted. When it comes to personal interests, group concerns, or especially the possibility that someone may have made a mistake, more effort is made at maintaining peace and using diplomacy than at tackling the problem as such.

As for the effectiveness of the process, there is no doubt that a large number of people are involved in making the decision and thus committed to fulfilling it. The decision thus has a very great degree of acceptance and legitimacy and most parties concerned will do their best to have it implemented.This makes the operation often more successful than Western decisions that are tossed out at some brainstorming session or imposed by the boss on his subordinates. Indeed, the thoroughness of the Japanese in putting their decisions into practice is admirable. A first problem arises, however, in that much of the decision-making was carried out with such decorum and care to maintain harmony that no one really knows what the others think. The very ambiguity of many decisions can permit opposing parties to leave the meeting with a very different interpretation of the decision. Worse, some may be dead against the decision without having said so. They will bide their time, perhaps undermine implementation, or try to discredit those who proposed it.

What, however, if the decision was wrong? It is true that it was studied by all and from every angle. But the conflicts were carefully hidden and the decision was often a subjective agreement among people rather than an objective analysis of things. Moreover, even if the decision was right in a given context, there is a tendency to use the same decision time after time although circumstances may change. Then the Japanese will keep on doggedly or pigheadedly (image at the reader's choice) implementing it, destroying rather than creating and forcing it down one another's throats because it was a collective decision. For, admitting mistakes is even harder than coming to decisions. It would involve a loss of face, which is no small matter, a shaking of one's self-image and shattering of the respect formerly enjoyed. It could also open a person to attack by his enemies and perhaps a loss of promotion. This responsibility reaches even further, for one's protégés are also sullied. However, by making joint decisions, there is a built-in defensive mechanism whereby the collective responsibility can become collective irresponsibility. For, if well arranged, a collective failure may have no effect whatsoever on anyone since everyone was so deeply involved that no one will raise his voice against the others.

Collective decision-making can also turn into the opposite process of collective indecision, with the matter being tossed around repeatedly because no one can come to a decision. This occurs most often where the vested interests are very great or the chance of conflict menacing. Harmony, more than a decision as such, is often the primary goal. Thus, when conflicts do break out and threaten harmony, the first step is not to make the parties come together and reach some agreement but simply to end the conflict. In this case, a person closer to a referee at a boxing match than an arbitrator, will step in and say "*ma-ma*" which roughly means "cool it." He does not decide who is right and wrong, ask either side to modify its view, or suggest a compromise. He simply urges the parties to stop quarrelling openly in the interest of society. This does restore harmony. However, the conflict will continue to exist and fester and will not just disappear for being hidden.

In such a society, it is obviously difficult to find leaders or for leaders to fulfill the functions of leadership. Fortunately, this mass of people, brought up to follow or conform with one another but finding it difficult to establish relations, seems to realize that there is a need to form larger units, linking them together, and place them under leaders of some sort. No matter how they may dislike it, most Japanese realize, perhaps acutely, that followers cannot exist without leaders and can only fulfill their function and role in society when directed. Thus, they are often receptive to leadership when it comes, and a good leader can attract unusually large numbers of followers in a shorter time than almost anywhere else. Although not adequately stressed, the *oyabun-kobun* relationship is not always one in which a dynamic "parent" goes out looking for "children." It is as likely to be one in which a "child," realizing its weakness, seeks a protector. Even in today's Japan, the need to find a master or a position remains in the odd form of modern *ronin*. Like the masterless *samurai* of yore, there are students without universities, busily seeking a college to enter, and employees without jobs, eagerly trying to get not just a job but a position. For, nothing could be more miserable than a person without a master in a society in which a person is judged by his place in some group.

This craving for a leader should not make one draw the conclusion that Japan is in search of a charismatic leader, a Napoleon or Mao Zedong, or particularly likely to fall prey to some such. There is no craving for a leader with a capital L. Leadership has traditionally been more subtle and attenuated. The emperor, as is well known, was usually just a figurehead, and even the *shogun*, or the man behind the *shogun*, wielded greater—but far from absolute—power. Under the Tokugawa, as well as most earlier rulers, power was limited to tight control over a rather small group of people and much looser control over other relatively autonomous but counter-balancing groups. Even General Tojo, the most absolute recent leader, bore little resemblance to Hitler. There was always some opposition, or resistance, or simply disregard of central authority, and when he had clearly failed he retired without dragging the whole nation down with him. Indeed, in Japanese history, the urge for leadership has only been overshadowed by the almost spontaneous resentment against anyone who did become a leader.

In early days, leadership was often crude. The warriors who ruled the land had a code of honor, ultimately known as *bushido*, which applied largely to relations among themselves but did little to take into consideration the needs of the lesser classes. Even then, the punishment meted out to enemies was usually rather harsh and final, as often as not death on the spot, or for a particularly valiant foe, death at his own hand. Death often followed for his family and whole household. The peasants were roughly treated and exploited to the point that there were periodic, and usually futile, riots and uprisings. However, during Tokugawa days, the relationships between classes of people were clearly and rigidly laid down and enforced, rule was hereditary for the leading families and the father was made responsible for the household. Only toward the end was there enough change and flexibility to permit the rise of self-made men in the form of successful merchants and large landowners. The Meiji Restoration permitted a partial overthrow of the old order, as the oligarchs came to power, younger sons launched successful ventures, merchants or even ex-peasants opened up new fields of endeavor. This was the era in which political parties, schools, newspapers, companies, etc. were founded. The only similar outburst has been right after World War II. Thereafter, the more dynamic forms of leadership were toned down to the gentler, more devious forms of today.

Over the course of history and up to the present day, Japan has had basically three types of leaders. The original leaders, the founders and creators, usually had what is essential in Japan, namely an ability to attract large numbers of people, to guide or direct them, and to make them work together. Once such a group was formed, it could be harnessed to any task. This is different from the leader who comes with a mission, and follows it no matter whether he wins people over or not. Japanese leaders deal more in people than ideas. Thus, for example, the men who founded political parties did not always do so on purpose. They were men with a clientele to represent who, if they were excluded from power, could turn this clientele into a political party. An entrepreneur was not necessarily someone with a brilliant idea or a new invention, he simply knew how to get people to work, had some government or bank connections, and set up a factory perhaps, whether it was steel or textile was almost fortuitous. The ability to attract people, to direct people, or to manipulate them was the key to success and, once this was accomplished, a leader might well succeed in almost any field.

The true or original leaders had something more than

this to distinguish them. They were dynamic. Among a nation of followers, they alone seemed to know what they wanted and where they were going. But they were careful to hide their ambition or power. For the Japanese have both a respect for and a distrust of leaders and are afraid of being dominated. They expect "sincerity," so combined with modesty and regard for others that it is appealing. Quite simply, the Japanese expect their leaders to look and behave like anything but leaders. The easiest way is often the traditional one of being the man behind the throne and today, in most companies and bureaucracies, it is not the president or director who rules. Thus, rather than pushing and shoving, a wise leader will often bow and scrape, sometimes to the most humble, in order to build up good will and support and set aside human capital for the time it can be used.

The succeeding generations of leaders—the follower-leaders—had a different approach, and indeed they were quite different types of men. After all, they just inherited their following and authority as heirs of the original leader. Often they did not even possess much leadership ability. For disciples are often chosen for their weakness or lack of scope, simply to repeat the old motions in a routine that is worked out thoroughly. The reason is that all Japanese leaders have a deep fear, and one founded on history and experience, of the third type of leader—the schismatic. This refers not only to founders of religious sects; the phenomenon is encountered everywhere. These are people who work their way up as followers within an organization until they know many of the people in it, have their own disciples and clientele, and then betray their trust, break away and strike out on their own. There are hundreds of such to each true leader. This can be a salesman who steals the clientele, the subcontractor who opens a competing business, or the politician who sets up his own faction. Since these people have often started half-way up, they can be a rapid success at least for some time, until their ability as true leaders is put to the test.

In addition to leaders as such, there are also linking persons, be they go-betweens, middlemen, fixers, or what not. Since groups are largely self-contained and somewhat mutually exclusive, it is necessary to seek someone outside of the groups to bring them together. This, too, requires special human qualities, like the knowledge of many groups, contacts in them, an idea of how they operate and how the system functions to permit manipulation, and finally much political finesse and diplomacy. This sort of thing is constantly going on. A person will need an introduction before he can join a new group, move into a new company as an accepted member, build up a clientele and so on.

For a marriage, traditionally a *nakodo* arranges the match by negotiating between the parties. In companies or political parties, where there are a number of competing factions, there is a need for someone to intervene and say "*ma-ma*" to silence any quarrels or, if the situation is ripe, become a peace-maker. And, when one faction head has to be chosen for the sole position of company president, or the Prime Minister, a king-maker will consult the factions, measure their weight, and make the proposal. In commerce, there are accepted professions of agent, broker, intermediary, etc; in social life there is a constant call for third parties to restore harmony; and, in shadier matters, there are also fixers to arrange a deal.

The key to many institutions thus remains the personal characteristics of the individual running them and a true "institutionalization" remains weak. This makes it extremely difficult to replace the original leader. As Chie Nakane points out: "The first leader of the group . . . stands far beyond comparison with the members of his group, in that he became leader by his own efforts and merit, so that all group members are *de jure* and *de facto* his *kobun*, and this makes him drastically different from subsequent leaders." Unfortunately, this does not bode well for his organization. For, who can follow the original leader? This is indeed one of any leader's primary concerns, assuming that he created his organization to last, as he seeks a successor and, if possible, places him solidly in control during his lifetime. If this is not done, the result may be catastrophic. Again Chie Nakane: " . . . a change of leadership leads to a very critical period for the continuance and stability of the group. In many cases groups split into a number of small and hostile segments after the death of the leader. The chaos thus created can rarely be repaired internally."[8]

So, the great tragedy of Japanese society is that the institutions that have been created with so much painstaking care and difficulty, and over such a long time, remain to the end a loose grouping of smaller units which can fall apart as early as the original leader's demise. It is perhaps for that reason that many leaders tend to stay on, at least symbolically, until a very great age, an age at which leaders in most other countries would have left room for fresh blood, since no one else has this store of personal relations that is so hard to transfer. Moreover, knowing that the danger lies in friction among those below or excessive ambition that could lead an inferior to rise as an upstart or break away with some of the following, most leaders have tended to be conservative in their choice of aides, preferring loyal, compliant, relatively docile persons. This will mean that the gap between the original dynamic leader and the tamer follower-leaders is even larger than necessary, and that they cannot possibly fill his boots or just keep things running by following established routines. At best, they may avoid serious disruption, but this does not give them the strength to move ahead. Indeed, as Chie Nakane states: "It is the general pattern that such enterprises lose some of their vitality under a succeeding leader; in the second generation there develops a bureaucratic stability which may readily spawn factions and blunt the earlier initiative of the pioneer. If an enterprise is not firmly established before the death of its founder-leader and has difficulty in deciding on his successor internal disorder and dispute may well lead, as has regularly happened, to bankruptcy and disintegration."[9]

Thus, the system as it exists is far from perfect. There is an unusual difficulty in organization which is generally centered on personal relations. Leaders can weld smaller groups into extremely large ones, often quite rapidly, but the larger units tend to remain very fragile. In addition, simply to keep up the personal relations that are the cement of the organization, it is necessary to spend a tremendous amount of time in consultation, meetings, friendly gatherings, so that the links may solidify. Less time is then available for dealing with objective problems. Finally, by centering all units on personal relations, there is a tendency to forget or play down so-called higher values. The possibility of forming groups for abstract reasons or ideal goals is extremely limited and many times a philosophy or ideology is just a window-dressing. Starting with a goal, and then rallying people to it, has tended to be less successful than attracting people and then finding a purpose for them.

* * *

The Japanese social system has many fine points. It inserts the individuals in groups, provides them with vertical and horizontal linkages to others, and harnesses them to the accomplishment of given tasks. Without this structure, it would be impossible for companies and bureaucracies, families and clubs, associations and friendships to be as strong as they are. But, this entails serious weaknesses as concerns the largest and smallest units. Most observations show the extraordinary strength of groups, usually small in size since they are based on personal relations. Any unit transcending such a small group is exceptionally weak, and this also applies to the broadest unit which is the nation. The group in Japan is simply too important. One must fit into it entirely, give of oneself fully, and accept emotional and other ties that make it hard to leave the group or even belong to two groups. Without people who are sufficiently free to feel at home in various groups it is hard to weld them together. Without people who can ignore the interests of their specific group for broader and national causes, it is hard for the Japanese nation—no matter how solid it appears to some—to be a reality.

This also leaves the individual particularly weak. By subordinating his interests to the group, it is hard for him to develop much character, initiative or drive. It is clear that the Japanese do not regard individualism as a particularly noble characteristic. This was summed up by Ezra Vogel in a very detailed study of a small community. "Individualism does not imply a sense of oughtness or responsibility. . . . Few people in Mamachi consider it a higher morality to be concerned more with one's own benefit than with the welfare of one's group."[10] But, there are more and more cases in which the individual is forced to function on his own. This may be before he has joined a group, or when he cannot readily consult with the group, or when the group comes up with inconclusive answers to his question or no answer at all. It may be just the banal fact of going on a trip or living abroad (or even in Japan, but surrounded by others). In these situations, a person should be able to figure out the proper behavior on his own.

More seriously, there is a definite trend in the younger generation to seek more individualism. Often these desires are crushed by society. However, it is clear that many young people are growing up as individuals and refuse to surrender a large part of their being to any superimposed group. This includes not only rebels, also artistic or sensitive people, some who grew up abroad or resulted from mixed marriages, and any number who were nourished on American and European films and novels and prefer that kind of life. Given the rigidity and painful depth of relations required of any group member, many just cannot comply. If there is going to be more and more of these people, then it would seem wiser to let them adapt to the requirements of individualism. There is no reason that should turn it into pure egoism rather than the creative thing it could be. If society rejects them, and if they are never taught how to express their personality in positive and acceptable forms, they would not only be a loss to society, they could constitute a danger.

Even within the recognized groups there is much individualism. We are told that in most companies or administrations the individual is such a weak link that he does not even introduce himself as a person but as Mitsubishi's or Mitsui's Mr. So-and-so. In that same sacrosanct unit, however, he is probably busy at work making himself the most comfortable niche possible. There are also plenty of employees striving to rise just a little bit faster than the others, often the petty jump of one grade, and others engaged in rabid fights to reach the coveted positions of section or department chief. Indeed, there are many who are trying to rise despite adversity and all the efforts to keep them down, and to pull off a *shussé*. Literally this word means "to go into the world." In practice, it means to succeed in life, to move ahead, to come out on top. Those with more modest ambitions, who sublimate their personal goals to those of society are often in fact doing nothing of the sort, they are trying to induce or manipulate the group into supporting their own unavowed personal goals. This is the ultimate distortion of individualism, in which a person harnesses a whole group to his own ends, which are made nobler and more acceptable by appearing to be group goals.

Finally, although in many ways the individual is regarded as small and insignificant, in other crucial ways he is in fact everything. For, in Japan, all relations are personal. The *oyabun*, the center of all vertical units, is not an abstraction, he is a human being with virtues and defects and his relations to others are very largely one-to-one, namely personal and individual. Every single group is based on personal relations and the nature of the persons involved is the foundation for every institution. Companies are formed around a person who can create or destroy them. In politics, parties and factions are formed around a person and not a platform. In religious sects, the kind of person at the center of the nexus of relations is decisive. It is also decisive in newspapers, theatrical groups, or ladies' sewing circles. The right person can direct the group wisely or perhaps galvanize the nation. The wrong person would lead them to their destruction.

Along the same lines, it might be better to accept the fact that, due to exceptional talent or ability, some persons may be able to rise more rapidly than society usually permits. There is an old Japanese saying that "a nail that sticks out must be hammered in." This precept has not disappeared, and by hammering back in persons who might be of great significance, Japan may be losing some of its finest elements. After all, nothing has proven that people who slowly worm their way into groups, accumulate human capital in not always honest ways, or manipulate society, are that much superior to people who openly state their goals and fight for them. Individualism is obviously a threat to the continued placid and smooth flow of events. For that reason it may be frightening, and for that reason it may be suppressed. But this cannot be done forever without creating equally serious threats to the ultimate success of Japan. Why not then accept the existence of individualism and find a role for it?

NOTES

1. Ruth Benedict, *The Chrysanthemum and the Sword*, pp. 99–117.
2. Chie Nakane, *Japanese Society*, p. 30.
3. Jack Seward, *The Japanese*, p. 56.
4. Ezra Vogel, *Japan's New Middle Class*, p. 139.
5. Ichiro Kawasaki, *Japan Unmasked*, p. 188.
6. Richard Halloran, *Japan: Images and Realities*, pp. 92–3.
7. Herman Kahn, *The Emerging Japanese Superstate*, p. 52, and Ezra Vogel, *Japan as Number One*, p. 94.
8. Nakane, op, cit., pp. 47–8.
9. Ibid.
10. Vogel, *Japan's New Middle Class*, pp. 147–8.

3

The Basic Cell . . .
The Harmonious Family

"In Japanese culture and society, there is a permeating sense of '*wa*'—or harmony. . . . In Japanese social organization, *wa* is also an overriding factor. The family structure reflects *wa*, in that each family member respects his elders and shares responsibility for the family welfare. Japanese corporate society follows the same principles as the family social structure."[1]

So runs yet another newspaper article explaining Japan to the unknowing outsiders and, if they are unknowing, all too often believed. There is, of course, no doubt that the family is a crucial unit of Japanese society and perhaps as the family goes, so goes Japan. Harmony is obviously essential to a good family life. But, it cannot be taken for granted, certainly not in present-day society. Rather, it would be much wiser to see what the family really represents and then check what its contribution to society is, a contribution that can be negative as well as positive.

For centuries, indeed, for millennia, the family was the basic unit in Japan, just as it was everywhere else in the world. This was not the nuclear family but rather the traditional three generation or even extended family or clan. In a farming or early village community, the older members gave life and sustenance to the younger, which the young repaid in respect (very deep respect in a traditionalistic society, systematically reinforced by Confucianism). This age ranking was often quite detailed among men or women and, in each family, the first son, who is often given a name that reflects his status, had his rights. Indeed, any older brother or sister had a higher status than a younger one. At the same time, women were subservient to men, an elder sister not always being treated as well as a younger brother. As they grew up, the younger were expected to look after the older as repayment (assuming that their own example would be learnt by their children, who would ultimately look after them). Even when they were quite old, the elders and males not only got respect but continued having a major say in all decisions. As the younger generations grew into their positions in this society, they gradually participated in it and then perpetuated the system.

Was this harmonious? Perhaps once upon a time it was. The family (*ié*) was made the cornerstone of the social, economic, and political life of the Tokugawa era, which lasted nearly three centuries. Although it was in some ways renovated, it was kept on as a foundation for the Meiji regime. Certainly, with the sanction of the traditional gods and the inculcation of philosophies like Confucianism, which foster the respect of age or subservience of women, there were few questions asked. Legally and in practice, as long as they were hale and hearty, the elders and men had the real power. They ruled the family, and outside of the family there was little hope of success or indeed survival. Still, this does not imply harmony nor that they were automatically obeyed if there was some way of getting around them. There was certainly little room for outright disobedience or differences of opinion. But this could not exclude bitterness and evasion. Moreover, as the society was increasingly modernized, harmony could only prevail through some accommodation to change and alteration in the family style itself.

Modernization came with the reforms of the Meiji era. No matter how tame they may look today, they were then a momentous break away from earlier customs. In the Civil Code of July 1898, for example, although marriage was still based on the approval of the head of the family and a man under 30 years of age and a woman under 25 had to obtain the consent of their parents, at least beyond that age they were legally free to act on their own. Women were still clearly treated as inferiors by the old Civil Code, and the wife had to defer to her husband's powers and her legal incapacity with respect to the disposition of property. The husband had the right to manage the property owned by the wife, and fathers alone exercised parental power over the children. Only the wife had the obligation of maintaining chastity. But, at least some laws were laid down to protect marriage as an institution as opposed to polygamy and common law wives or just mistresses.

The updating was carried out sporadically, if far from thoroughly, until nationalism arose and a reactionary regime imposed a harmony on the country that included a constriction and retrogression in relations among family members. At the same time, by following an imperialist policy that involved sending millions of men abroad and then entering a war that drew just about every male and many females into a long and painful effort, the family fabric was rent asunder. After defeat in the Second World War, a new Civil Code was adopted in 1947 at the behest of the occupation forces. Under this, the legal system of the "family" was abolished, enabling adults (20 years of age and older) to marry based only on the mutual consent of both partners. For women, equality of the sexes was established by law. A separate property ownership system was adopted under which, unless a contract made before marriage provided otherwise, the property owned or acquired by the wife was her own. The widow inherited one-third, now one-half, of the estate of the husband (the children getting the rest). And parental power was joint. Far from rejecting this imposition, the Japanese talked of new ways and new freedoms and sought to create new relations between husband and wife, parents and children.

The first Civil Code was an edict of the Meiji oligarchs to show that Japan was a civilized country; the second was a model suggested by MacArthur's advisors to bring it further into line with Western standards. In neither case did the law, nor could any law, completely overturn the previous situation. But, what law cannot do, in many cases material circumstances can accomplish. For example, with the increase in urbanization, it was far easier for a younger son to break away from the family group and come to the city to set up on his own. With the increase in modernization, with new talents and skills required, it made increasingly less sense to turn to the elders for advice on things they knew little about. Also, with economic de-

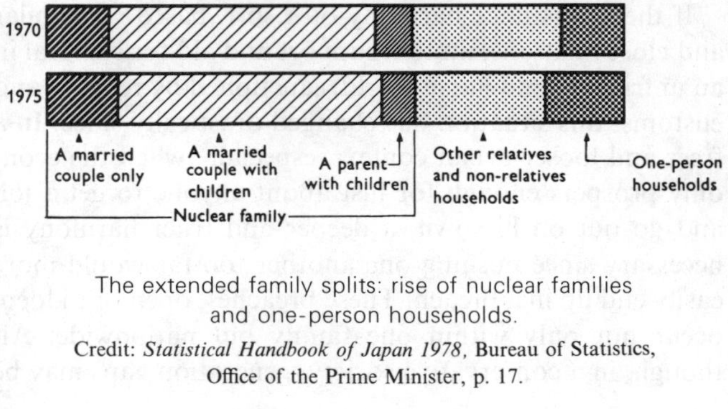

The extended family splits: rise of nuclear families and one-person households.

Credit: *Statistical Handbook of Japan 1978,* Bureau of Statistics, Office of the Prime Minister, p. 17.

velopment, there were many more sources of income outside of the family farm or shop, which meant that the sons and eventually the daughters could earn salaries that would—if need be—permit them to lead their own lives. As extended families split apart, there was a trend toward the nuclear family. Already by 1975, the number of nuclear households in the total was 64%, although it was particularly widespread in Tokyo and the larger cities. However, this was not a constant flowing movement; there were also signs of regression. True, the first generation did break away and was not exposed to the constant demands of humility, gratitude, and obedience. It showed a rather free and dynamic spirit. But, already the children had it less easy. For, they were brought up under constant parental control. Another generation later, the children of the children had to listen repectfully to the gratuitous advice of their grandparents, swallow it and also congratulate them on their courage in coming to the city to set up the family branch there. Indeed, the hardy peasant become city dweller tried to force the succeeding generations into greater submission than he had been subjected to (although nothing compared to what was still going on in the more unbroken traditions of the countryside).

If there was once harmony of a sort, based on regular and close relations, mutual support and aid for survival in an unfriendly and harsh world, sanctioned by religion and customs, this situation has changed drastically since. In a freer and looser urban context, especially when the economy prospers enough for just about anyone to get a job and go out on his own, a deeper and truer harmony is necessary since pushing one another too far would more easily end up in a breach. These breaches, open or hidden, occur not only within one family but nationwide. Although, in a conservative society, generation gaps may be smaller, they do exist nonetheless and will not cease growing. So, let us take a closer look at the "harmonious" family unit of today.

* * *

In traditional Japan, child rearing occupied a major position in family life and the mother, father and grandparents played a determinant role. Each, in a different way, was helping to form the child and mold its character. They all knew their functions and the ultimate result could almost be predicted.[2] Nowadays, the roles and degree of influence of mother, father and grandparents have shifted and their actions are anything but coordinated. The traditional forms were often carried over into a very different postwar environment where they made less sense or were not entirely accepted. More important, changes in the family and generational differences have confused the signals and the outcome is far from certain.

Basically, it is impossible to bring up Japanese children properly without the father playing a leading role, and this applies almost as much to the girls as the boys, since the latter must know how to behave as a man and the former how to respond to a man. Yet, all too many families are still "fatherless" much of the time. The father leaves home early in the morning, returns late at night, and is usually only accessible on Sunday. Many men are posted to the provinces or abroad for some years, and do not always bring along the family, or leave children back home so as not to upset their schooling . . . as if the experience of living with one's father were not also an essential part of education. Of course, the father must have something to teach. If he only plays with the children, spoils and pampers them and then when the children have overstepped some invisible social boundary, he gets angry and punishes them or mutters some words of instruction and disappears for another week, he is not of much help.

The weakening of the father's status has been accompanied by an enhancement of the mother's position. Due to the closeness of relations and especially the greater ease in dominating the one or two children in modern families, she is the one who makes the strongest impression and shapes the children to her will. This is reinforced by her important role in the children's formal education where mother has become an adjunct to the teacher, to make the children study harder, to achieve more and more. This has earned her little love and much notoriety as the infamous "education mama" (*kyoiku-mama*) or even "mother-monster" (*mama-gon*), as some children have nicknamed her. This could not help but distort the traditional patterns and create what in the past would have been regarded as deviant types. This is particularly so when the mother, as often happens, devotes too much attention to the son's upbringing (more than the daughter's) thereby creating a growing category of boys known for their weakness and dubbed "*bon-bon*" or mother's pets, who find it hard to function on their own and call most often to mother for advice even into their teens and much later. Meanwhile, many fathers have shown less interest in bringing up their sons and more concern about their daughter, with the doting father protecting her at home and sometimes also after marriage.

A second problem arises from the clash of views between the parents and the grandparents, who also play a considerable role, and more particularly between the mother and the mother-in-law with regard to child rearing. Having grown up in very different settings, the wartime experience being a decisive border line, they have very different ideas about how to bring up children. Whereas once the grandparents tended to be more on the pampering side, spoiling the child, increasingly as society itself changes they have swung back to a more traditionalist and disciplinarian tack. Now it is the grandparents who tend to be harder and more demanding task-masters. If they chide their own children on anything, it is on not being stern enough with the grandchildren and not teaching them their proper position in society nor giving them an aim in life, one which would include keeping society on the right, usually preordained, track. The younger generation, they so often say, is too soft. Perhaps they are right. But, it is their own fault. For many of today's parents grew up in strictly regimented schools, with the father away to build a strong Japan, and the mother forced to run the household. Later on, they hid in the bomb shelters and saw Japan's supposedly superior culture collapse all around them. How should they know how to bring up children?

The gap in mentalities between the grandparents and parents has not ceased growing, since the postwar generation, which was a bit soft itself, was extremely confused about what was right and wrong, about imposing discipline as such, and sometimes tended to adopt the gentler American methods of rearing children. Moreover, rather than lay down the line, they do not hesitate to buy their children's obedience rather than impose it by giving them a little gift here or there. Affluence has arisen even among the teenagers and younger tots. Aside from modest allowances, they also get considerable gifts for birthdays and especially New Years. Most of them have all the toys and sports gear they need and usually radios, cameras, or TVs. If they pass the exams to college, many are rewarded with comfortable allowances, fancy clothing for the girls, even a brand-new car for the boys. Most parents also devote much of their lives to the "success" of their children. A recent poll showed that well over half the parents were willing to make the necessary sacrifices to put their children through college, pay the costs of their marriage, and then leave behind property or assets as an inheritance.[3]

This self-sacrifice by the parents, they assume, gives them the right to direct their children's lives in certain crucial matters. While giving in for all sorts of minor things and often spoiling the children outrageously where it does not count, they will show incredible tenacity in pushing their children in the right direction for the essential things in life. One of them is certainly to have the children study well and enter the right schools. The parents, from the Emperor on down, often decide to which level the children will study and even at which school. They may also have a word to say about the courses taken. Later, the parents will guide the children into the right careers and perhaps help them land the job in which their sons at any rate may well spend a lifetime. They also interfere in the much more personal and intimate matter of who the children will ultimately marry. Even those parents who want their children to marry for love also want the person to be "someone who we can agree on." If there is danger of a mismatch, they will exert considerable pressure. Then, many continue imposing themselves even as the children form their own families, expecting perhaps payment in return for services rendered in the form not only of respect but of dutifully following advice.

Yet, even while trying to impose their will on the children, they may have been sowing the seeds of rebellion against society and ultimately themselves. The best laid plans, as they say, sometimes go astray. Among other things, since the war few parents (or schools) dare inculcate moral values of any sort, perhaps because of their own uncertainty, and thus a basic foundation for reasoned action is missing. Although demanding obedience, when he does so, by being absent so often the father cannot see that his bidding is done. And the mothers are left very much in charge. They may be strict disciplinarians when it comes to education, perhaps to attain through their children what they once desired. But their old stirrings can also carry over into what little moral training there is. A very strange and far from traditional mixture is reflected by an NHK survey on the way of life mothers desire for their children. Over 75% taught them to put personal life before society, about half not to help others (but not to inconvenience them either) and the number telling the girls (54%) and boys (32%) to relax and enjoy life rather than try hard was surprisingly large. At the same time, most children were warned to follow majority opinions.[4] Thus, the personal and self-centered pursuits should be suitably disguised.

*　　　　*　　　　*

In this social context, it must be expected that tremendous changes will be taking place, perhaps even a complete transformation of what had been hitherto regarded as typically Japanese behavioral patterns. At any rate, it cannot be denied that the old order is still crumbling although it has not been replaced by a new and generally accepted one. There is still much confusion and conflict over what is right and wrong and it is pointless to expect anything but a superficial harmony until there is greater agreement on society's aims and the individual's role therein. The movement is so rapid that each generation seems to differ from the last and bring up children that are bound to differ from it. One of the few clear trends is away from the old Spartan conditions and strict ethics towards something softer and more pliant and a weakening of the will. The younger generations are often spoiled by their parents and at the same time overprotected. They get what they want almost without asking and are shielded not only from danger but even discomfort. Meanwhile, despite any inner strivings to shape their own lives, they are clearly other-directed. The most striking phenomenon has thus been a marked feeling of dependence or *amaé*.[5] Many young people expect that things will be done for them rather than doing things themselves, they accept to be directed by others as long as their needs are met.

None of the changes should come as much of a surprise to anyone, for they have been charted by a vast array of polls and surveys for years. Yet, there is often a shocked disbelief among elders when the results are announced. For example, back in 1958, the White Paper on Youth found that most young people wanted to "live a clean and righteous life" or "devote themselves to society." That is hardly the goal nowadays. Instead, the 1977 White Paper found that youth wanted to live "in an easy-going manner" or "in a manner best fitted to personal tastes." Although it felt "free" in society and enjoyed the fruits of affluence, only 5.8% replied that they wanted to contribute to society within their own limits. Moreover, although youth was prepared to learn from the experience of their elders, they would resist any high-handed attempts to make them follow in their footsteps.[6] Yet, even while rejecting society and discipline, they yearn for *amaé*. This extends to their parents as children, their teachers at school, and even their superiors at work. There has always been a strong preference "to work under a chief who takes care of his subordinates kindly," but recently as many as 87% of the youngsters chose this in an Education Ministry survey, the highest in 25 years. This led the *Japan Times* editorialist to speak of a "hothouse generation" and ask: "If so many workers want only to be taken care of—their bosses substituting for their nursing mothers, it seems—where are the leadership and initiative going to come from?"[7]

Despite the fact that there is an increasing rejection of imposed values and a clear trend toward individualism,

Image of Young People **(multiple answers)**

General public	Young people	Favorable	Unfavorable	General public	Young people
6 %	10 %	Firm beliefs	Lack firm beliefs	23 %	19 %
12	17	Highly motivated	Weak-willed	16	25
25	36	Dreams and ideals	No dreams or ideals	12	15
45	47	Free	Restricted	3	7
8	10	Strong interest in society	No interest in society	25	33
4	5	Considerate	Selfish	48	37
4	7	Warm human ties	Lonely	11	21

Image of Middle-Aged People (multiple answers)

General public	Middle aged people	Favorable	Unfavorable	General public	Middle aged people
36 %	43 %	Firm beliefs	Lack firm beliefs	3 %	3 %
28	31	Highly motivated	Weak-willed	3	4
10	16	Dreams and ideals	No dreams or ideals	10	6
3	2	Free	Restricted	20	20
44	52	Strong interest in society	No interest in society	5	6
20	27	Considerate	Selfish	7	3
25	30	Warm human ties	Lonely	8	7

Image of Elderly People (multiple answers)

General public	Elderly people	Favorable	Unfavorable	General public	Elderly people
22 %	19 %	Firm beliefs	Lack firm beliefs	3 %	3 %
4	4	Highly motivated	Weak-willed	12	10
3	4	Dreams and ideals	No dreams or ideals	18	14
6	9	Free	Restricted	9	3
16	18	Strong interest in society	No interest in society	10	8
23	30	Considerate	Selfish	9	5
25	30	Warm human ties	Lonely	33	19

Source: NHK Public Opinion Survey Office, February 1976.

How the three ages think of themselves and of one another.

few positive alternatives or outlets exist. This may help explain some rather odd results from a comparative study between Japanese youth and young people in such diverse places as the United States, Europe, and Asia. The percentage of young Japanese who expressed pride in their nation was just about average. However, those who said they were willing to put the interest of the state ahead of their own was the lowest of all (20%). Fewer Japanese found that life was worth living when they were contributing to society (12%) or when they were with their families (21%). Only 14% of the Japanese youths regarded education as an important factor for succeeding in life, as opposed to about 40% elsewhere, while 44% of the Japanese (the highest figure) believed that they needed luck more than anything else to succeed in life. Again we have the complete opposite of the traditional picture. Although everything is going well materially, Japanese youth seems to be among the most frustrated. The only reason this is not openly shown was revealed by another question, namely, what they would do to change this state of affairs. The Japanese were not only among the most dissatisfied, they were also the least willing to do anything about it.[8]

Nowadays, this frustration is being expressed more often and openly than before, and is taking increasingly antisocial forms. The most conspicuous of the "bad" elements have been the gangs of hot-rodders, who delight in creating traffic hazards as they speed along the highways and more recently began invading the city streets to frighten passers-by. Now violence is breaking out in the schools, as older students victimize the younger ones and some even insult and beat up the teachers. There are also many drop-outs among the students. From glue sniffing, more and more are graduating to drugs. Crime has also broken out among youngsters. Children from good families engage in shoplifting "for fun;" girls are picked up for prostitution (and then blackmailing their clients); there have even been cases of murder. The trends were far from encouraging and the 1979 Police White Paper reported a number of "records" for the previous year. These included the largest number (136,801) and highest proportion (1.4%) of juveniles taken into custody for criminal offenses, major increases in teenage and female delinquents, sexual crimes by and offenses against youths, use of drugs, and the most runaways ever, some 58,375.[9]

This, of course, is nothing compared to the vast majority of "good" elements in society. Or is it? The good boys and girls are not rebelling openly. If anything, their will to rebel was crushed at an early age. Many of them are overly protected, they rarely face any hardship, danger, or even unpleasantness. Their parents look after them too much, handle every aspect of their lives, and take most of the decisions. Any time a difficulty arises, they will refer back to mother (more often than to father). However, if no one is there to help them out, what would be a minor problem for tougher or more practical-minded youths becomes a major one for them. No matter how many facts and figures they may learn, they have little experience with the real world. They don't even have enough time to develop physically and socially. Although tests show the physique has developed due to a better diet, the muscular functions are very poor and strength decreases with age. Social activity takes up a minor part of their lives as compared with children elsewhere. After returning from school, they only want relaxation, which usually assumes very passive forms; rather than playing with other youngsters, they recuperate by reading comic books or especially by viewing TV.

Sometimes, trying to play the game and be a good boy or girl is just too much for them. Suicide has a noble tradition in Japan—but not for children. Yet, over the past ten years, the number of suicides among those under 19 has fluctuated between 750 and 900 annually. Worse, the number of suicides in the under-14 group doubled.[10] The causes were often underachievement at school, followed by domestic discord, and then trouble with or about boyfriends or girlfriends. Yet, the causes were usually out of all proportion with the outcome, a rather petty matter such as a scolding from the parents, a test failed, or refusal to buy them a tape-recorder being enough to destroy the fragile balance of attachment to life.

"Bad" and "good" are used here to express traditional value judgements. However, when values change so radically, it is necessary to reexamine the value judgements. If so many young people disapprove of their situation, if the striving for a personality of their own is so great, rebellion is a very natural phenomenon, and in many ways a healthy thing. If anything, it should be permitted, almost encouraged, and if possible channelled into positive forms. Denying or blocking change can only increase the frustration and make the explosion or collapse of the personality that much worse.

* * *

Once upon a time, men were men. Thinking back to earlier days, stress is placed on the *samurai* who represent the manly virtues of strength, courage, discipline, sacrifice, and so on. To be perfectly fair, the peasants and merchants of earlier days were also hardy and disciplined men. However, over the Tokugawa period, although Confucian philosophy constantly preached the elevation of men and the degradation of women, society was more peaceful than it had been for centuries. And, modernization and peace have turned Japanese men into much the same as men in most other modern societies . . . people whose physical prowess is of much less import than other "virtues."

Nevertheless, in Japan, a man must still behave like a man. The thousands of employees and workers walking around in their nice neat suits or huddling together over a drink are not left in peace. For some reason they cannot come to terms with a new status and are driven on by a traditional "machismo" that insists that men behave like men, although the code of behavior has disappeared and no new one come to replace it. So, even the meekest of men puts on a big voice when he talks, uses the rougher, coarser men's language, indulges in men's jokes and men's activities. Each tries to prove he is a man—whatever that means—by copying his colleagues or perhaps some quaint traditional image.

Until a few decades ago, it was not very difficult for the little boy in the family to learn the role of a man in the family. Daily exposure to his father's behavior vis-a-vis his mother or sister told him that the male is different as well as superior to the female members of the family. This was systematically built into the language, the customs, the life of the family and society. The little boy saw that his father is, or at least should appear, superior to this mother. However, the little boy in today's family is not as fortunate. In many families now, the mother has become so strong and the father so much weaker (although it is hard to tell which came first), that it is not uncommon for the young son to see his father spoken down to or scolded by his mother. Yet, on the other hand, he will be told by his mother or by any number of people that he must act like a man. He may also witness a different situation in his friend's family where the "father is superior" relations still exist. The result is that he is totally confused. And since there is usually no one who can tell him exactly what a man's position or role is—because everyone else is just as confused as he is—he grows up not knowing exactly what he is or how he should act, which by any standards is far from being masculine.

What then remains of being a man? Once feeding one's sexual appetite was regarded as manly. That is increasingly less so for a younger generation, brought up quite puritanically by mother, school, and TV. Where awkwardness or fear do not quite repress the instinct, young men are put off at any rate by the difficulty of such relations with "good" girls and the high price of sex commercially. These sexual hang-ups may have contributed to the rise of that other manly characteristic, drinking. The craze for drink has spread at an incredible pace. The frequency and intensity are boosted by the many social occasions for drinking and courtesy, which dictates that each party fill the other's glass and almost makes it a duty to empty it. Thus initiation in drinking is one of the primary requirements for any "man."

In such ways, men manage to distinguish themselves from women. A healthier form would have been through sports. Although "sports" are very popular in Japan, they are often merely friendly and social gatherings, as with golf, or status symbols, as with tennis, and not a passion or love. The amount of time spent and the physical results are notably lacking. Sports today often degenerate into a spectator activity, with incredible numbers of men packing baseball and other stadiums and following the exploits of their idols on television. Mixed with this is gambling, once again partly regulated and sometimes illegal, but flourishing as well as if it were not. There are no gambling casinos in Japan, heaven forbid! There are, however, pachinko parlors with vertical pinball machines in almost every neighborhood, usually packed to overflowing. There is also gambling on horse racing, bicycle racing, motor boat racing, with enormous sums of money changing hands and equally fabulous sums going to the organizers.

The attempt to have men and women mix, even to have

husbands and wives get to know other couples, has not been particularly successful. Obviously, if both are brought up differently, have different interests and rarely see one another, there are many barriers to be broken down. When something is done, it usually centers around the children, who form a common interest. But a look at what men tend to do in their free time, and later what women tend to do, will show why mixing is so hard. According to a survey by Suntory, when salarymen get together with friends or colleagues, what they discuss is hobbies, sports, and gambling 36% of the time, work 34%, and rumors about people in the company almost as much, while general subjects like current affairs and politics only account for 3.3%.[11] There is no room for women in all this.

Relations with the family do not occupy the major part of a man's time. In addition to leaving early for work, and putting in long hours, there is the sheer problem of getting back home again. In earlier days, when the economy was booming, it was considered natural that everyone should do a few hours overtime. Today, that is usually not necessary. However, with the recession and need for more money, many men manage to arrange some work or a meeting for at least an extra hour or so. Then, they have to face the thought of being packed into the subways and trains or peak hour traffic jams and movement at a snail's pace back home. So, why not stay on a bit longer and chat with the colleagues, or go for a drink, or have something to eat before facing the ordeal of return? Even today, when the office no longer holds them, most men manage to tumble home after dinner has been served, the kids are in bed, and the wife is watching television.

Unfortunately, the wife may not be the person he wants to see most when he returns, tired, a bit inebriated, perhaps depressed. For she may be having troubles with the children or in making ends meet with a family budget that grows slower than the prices. Moreover, personal bonds between them, socially and sexually, may be lacking. Be it a "love" marriage or not, men repeatedly express their preference in polls and through marriage for a wife to look after the house and children, and not one with any particular intellectual level or even as a sex object. If anything, the wives find themselves relegated to the position of a housekeeper to do the domestic chores and an effort to remain sexually attractive after marriage would more likely than not draw criticism, especially from the in-laws. Thus, the sexual element does not serve as a cement to hold the couple together in all too many cases. Worse, this aspect of the relationship is often likened more to a duty or chore than a pleasure. According to present folklore, only Saturday night is officially designated by many married couples for that activity.

Still traditionally, and even today, a man is expected to obtain respect from his wife and children. Indeed, it is expected by society that a husband should behave in a *teishu-kanpaku* manner. In essence, this means that the husband is the ruler of the family, in practice, that he act "bossy." Of course, the husband should act bossy, After all, he's a man, isn't he? And no man could afford to lose face by not acting bossy to his wife and children! This concept may have been propagated so well due to the traditional and still existing system of arranged marriage, where the husband and wife form a relationship not necessarily based on love and the husband is usually much older than the wife. Alas, nowadays it is not so easy to be bossy, and some husbands appear rather more hen-pecked than otherwise. So, big voice and manly airs or not, the husband does not always manage to impose on his family when he is there . . . which is rare enough. Often, he may leave the family pretty much alone. After all, outside of the home, it is still very much a man's world.

* * *

During the Tokugawa period, many of the traditional patterns of behavior were constructed on Confucian thinking and, despite the Meiji Restoration and the instructions of the Allied Powers, there are still many people who believe there should not be equality of the sexes, even more who doubt the advisability of a greater similarity in sex roles, while there are few who really believe that women today are treated the same or as well as men. Obviously, there has been much change and progress since the days when a woman was taught that her life should consist of obedience to her father as a girl, obedience to her husband as a wife, and then obedience to her male children when she was old or when wives had to walk a few steps behind their husbands. But there are still definite limits to the change.

Thus, in 1972, when the Prime Minister's Office held a poll on the question of "how should children be brought up?" nearly 80% of the respondents felt that "boys should be brought up in a manner befitting boys and girls should be brought up in a manner befitting girls." A perfectly noble and thoroughly ambiguous statement that is quite unattackable without knowing what is meant by a "manner befitting." A slight indication of this was provided by another survey, this time by NHK (the public broadcasting company) more recently in 1976, where 66% of the respondents hoped that their sons would acquire knowledge and skills and enter a specialized profession while their daughters became "happy family women." This is our first lesson in what is befitting for a woman.

However, a girl's education begins much earlier, and her lessons never seem to end. They drum in the simple message that a girl should speak like a girl, act like a girl, and preferrably think like a girl. Women's language is more melodious, more attractive and softer; it is also full of honorific *o*'s in speaking before men or even referring to all sorts of everyday objects. It is full of self-demeaning words to express modesty, and it has no suitable words for many of the cruder things of life a girl is supposed to know nothing about. In addition, there are dozens of womanly movements and gestures a girl picks up, such as putting her hand in front of her mouth to giggle when something is confusing or embarrassing, or holding her hand in such and such a way with the charm once associated with *geisha* and now transmitted to the public by female TV stars and teeny-bopper singers.

This, however, is only the form, for the linguistic formulas were created to comply with the social substance. The basic rule is that women should show clear respect and obedience to men in general. A woman is expected to act meek, to appear subservient, and to seem more ignorant than any male she may be with. No matter what the issue—aside conceivably from child raising and household expenses—the man is always right. Thus, the task of learning a woman's role is never quite finished, since the men she is dealing with can always come up with one more demand, one more order, or one more humiliation. No matter what the law may say, this customary rule has never really been cast out and any degree of equality is the result of social arrangements and compromises or perhaps strength of personality, especially now that so many men are uncertain of their own position.

If this is still a woman's lot, one may well wonder why girls are being sent to high schools and colleges in such numbers. By 1979, the percentage of all female students going on to receive higher education was 34%, as opposed to 44% for male students. But, this is not as much of a contradiction as it may seem, for many were not really preparing for a career or seriously committed and only

58% proceeded to get a job.[12] This is already reflected by the courses they take: home economics classes are 99.6% female and 60% of those taking liberal arts and education

Bridal training: how can you hook a man if you can't play the koto?

Photo credit: Foreign Press Center-Japan.

are women; in engineering, social sciences, and agriculture, women only represent 10% of the total. In addition, most of them also take outside courses such as sewing and cooking (Japanese, Chinese, and European) or study feminine accomplishments such as flower arrangement, tea ceremony, playing the piano or some other instrument, which is part of the curriculum of any "bride trainee" (*hanayome shugyo*). Actually, a lot of the "students" seem to be simply filling in time and picking up essential know-how for the career almost all will ultimately enter into: *eikyu-shushoku* ("eternal employment") . . . the recognized profession of housewife.

Just before this, however, there comes a rather unusual period when the girls seem to blossom into womanhood without yet accepting the responsibilities of wife and mother. This is when the young women (and also men, although much less visibly) leave school and enter a company for the most part or are looked after in style by their parents. Now, they are earning a reasonable salary or drawing a comfortable allowance while still usually living at home. This leaves a big margin with which they can do more or less as they please, either put aside some for the future, and all girls do this a bit, or splurge . . . They do not hesitate to spend a big chunk of it on fancy clothing, cosmetics, and perfume, visits to the tea salon with friends or a little trip to Hawaii. They wear the latest Paris fashions, to a degree never seen in Paris, and have nothing but the finest accessories, often made specifically for the Japanese market. Today there is a veritable orgy of expenditures in this 20 to 25 age bracket, called by the rest of the population the "bachelor aristocrats."

All this is not seriously begrudged them by their parents, for it is their fling. Moreover, this money is also an investment of sorts. The young ladies are on the marriage market; they must marry soon, and they must marry well.

And thus they are decked out in finery and presented elegantly yet correctly, like all Japanese consumer products on the luxury end of the scale. Moreover, this is just a passing phase and not taken too seriously. For girls are expected to marry during the *kekkon tekireiki*, or ideal period for marriage, which peaks at 25 and then falls off rapidly. In Japan, marriage is somewhat closer to a duty than an option, and no girl would like to end up an old maid. Indeed, almost all the kindly suggestions to her, from family and friends, sometimes even from total strangers, push her in that direction (as happens to the boys, though less intensely). Ultimately, some 98% of the people are married off.

But, what kind of marriage does one make? For, there are now two basic types, the more traditional Japanese "arranged" marriage and the modern, Western-type "love" marriage. This, too, has been the subject of polls, this time from the Ministry of Health and Welfare, under whose competence the reasons for marriage seem to fall. Surveys showed that in 1966, marriage for love represented 50% of the total, whereas by 1973, it had reached 63%.[13] But, there is a lot of overlap. Often, a couple that was introduced by a go-between falls in love. The love couple, to make the family happy, will appoint someone as go-between to make the traditional speech at a Japanese style wedding ceremony. Moreover, love or arranged, most marriages are made with the approval and support of the parents. Otherwise, there would be a terrible battle in which it is more often the parents who win. The number of marriages that represent "love" in the sense of passion and refusal to compromise with the parents or society is infinitely small.

Why are there still so many "arranged" marriages? Because the parents still impose them on weakling children. Also, many children, especially the girls, have been brought up so highly sheltered that their choice of potential husbands is small. Some of them hardly know any eligible bachelors and the chances of meeting acceptable men on their own are limited. So, if one of the men around (perhaps a college or office chum) seems to suit them without upsetting their parents, that is "love" or at least inclination. When that fails, the girls can resort to the tradition of *omiai* or match-making. The matchmaker or go-between, the *nakodo*, can be any more experienced person (daddy will often suggest names) who will introduce suitable young men. Just make a snap shot and a full-size color portrait, write out your own resumé with all the pertinent information, don't forget to add data on your family up to three generations back, and prepare to meet the man of your dreams, with your parents and his, at some expensive hotel lobby or restaurant. Dress not too fancy, not too casual, engage in a bit of harmless conversation in the presence of the *nakodo* and, if you are satisfied, call up the *nakodo* a few days later to thank him, and, oh yes, don't forget to keep him up-to-date on how things progress with your potential husband. If you weren't turned on, let the *nakodo* try again. Nowadays, along with the traditional *nakodo*, college professors hold parties and companies form clubs to bring people together with a view to matrimony. Mitsubishi has its "Diamond Family Club" and the Dai-Ichi Kangyo Bank its "Heart Family Club." There are also about four hundred private agencies to help lonely hearts and untold thousands or perhaps millions of volunteers. Indeed, *omiai* seems to be making a comeback as people are increasingly concerned with a "good" match.

However, as soon as they are married, once the wonderful period of courtship is over, when the two can freely talk together, eat together, go out together, they are separated again. The man goes to work early every morning. If he rushes home in the evening, his friends and colleagues will make fun of him. So he goes out for a drink with the boys instead. Gradually, as he assumes more and more importance in the company or administration, he works longer and longer hours. Meanwhile, his wife stays at home and looks after the house and children. From the peacock she was, she becomes a raven. Her allowance, for her own personal needs, is drastically reduced and hardly enough to afford even a little luxury or entertainment. She knows how to cook Japanese, Chinese, and Western dishes, but aside from Sunday her husband is not at home to eat them. She can do flower arrangement and tea ceremony, but then some Sundays he is out playing golf and she sits at home. Or he watches the TV and not the flowers.

So, a woman's first struggle after marriage is to hold on to her man, which she may make some effort at in a "love" marriage but requires both a great deal of diplomacy and a greater degree of tenacity, a rare combination in anyone and particularly in Japanese women trained for neither. The following case is hardly exceptional, for current Japanese folklore has already come up with a special name for husbands who work late at the office, entertain customers, or just have a friendly drink with the boys and come home in the wee hours of the morning: *gozen-sama*, or roughly the gentleman who comes home after midnight.

"During our engagement period, I told him over the phone: 'A man's life is in his work. In the future we will always be with each other, so please concentrate your energy on work.' With a child less than one year old and another baby in my womb, I prepared midnight snacks for my *gozen-sama* husband without a word of complaint. There were twelve months of bathing my one year old child and putting him to bed and then rewarming the bath and washing the baby. At this stage I stopped shining

Flowers for my husband . . . if only he gets home on time tonight!

Photo credit: Foreign Press Center-Japan.

shoes for my still *gozen-sama* husband. (Since then, he has been shining his own shoes.) And now, my four year old and three year old children are growing up nicely fighting together, playing together, and caring for each other.

Every evening, without exception, they ask 'Will Daddy come back tonight?' . . . Once or twice a week, I don't bother preparing supper, or rather the midnight snack, and go to bed with my children. (My husband in such a case seems to be taking food out of the refrigerator himself.) Every year, increasingly, my husband is becoming more and more of a 'salary bringer.' I am really to be pitied. Or is it him?"[14]

Her next task is to bring up the children. The set pattern is not by any means to put off having children so that the couple can first develop their own relationship or the woman can work, but rather to have them promptly: in two or three years. This keeps the mother busy for the first years before the children enter the school system. With only two children on the average, the task of a mother is much less of a grind than in the past. The same applies to looking after the house. Before the war, most housewives spent a tremendous amount of time cooking, scrubbing, washing, and so on. Nowadays, many homes have modern conveniences that take away much of the time-consuming labor: washing machines, rice cookers, refrigerators, vacuum cleaners, etc., etc. Fast foods have also made their appearance. According to statistics, the Japanese housewife only spends six hours a day on house-keeping—and can get by on three if she's a working woman. Among her spare time activities are dressmaking, knitting, handicrafts, lounging about for rest, or watching TV. Next come "prettying oneself up," reading, and shopping. The last category, less often engaged in, includes tea ceremony, flower arrangement, music and art appreciation, calligraphy, theater going, and various sports. So, here we have a rather different picture from the traditional image of the Japanese woman, but a very clear order of priorities: caring for one's person, one's clothing, one's exterior, before one's interior; far more domestic and banal than intellectual or aesthetic. The prime activity of the Lady of Leisure (*Yukan Madamu*) seems to be watching TV, while doing other things or for its own sake, almost five hours a day.[15] Sadly enough, the statistics show no particular commitment to charitable, community-centered, service or other voluntary activities. Continuing education, now paid some lip-service, usually consists of another cooking or sewing course.

However, what seems to really use up the energy of modern Japanese women is coping with their unmodern in-laws. Traditionally, the daughter-in-law was regarded more or less as her mother-in-law's maid, and thus even kindness between husband and wife was not regarded as in order. "Don't spoil your mother's maid" the old saying goes. But, in modern Japan? Apparently, in all too many cases, there has been little change. Even at the age of 25, or 35, or 45, it often happens that the wife really is not running the household by any means. The mother or mother-in-law gives pointers on how to bring up baby, how to instill discipline, how to cook the son's favorite dish, and how to behave in general and towards one's elders in particular. The number of women living with their in-laws has fallen, but, as long as they are in commuting distance, the problem has not died out. An idea of just how serious this can be is conveyed by the unending stream of letters to the editor of women's magazines from dissatisfied daughers-in-law (*yomé*).

"I have been married for five years now and I am sick and tired of the relationship with my mother-in-law. Before we were married, I used to think foolishly: 'What an understanding mother. With her, I can be on good terms. The hard feelings between the *yomé* and mother-in-law you hear about so often will not exist between us two.' However, the minute my husband and I were married, she revealed her true nature and she grudges every little thing I do. For example, if the meat of the fish stew I make falls apart, she complains: 'I only get people's left overs.' If I go to visit my parents once in a blue moon: 'My goodness, you go there often. I bet you like your parent's place more than my house, don't you.' And she never says a word when her own daughter comes and stays overnight for many days. My husband is a coward, too, for that matter. For god's sake, he is a grown man with a family of his own! Why doesn't he say something to his mother. Who was it who said, before marriage, that he would definitely make me happy? It seems that he is a dynamic section chief at his company with twenty people working under him. But, once he sets foot in the house, he is a blockhead. He is like a rotten weak-minded woman. If he would only shift one-tenth of his power at work to home, my mother-in-law would not pick on me."[16]

This does not mean that women are defenceless. They may do what is asked. But, they can always get back at their husbands, parents, or in-laws with dozens of little tricks, like not doing the bed, serving cold food, misplacing things, or forgetting to look after the household altar when the elders die. They try to avoid any head-on conflict but, should one arise, there is still the possibility for the women—who cannot answer back—of retreating into an icy silence that will rattle even a strong man's nerves. Indeed, this sort of guerilla warfare is often going on intermittently. Even if a daughter, wife, or mother has to be docile, she may be anything but "supportive" in the present sense. Within the home at least, she can frequently have her own way, by hook or by crook. All of this gives women a considerable standing and authority within a somewhat restricted realm.[17] However, most women seem to encounter their biggest problems with other women, and the modern woman in particular often has less trouble with men than with the older and unmodern women around her. Having been broken in early in their own lives, these women cannot always accept that the next generation should have it easier. This gives rise to an even more pervasive and tenacious pressure to perpetuate the system. Here is an example from the life not of a newly wed but a 37 year old woman whose husband suggested she go back to her parent's home while he is away on business.

"I really wanted to see my mother and thus I ran back to her. My mother is 71 years old. 'When the husband is away, it is the wife's role to stay home and look after the house. And you came back here directly without even stopping over at his mother's place!' My mother was in a bad mood. The next morning, my mother made me go over to my mother-in-law with incense and flowers for the house buddha. My mother-in-law said: 'The minute you got married, this became your home. Isn't it proper to come back here first and then go and visit your mother's place? If you think I'm wrong, please say so.' I was not happy at all. Who cares which place I go to first? That's why I don't like old people, I thought. But I calmed myself and told myself that I can complain to my real mother, and so to my mother-in-law I bowed and said: 'I am sorry. I will not do this again so please forgive me.' When I went back to my mother's place, I told her the whole story and complained that my mother-in-law was a very difficult person. But my mother said: 'A very fine person she is. What she says is completely logical.' And she scolded me for not having the right attitude of a daughter-in-law."[18]

A woman's place would definitely seem to be in the home, but not a very congenial or cheerful one.[19] What is her place like outside of the home?

More and more women have been entering the labor market, rising from 13.76 million in 1950 to 20.83 million in 1978. Nevertheless, the increase in female workers simply kept pace with the increase in male workers, and the share of women in the total remained about 39% until the recession, when women's share in the working population began to fall off, only to resume its growth because many women were hired on a part-time basis. Most of these women were engaged in office 33.8%, production work 26.8%, and services 13.3%. Very few were in specialist and technical occupations, a mere 1.41 million. Even fewer women climbed high in the business world. A government survey on women's participation in the decision-making processes, which covered nearly 1,000 top companies, revealed that, although women made up 23% of the work-force, only 0.3% of the decision-makers were women. With regard to the matter of money, the situation is even less attractive, with women's wages only averaging out to 56% of men's wages.[20]

These figures gloss over certain other peculiarities in the employment of women. A tremendous number are running Japan's farms while their husbands are off working in nearby factories. Another massive block consists of so-called "family employees" helping out in family firms or tending shops and stores. And many of those in industry are just temporary or part-time labor and not regulars under lifetime employment. In fact, most women seem to shun such total commitment and seek casual labor. This is clearest in the phenomenon of *arubaito*, derived from the German word for work, but involving part-time, short-term or periodic jobs such as work in a factory or farm during the busy season, putting in some time as a salesgirl or translator, or giving music, language or flower arrangement lessons. In addition, companies hire girls as "office ladies" or OLs for short. They often wear cute little uniforms and flash big artificial smiles while directing customers to the right department or ushering visitors in to the boss. In the many offices, they assist the male employees by neatly rewriting documents, filing papers, answering phones, running errands, making photocopies, and especially preparing and serving tea. Usually they do not even have any skill such as typing or bookkeeping or the ability to act as secretary. As one potential OL pointed out: "OL has a nice ring to it, but what it really means is someone to take care of pretty things in an office."[21]

This leaves us with a rather uncertain view of women's place in the business world. True, they get fewer good jobs, rise less quickly, and are paid less. Still, despite any pressure from society, they are the ones who decided to study liberal arts or home economics, although they knew it was a professional dead-end. In an economy in which pay is based very largely on seniority, it is also partly their fault that they can be employed for such a short time. Compared to men, most of whom are expected to spend their life with the same company, the average length of continuous service of female employees was only 3.2 years in 1949 and 5.8 years in 1978. With ever more going to college, and starting work later, the figure is not likely to rise much. What is less comprehensible is that retirement time for most women is not just prior to birth of a child but much earlier, at marriage or even upon starting intensive bridal training. With a bit of will power the working life could be increased somewhat. Instead, the women retire to their homes, where they often have little to do, just so that they can be present when their husband returns and the family will not lose face because the wife "has to earn a living" rather than be supported by her husband. More recently, however, there has been a trend for women between the ages of 40–49 to return to work, usually because they have to earn money, have become divorced or widowed, for starting a real career at that age is unlikely in Japan.

In the nation's social, intellectual, and political life, the

Is there equality of the sexes in the home?

	Yes	No	Undecided	Don't know
Male	42 %	37 %	17 %	4 %
Female	29	49	16	6

Is there equality of the sexes in the area of social norms and traditions?

	Yes	No	Undecided	Don't know
Male	16 %	64 %	14 %	6 %
Female	10	70	11	9

What you think about the discrepancy between the status of women and the status of men?

	Natural	Unavoidable	Not good	Don't know
Male	23 %	54 %	14 %	9 %
Female	18	51	20	11

Are men and women treated equally at work?

	Yes	No	Undecided	Don't know
Male	21 %	57 %	13 %	9 %
Female	13	59	10	18

What do you think about women quitting work at the time of marriage or the birth of a child?

	Natural	Unavoidable	Not good	Don't know
Male	22 %	58 %	12 %	8 %
Female	17	61	13	9

Source: Office of Public Relations, Prime Minister's Office, July 1975

What men and women think of equality of the sexes is not quite equal.

situation is even less encouraging. For example, in 1977, in all the local assemblies which deal with the daily lives of the population, the lowest or grass roots level which should interest women directly, be they prefectural, city, town, or village assemblies, the share of women representatives was only about 1%. Few serve in the civil service, even local ones, except at rather low levels. The only outlet seems to be the Parents-Teachers Association at all schools. Yet, even here, the women seem to accept what is dished out to them and fall all over themselves to avoid assuming responsibility. Women play a minimal—and declining—role in party politics. And, there is the paradox. For, in the first postwar House of Representatives, there were 39 women, whereas only 11 women were elected out of 511 members to the present one. Is it possible that the "modern" Japanese woman has achieved even less than her predecessors? Let us look back and see.

Women, although few, played an active role in the ferment of the Meiji era, even though they had to fight a battle far harder than any man's. Some were in the arts and literature, others in politics. In 1911, Raicho Hiratsuka launched a magazine entitled *Seito* in favor of women's emancipation. In 1920, along with Fusae Ichikawa, Mumeo Oku, and other leaders of the women's movement, she set up the Shin Fujin Kyokai (New Women's Society) to promote democracy and universal suffrage. In 1922, Japanese women won the right to engage in all sorts of political activities, but not the right to vote, not even under the law of 1925. Yet, they continued their struggle until the women's suffrage movement was also crushed by the nationalists. Then, in 1945, without lifting a finger to attain it, suffrage and equality were granted by the new Constitution.

After the war, many women's organizations were founded, often headed by prewar leaders. Shigeri Yamataka, for example, who served twice in the upper house, founded the Tokyo Federation of Women's Organizations in 1948 and became chairwoman of the National Federation of Regional Women's Organizations. Shufuren, the Federation of Housewives' Associations, was also organized in 1948. It grew rapidly, with its own headquarters, hotel, monthly paper, and a nationwide chain-store network of "honest shops" chosen, supported, and sponsored by the union to sell a wide variety of reasonably priced, good quality products. It claimed to have hundreds of groups and as many as a million members. There were also vast numbers of women's organizations in all sorts of fields, labor, farming, consumer protection, etc. But they gradually dried up, as the older leaders disappeared without being followed by younger ones, and few young ones had the initiative to found their own kind of grouping or move in new directions. In politics the situation was particularly bleak. Few women regarded that as a matter of concern to themselves or had the courage to stand up for their rights in any way. Now, women of twenty had the right to vote and those twenty-five and over were eligible to run. From election to election, the number of women voters rose until, in 1968, it passed the number of male voters. Yet, recently the share of women in the lower house has only been about 2%.

For the first time in Japan's history, women have equality within their reach. There is no law preventing them from exercising any activity that a man does, there are no pressure groups keeping them from voting, there is nothing to prevent them from working in any profession and the law guarantees equal pay for equal work. Moreover, their husbands are now physically and intellectually too soft to really oppose them. Yet, the same weakness has overcome the women. They have been brought up more docile than the men, their will and backbone bent. At the same time, they have been spoiled more than the men. This flood of household conveniences that make their lives easier, the streams of consumer goods that make living more attractive, and especially the tidal wave of luxury fashion goods from all over the world have sapped their morale. The only field in which women really push nowadays seems to be fashions, the new horizon, rather than art, culture, or social affairs. Worst of all, the natural spearhead of a women's movement, the more educated university graduates, frequently show little interest in the state of affairs of others once they have entered their gilded cage of a relatively luxurious home with a reasonably well-to-do husband.

Fortunately, not all have sold out. There are still some who fight their individual battles or band together with a few close friends. There are those who choose a career or a modern family life, and impose it on their husbands or at least work out a private arrangement. Others just break away from straight society and enter more off-beat professions. A fair number go off to study, and then live abroad, often marrying a *gaijin* (foreigner). The rest keep up a futile and pointless guerilla warfare of cold dinners and unshined shoes. However, the more isolated and alienated one becomes, the more bitter and extreme the fight, and the fewer who will see it through to the end. Just how isolated women can be in their struggle is shown, for example, by the fact that the most prestigious movement, Shufuren, claims a million members but only five hundred "activists" and that only the Communist Party puts up many female candidates.[22]

Women's lib (*uuman ribu*), which managed to spread around the world and was widely read about in Japan, has only generated rather few groups there, and the fate of the most prominent may be instructive. Although society hesitates to concede this, most divorcees have insufficient alimony, many mothers are deprived of the custody of their children, men still have mistresses (*nigo-san*) or indulge in extramarital affairs of some sort, and illegitimate children do occur. More generally, although use of the "pill" has become widely accepted, in Japan women still have to use awkward contraceptive devices, undergo operations, and frequently have abortions. Thus, Misako Enoki formed a group known as Chupiren, short for "Federation for Free Abortion and the Liberation of the Pill." Rather than tackle the more general problems, and one would hardly know where to start, she chose to help individual women. Forming a small group of activists wearing pink helmets, they hounded the men involved in such cases, not hesitating to storm into their offices or disrupt stockholders meetings to complain. In the highly correct atmosphere of Japan, a man would do anything rather than lose face before the company and nation (for newspaper reporters were always on the spot).

In specific cases, this action was effective, and Mrs. Enoki's group did win. How to spread the movement was another problem. Pink posters on university campuses only recruited a few members. An invitation to fifty women of high social status, including the Prime Minister's wife, was accepted by only one. Rather than move slowly, Mrs. Enoki took page after page from the world book of women's lib. She trained women for a Women's Liberation Army, talked of a new religion for women, and staged shock actions like those above. Ultimately, she decided to form a political party for the elections and, rather than campaign for equality and justice, she spoke of women's superiority. Then, tearing a page from the Japanese politician's book of rules, she demanded that the women running under her banner in the various constituencies should campaign not as individuals with a given platform but under her name. By now Chupiren had gone too far, her party was taken as a joke, and the whole thing fizzled. What's more, Mrs. Enoki had borrowed the money to finance her campaign from her husband, promising to return to the household if she were not successful. And this she did. Her movement folded, without having attained much in its few years aside from some publicity (positive and negative) and helping some individual women, leaving a vacuum presently filled with Dior scarves and Nina Ricci perfumes.

* * *

Then, almost before one knows it, one is old. In traditional Japan, this was no real problem. The aged were treated with respect, there was a place of honor for them in the family and in society. The children they had brought up would look after them in the autumn of their lives. Even old, they would not be treated as a burden; rather, they continued to rule supreme. Since then, the web of tradition has been torn to pieces at all age levels, but nowhere more thoroughly than for the elderly. For the men, much of whose lives had been spent with friends and colleagues at work, retirement is not only a financial blow, it removes their role in society as well. Their wives can continue to look after the home. But over all these years some have never really jelled as a married couple. In earlier days, they would have gone to live with their eldest son or another child. But there is little room for them in the new apartments and houses, nor often in the hearts of the modern "nuclear" families.

One reason the situation is particularly acute is that the increase in this category of the population was so rapid it almost came as a surprise. After the war, life expectancy was rather low and Japan had huge numbers of young people. Today, life expectancy is among the highest in the world, 73 years for men and 78 for women. The number of

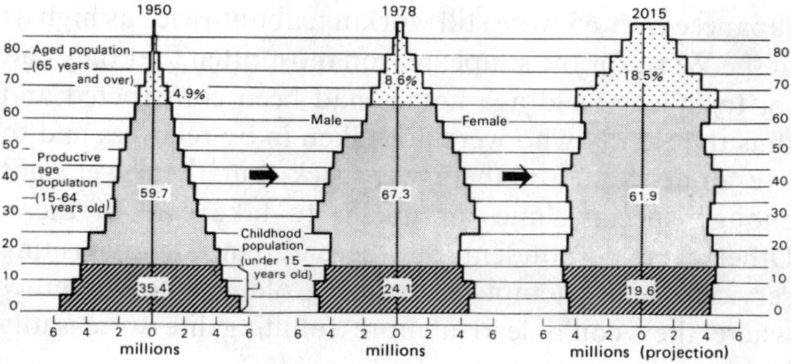

The greying of Japan.

Credit: '79 *Japan*, Prime Minister's Office, p. 43.

those over 65 years of age has thus swollen rapidly, from less than 5% after the war to 8.6% of the population in 1978. It was expected to reach 10% of the population in 1981, and 15.5% in 2005, at which point Japan would have caught up with the West. This tremendous achievement, for that is what it is in one sense, was also a disaster to the extent that it was not expected or prepared for.

For where Japan failed to catch up with the West was in the fields of how to care for the aged and how to deal with them. The old age insurance and pension schemes, social security, and charity, had hardly kept up with the needs. Pensions only averaged out to about 40% of former earnings, in some cases higher, in many much lower. Since the schemes were often recent, many of the aged could expect no pension whatsoever. In general, Japan was only devoting 13% of national income to social security as compared to about 15% in Britain and the United States, 20% in France, Italy, and Germany, and 30% in Sweden. One recent survey of the aged showed that the average pensions amounted to about ¥70,000 a month, while the average living expenses ran into ¥131,000 per month.[23] Thus, it was not surprising to find that about 27% of the

Japanese over 65 were still working, about twice as high as in the West, for the simple reason most often that they had to. Insufficient old age homes had been constructed and thus the elderly who were not taken in by relatives had to live alone. Some of them were sick, but there were not enough special clinics or nurses to take care of them. Others were despondent, but there were not many visiting services. And attempts at forming old age communities where they could lead a more fulfilling life were sadly lacking.

Improvements were certainly coming. But the question was whether they would reach the aged on time. More and more people were qualifying for the better private and government pensions schemes and the amount of money flowing into them is rising. The present younger generation can look forward to reasonably good conditions as of the age of 60. But this does not help those who are now 60 and over but could not contribute the necessary 20–25 years because they were too old when most pensions were launched in the 1960s. Instead, they have to wait until the age of 70 for modest public welfare. At the same time, they usually came under compulsory retirement as of 55. The fact that the retirement age is rising does not help them get through a very painful 5, 10 or 15 years. Thus a special effort is needed to help today's aged, namely the ones who created an economic structure all later generations will benefit from. Another question which might be raised is whether the promised social security and medical systems of the future will ever become a reality. It takes more than just legislation, they must also be funded, and it is increasingly difficult to finance these schemes in a period of slow growth and reluctance to increase taxes. Yet, if sacrifices are not made now coming generations will find themselves much less well provided for than they thought when they get old.

The final problem is that mentalities have not changed quickly enough. It was clear with the growing generation gaps that, even if the aged were taken in by their children, the atmosphere might not be the best. There were still too many sources of friction as well as the very central issue of who would rule the family unit, the aged parents as in olden times, or the adult children. It was necessary for a great change to be made on both sides if living together were to be successful, as indeed it has to be, with 75% of the elderly Japanese still living with their families. A contribution by the aged might be to accept a new role for themselves; for their children, to treat them with more warmth; and for society, to make them "senior citizens" rather than despots or just old people. None of this would be easy or rapid.

Just a few comments from the aged will make their plight clear enough. Financially: "I get a monthly welfare pension of a little over ¥30,000. The amount is to be increased in proportion to price rises but our life gets harder each year, and the savings I had managed to make by economizing on everything while I had a job are swiftly dwindling. What I don't understand is that the increase rate of our pension and that of civil servants are different." Or: "Since the pensions we get amount to only about ¥80,000 a month, the rent (¥30,000) is a big burden for us. We want to move into public housing. However, we have never been successful in the lotteries." Socially: "Although I have grandchildren, I feel I'm still an active, working housewife. But wherever I go, people call me '*obaachan*,' meaning old lady. And yet when I get on the train, people won't give up their seats for me. I feel that this society is made so that older people feel and behave like they are old. I don't think it's right that old people should feel old and become inactive." And morally: "People started greeting me with, 'You look so healthy,' or 'Aren't you sprightly!' and so forth. They say so probably in order to cheer me up, but what they say really hurts me. Sometimes I feel the people really mean: 'Oh dear, you are still alive.' "[24]

By now, there would almost seem to be a crisis with regard to the aged. The government admits this and, on the occasion of "Respect for the Aged Day" every year, speeches are made by politicians and resolutions adopted by young and old. But this is rarely followed up with legislation and, what is far more important, budgetary outlays. It is a bit surprising that more is not done in a country where ministers are usually in their sixties and seventies anyway, and could be expected to take the matter to heart. Perhaps they, like the bureaucrats, have already worked out their own salvation or are under insufficient pressure. Such pressure could only come from the aged, as voters, and indeed as a very large portion of the voters. But like youth, and women, the aged have not united and they lack political clout. Some time ago, a group of senior citizens planned a sit-in at the Welfare Ministry to demand larger old-age benefits. This Japan Federated Activists for Old Age Security was formed in 1962 by Toshio Furuya, who started it after seeing his aged mother die in poverty. Thirteen years later it had 30 chapters throughout the country and 5,000 members: much for a Japanese group, few compared to the number of aged, certainly not enough to get the trade unions, political parties, or government to do anything for them.[25]

So, the problem of old age has remained a "family" problem of sorts, and the elderly are usually forced to turn to the children as the ultimate resort. But they are not always welcome. And, given the earlier relations between young and old, how could it be otherwise? To make things that much worse, the most common case is the hardest. Since women tend to live longer than men, after all these years it is the mother-in-law who comes begging, or stamping into the house, to live there with the *yomé*. How she is received by the daughter-in-law may well be imagined. One elder son recalls how his wife did all the cooking, laundry, and housework for the mother-in-law. Then, three months after the marriage, "my mother yelled at my wife: 'I haven't received the meal expenses from you yet!' " Thus the young couple moved into a house of their own but, after his father died, his mother came to live with them again. "However, my wife's hatred towards my mother had not relaxed over the twenty years and she refused to take the meal expenses that my mother offered to pay and she not only refuses to do my mother's laundry but does not even make satisfactory meals for her. I without a word, prepare my mother's meals in the kitchen. Personally, I feel embarrassed and depressed but I take it as fate that I have a mother like this and thus I cannot scold my wife. In fact, I even feel apologetic towards her."[26]

* * *

The traditional Japanese family, sanctioned by religion and custom, with its close and often regimented relations, was by and large a success. The same cannot be said for the so-called "modern" family system. The sanction it derives from cold legislation and its material and social foundations are still insufficient to overcome the effects of the earlier order. The fact that some family members grew up under the old order, others during the confusion of the war, and yet others during the postwar groping makes it even harder to construct a solid new model. Not all of the effects of modernization and Westernization have been positive, and some forms of "progress" have created more problems than solutions. It is thus perhaps more correct to refer to the family system we described as a "transitional" one. Japan has cut itself off, or been cut off, from its roots and is floating towards something new. Until this new system strikes roots and gains acceptance there is little reason to expect it to be successful.

Regarding *wa* as the guiding principle of Japan's families is a bit ludicrous to anyone familiar with these families and probably only the old people proclaim the goal of "harmony," which will work in their favor, while the younger ones smirk or evade it. Conflict would seem to be as natural a state of affairs. There is conflict between old and young, heirs to different values, living almost in different worlds, but in which the elders are burdened under experiences that are meaningless to the juniors. The younger people may suffer due to the pressure on them, but so do the elders who do not grasp the incomprehension nor understand why the honor they once paid is not returned to them. There is conflict between men and women, forced into different roles and different worlds although modern society and a similar education make most of this pointless. By now the women have ceased accepting discrimination or oppression and give as many blows as they receive, although little of this serves much purpose. For, the conflicts are usually blind; young and old, men and women, form their own groups and communicate poorly, if at all, with one another. The other side does not really know what they want (even when they do themselves).

Where there is little conflict, the alternative may not be harmony, it may be that the family members are leading parallel lives, an official one for the family and a secret one for themselves. Young people who rebel usually do so internally or away from the family. Those who become passively alienated, who lead dream lives or form small friendly groups with colleagues, hardly regard family life as "real." The ones who strike out against society, be they student radicals or juvenile delinquents, always bring about responses of surprise from their parents: not our son, not our daughter, they are not like that! Husbands while away their time quite often with their friends and colleagues, seeking fulfillment at work or the club. The wealthy still have mistresses, the more modest an occasional night out or flirt. And the number of women who have "secret savings" in order to run the household on their own is most impressive, only overshadowed by the small but growing number of women who work as hostesses or even engage in prostitution to earn pin money or simply have sex. Although taking out loans still involves the whole family, each member is more likely to do this on the sly without explaining the needs to the others. Finally, when the real life becomes too depressing or the parallel life collapses, and suicide becomes the only solution, there is often no one among the living to explain why it happened.

Some observers insist that family life is still strong and sound because there are so few divorces in Japan. True, the divorce rate is particularly low in Japan, only 1.09 per thousand persons in 1975, compared with 3.08 in the USSR and 4.80 in the USA. But, the figure is rising, from only 0.79 in 1965 to 1.15 in 1978. Moreover, the social context casts some doubt on the value of the figures. In Japan, divorce is still regarded as a shameful matter, more so for women than men, but at any rate something everyone should try to patch up for the couple concerned. Thus, many couples who would like to separate and indeed would be better off that way come under considerable pressure from parents and children, relatives on both sides, perhaps the religion or cult, and also the company, which does not think highly of divorced personnel. Although the wife is more often the aggrieved party, the initiative rarely comes from the women. Many accept that their husband should have extramarital affairs or even keep a mistress as long as it is done relatively discreetly. This is not indulgence or disconcern, the women would simply not be able to fend for themselves in most cases, since the alimonies are low if obtained at all and few women have independent sources of income or any access to sufficiently gainful employment. "A man and woman living together under one roof" might be a better description of some married couples.

If the Japanese family is to remain a viable unit, it will be necessary to exert exceptional efforts to find a new format and create more positive, or at least tenable relations, first between the couple, then with the children, and finally with the grandparents. None of this will be easy, and the attempts that have been made are not always conclusive. Yet, there has been a lot of experimenting with what is referred to as the "new family" (*nyu famirii*). This style has been given a name, and much publicity, but the details remain to be worked out. For the moment, it is simply the reflection of untold thousands of individual cases with only a vague similarity. The couple is more often a "love match" and the husband and wife usually met at school or work. They went out more informally and knew one another much better before marriage. The wedding was a rather modest affair to which only close friends and family were invited. The honeymoon was also less often the gala trip organized by some travel agency for a batch of newlyweds. They live more often in apartments, but still hope to buy a house. They dress more simply, this sometimes meaning largely in blue jeans.The furnishings are frequently Western, so is the food, and long hours making a Japanese meal may be short-circuited with frozen foods. The husband is less achievement oriented and a position without status, but enough money to get by, is acceptable. He may even let her work. The major innovation, however, is that the husband and wife try to remain a couple, to see one another more often, to bring up their children more frankly and informally and to create a closer unit.

It is too early to tell whether the "new family" will succeed, or whether it will even become widely accepted. After all, it might be just another fad. But, it is still one of the most promising attempts at overcoming the atomization of the individual and the conflicts between ages and sexes. It could even restore some degree of harmony. Until then, however, there are more causes for concern than satisfaction regarding the Japanese family.

NOTES

1. W. S. Egekvist, "'Wa' Holds Key to Japan-U.S. Trade Problem," *Japan Times,* January 4, 1978.
2. See Ruth Benedict, *The Chrysanthemum and the Sword*, pp. 253–96.
3. *Shukan Yomiuri*, August 20, 1977.
4. *Katei To Kyoiku* (Home and Education), NHK, 1976.
5. See Takeo Doi, *Amae no Kōzō*, and Robert S. Ozaki, *The Japanese: A Cultural Portrait.*
6. 1977 White Paper on Youth, Youth Bureau, Prime Minister's Office, November 1977. See also Haruo Matsubara, *Nihon Seinen no Ishiki Kōzō* (Attitudinal Structure of Japanese Youth), Tokyo, Kōbundō, 1975.
7. *Japan Times*, October 7, 1979.
8. *Japan Times*, August 1 & 5, 1978.
9. *Police White Paper,* National Police Agency, July 13, 1979.
10. *Japan Times*, October 16, 1977.
11. *Sunday Mainichi*, October 9, 1977.
12. *Japan Times*, January 11, 1978.
13. *The Rising Younger Generation in Japan—1976*, National Assembly for Youth Development, p. 49.
14. *Shukan Asahi*, November 11, 1977, p. 124
15. Mariko Bando, *The Women of Japan*, p. 18
16. *Sunday Mainichi,* "Pen Salon," September 11, 1977.
17. See Ezra Vogel, *Japan's New Middle Class.*
18. *Shukan Asahi*, "Housewife's Corner, " October 14, 1977, p. 72.

19. For a counterview on the nobility of the housewife's calling, see Suzanne H. Vogel, "Professional Housewife: The Career of Urban Middle Class Japanese Women," *Japan Interpreter*, Winter 1978, pp. 16–43.
20. Bando, op, cit., p. 11 ff; *Japan Times*, September 23, 1979; and *Outline of Survey Results Concerning Women's Participation in the Decision-Making Process*, Prime Minister's Office, June 1979.
21. *Asahi Shimbun,* "Reader's Corner," October 6, 1977.
22. Michael Berger, "Japanese Women—Old Images and New Realities," *Japan Interpreter*, Spring 1976, p. 66.
23. *Japan Times*, September 18, 1977.
24. Ibid.
25. See Erdman Palmore, *The Honorable Elders.*
26. *Shukan Asahi*, November 4, 1977, p. 153.

4
The World's Best —and Worst— Educational System

Together with the Japanese economy, no other institution has reaped as much praise as the Japanese school system. For example:

"Perhaps equally important for a sustained rate of production is the second factor on my list, education. Among the large countries of the world, only the Soviet Union and the United States compare with Japan in the percentage of their population with high school and post-secondary education of various kinds. One can even argue that the Japanese situation is probably better than that of those two countries. As far as 'objective' tests can tell, at least at the high school level the Japanese indeed seem to have achieved American mass education combined with European quality."[1]

A very high compliment indeed, even from the generally lavish Herman Kahn. This is also the view of the Japanese government, the Ministry of Education, and the public in general. They are all extremely proud of the progress that has been made: new schools are opened regularly, there is a rapid increase in enrollment at all levels, and the number of graduates is already impressive. As for quality, without checking further, this seems to be proven by the much publicized phenomenon of "examination hell." However, oddly enough, when one discusses the educational system in greater depth, especially with the students and teachers, one gets a rather different story.

First, a few notes on quantity, something which is far easier to demonstrate than quality. Japan provides compulsory education for very close to 100% of the population. This consists of six years of elementary school plus three years in lower secondary (junior high) school, free of charge. Although the higher levels are not compulsory, and often involve considerable expense, by 1980 some 94% of the children moved on to three years of upper secondary (senior high) school. Parallel to this, there has been a constant increase in the number of high school leavers attending either a two-year junior college or four-year university. At that time, it was already 39% of the total, 44% for boys and 34% for girls. This increase in school attendance has already brought Japan close to the American level, and well ahead of Europe, and the figures keep on rising.

One would therefore expect that, as elsewhere in the world, there would be a trend for post-graduate education to swell. This has not been the case, and only some 5% of the college graduates continue on. Nor is there any particular eagerness either among the students or their potential employers for more. There has also been no serious trend toward continuing or "permanent" education, or of people leaving work to return for further education, or for married women or older people to attend courses. There are very few evening courses and just about no chances for workers or former drop-outs to obtain a diploma later. On the other hand, there has been a very striking trend in Japan to send children to kindergarten prior to elementary school, and not because the parents work, as this trend is most noticeable among the better off and involves quite some financial burden. In 1960, only about 29% of the

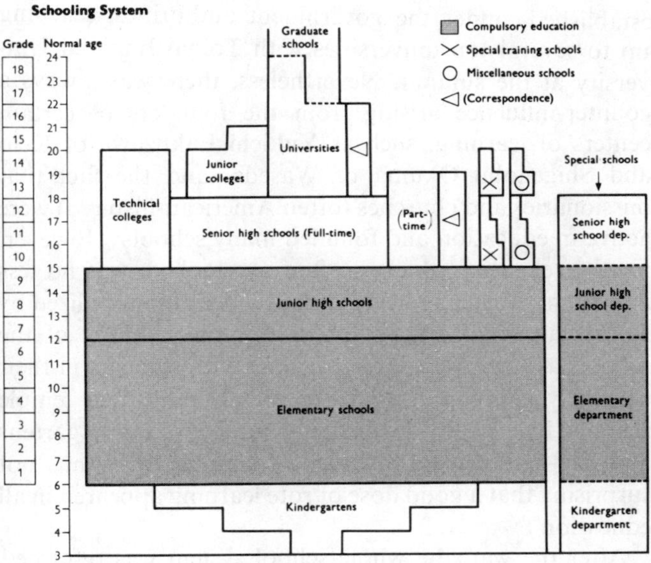

A bottom-heavy educational pyramid: kindergarten wins out over graduate school.

Credit: *Statistical Handbook of Japan 1978,* Bureau of Statistics, Office of the Prime Minister, p. 125.

children went to kindergarten; by 1978, it had reached 64%. Thus, Japan's educational system is extending downward with children attending schools at ever younger ages rather than upwards with education reaching into later life.

Japan's early educational system, after some fluctuation, was patterned on the German system. This was due to elements like discipline, patriotism and moral attitudes more than any question of academic excellence, since such virtues were highly evaluated in the Meiji period. Later, as nationalism grew, any academic freedom was further restricted and a rather rigid hierarchy was established, under the government authorities, reaching up to several top universities with Tokyo Imperial University at the summit. Nevertheless, there was always a counter-influence arising from the founders of certain centers of learning, such as Yukichi Fukuzawa of Keio and Shigenobu Okuma of Waseda, and the fact that missionaries and churches (often American-inspired) were active in education and founded many schools. However, another element, which is often overlooked, was no less important. Teaching had previously been monopolized by Confucian scholars and Buddhist monks. Many of the schools at the lowest levels, dealing with students in their earliest years, continued to be merely renovated temple schools. Even today, an amazing number of kindergartens and day-care centers are run by temples. It is thus not surprising that a good dose of rote learning appeared in all education.

After the war, the whole school system was reformed along the lines of the American system and the "moral education" and elitarian element played down, leaving room for greater democracy. Still, no reform could entirely wipe out the heritage of the past. It is also necessary to remember that this latest "reform" is already over thirty years old and little has been done to accomodate more recent innovations.

*　　　*　　　*

Now, to quality. Japanese elementary and secondary schools are justly proud of the amount of knowledge, i.e. facts and figures, they cram into the brains of their pupils. Indeed, the results are nothing short of phenomenal, certainly as compared with other countries. Japan boasts a literacy rate of 99.3%, second only to the Soviet Union. Its students at high school level also perform extremely well in fields like mathematics, chemistry and physics, and, although this is hard to compare, history and geography as well.

The first task of school is to teach the Japanese their own language, and this is no minor matter, eating up a goodly portion of school time. The Ministry of Education has adopted a standard vocabulary of 1,850 Chinese characters (*kanji*), about half of which must be learned in the elementary school, the rest later. These characters consist of as many as twenty strokes and require a fantastic amount of memorization. In addition, there are two other syllabaries, *hiragana* and *katakana*, used for grammatical purposes or writing of foreign borrowed words, each of them with 48 symbols. For good measure, the Japanese also use the Latin alphabet, which is referred to as *Romaji*, for writing Japanese names and words in English or other European language texts as well as both their own numbering and Arabic numbers. This makes the attainment of "literacy" something that bears comparison with no other country in the world. Still, many feel that at least 3,000 characters, well above the official level, are needed to be a "cultivated" person. In addition, anyone going into a specialization, especially scientific or technical, must know a tremendous number of foreign words, and more and more of these words are becoming essential even in daily life.

The Japanese then have to learn about their country, which has its own complications. History involves more than just an understanding of events and reigns of emperors, plus *shoguns*, plus others. For, the writing of any *kanji* name gives little clue as to how it is pronounced, which becomes another task for rote learning. In addition, since years are indicated in terms of the year of a given emperor's reign ("imperial year" or *gengo*), it is necessary to learn the whole year system plus perhaps an A.D. year to convert to so as to hold things together chronologically.

More rote memory. Then comes mathematics, chemistry, physics, biology, all sorts of scientific subjects, which are again memorized. But at least they all contribute to one's general education. Where memorization really comes into its own is in the preparation for college entrance examinations, which consists by and large of learning the questions and answers to as many past exams as possible.

This keeps the pupils terribly busy during their formative years. They have courses at school, and then two hours or so homework a day in elementary schools, and three or four in high school. They may also have tutoring and cram courses in the evening and weekend and prep schools during vacations. At home they strive under the watchful eyes of their parents and especially mother; at school discipline comes from the teacher (*sensei*) who must be treated with the utmost respect. There is little room for socialization or just relaxation in the system. It is an unremitting grind that starts in early childhood and goes on and on . . .

* * *

What is the purpose of this education? Is it to obtain knowledge that will be useful in later life? Is it due to some abstract love of learning? Is it, as one observer suggested, that "the most characteristic Japanese trait is the eagerness to learn" and that "it's an honor to get ahead, and education is known to be the key?"[2] Perhaps, it may be all of these reasons, but in small doses. The overwhelming purpose in each level of education is quite simply to get into the next level, and then ultimately the university. The whole purpose of nine, twelve or more years study is to pass the entrance examination to the university of one's choice (or that of one's parents choosing). As we have seen over 90% of the pupils proceed to high school, which gives them no particular qualifications for a job or promising prospects for future life, and just about all of them hope to get into the 40% (at most) university seats available. This creates quite a crowd trying to push through what is commonly called the "narrow gate."

Of course, in every school system, it is necessary to have some weeding out each time schooling enters a higher level, but the almost automatic passage from junior to senior high school and the impossibility of receiving too many in college means that the basic screening is concentrated there. Moreover, although there are indeed enough places for nearly half the potential students, society has created an artificial pressure. For, if it were nothing more than a question of getting into any college, there would be little trouble. Rather, the students are trying to get into, first of all, about a dozen top ranking state universities, and then perhaps two dozen lesser, but still rather highly evaluated, colleges, both public and private. This means that in practice there are often ten candidates for one place in the top level colleges, and five to one for the second group, while a person would have little trouble getting into the others. Moreover, if there were just one nationwide examination to pass, as happens in many countries, then a person would prepare once, take one test, and see which college he could get into on that basis. Not in Japan: one has to take a test for each college; and many students end up taking half-a-dozen or more. Those living outside of Tokyo are particularly disadvantaged in having to spend days in a hotel just for the test taking season.

It is this artificially heightened competition that creates the well-known "examination hell." In order to pass, the high school students spend years doing little more than preparing for tests. In addition to the normal school work, they often receive private tutoring or attend cram schools (*juku*). The Education Ministry has indicated that about

40% of the elementary and junior high school pupils were doing this, in addition to virtually every senior high pupil who intended to get into a university. This artificial barrier sets off a rather odd reaction backward. In order to get into a "good" college, one should attend a "good" high school, and for this a "good" elementary school, and on down to a "good" kindergarten. Some children are apparently exposed to "teaching" at the age of three or four.

What is the result of this? With little time to do anything else but learn and study, the children become physically weak and mentally fragile. They may have any number of facts and figures in their brain, but they are socially poorly adapted and integrated, and uncomfortable in many situations that would not concern children in most other places. They are robbed of their spontaneity when young and, more seriously, the crunch comes at the age of about sixteen or seventeen, when the late maturing Japanese also have the growing pains of adolescence and young adulthood. This is the time they would like to live and breathe, discover what life is about and perhaps enjoy it to some extent, show natural signs of rebellion and form a personality. Instead, they are locked up at school, drummed into further study at home, and sent off to cram during evenings, weekends, and vacations. "Eagerness to learn" among the young Japanese is a sad joke; the actual situation is one of tremendous pressure to "suceed." An inkling of the desperation and alientation felt by some can be gathered from the anguish of this student calling out from "examination hell."

"Studying to pass the entrance exams sometimes destroys our friendship or we must abandon the springtime of our life. It is a sad and foolish thing! What is our object for studying? Most Japanese students will say, 'Passing the examination.' But when they pass it, will they be happy? The answer is 'no' as they have lost the object of

Pay attention, children . . . only eight more years to go until college entrance exams!

Photo credit: Japan National Tourist Organization

their life. Their only object is passing it!! But I, who think it foolish, am studying for the examination, too. I am weak. Japanese students are weak. I am a fool. Japanese students are fools. Japanese teachers who teach the techniques of passing a college exam are crazy. Japan is crazy. But I am studying hard for the entrance examination."[3]

A few more particular results may also be mentioned. Since it is so important to get into specific schools, or at least certain colleges, there is a large class of *ronin* students, named after the masterless *samurai* of earlier days, who, having failed their test, or not accepting to attend a lesser college, continue to study for one or more years at prep schools (*yobi-ko*) until they pass the test or finally give up. At a usual examination period, which comes in February and March each year, there are as many as 200,000 students making a second or third try. Those who fail, especially the *ronin*, tend to become warped and twisted psychologically, develop a considerable hatred of society, and certainly no love of learning. Even the *ronin* who make it may feel the shame of falling a year or so behind their age group.

Things are sometimes worse. Professor Masayoshi Namiki of Asahikawa Medical College, who has been studying ulcers in children for some fifteen years, found relatively few cases at first, although there were very few colleges and much more difficulty in getting in. By 1976, he had twenty cases a year. The increase came not as a result of ordinary studies at school but rather stress arising out of the growing pressure placed on children to succeed. For example, 69% of them were attending cram schools and one, a 9-year old boy, was forced to attend three cram schools plus an English conversation school.[4] Then, as the exams approach, one increasingly finds notices like the following in the newspapers: 14-year old boy jumps into the path of oncoming train and is killed instantly."The boy was preparing for his entrance examinations for senior high school. Being the only son, with two sisters, the burden of carrying all his parent's hopes was apparently too much for him, police said."[5] This is no rarity or fluke. According to a recent survey of the Ministry of Education the number of suicides among primary, junior and senior high school students reached a record 335 in 1978. The main reason for those in senior high, and the second cause for those in junior high, was poor scholastic achievement. The suicide figures for these categories have risen steadily over recent years and are expected to climb yet higher in the future.[6]

There is, however, one more side effect that is rarely mentioned, yet has as baneful an impact on society. Japan's whole system of meritocracy and equality of opportunity assumes that every child has the same chance of getting an education which is regarded as the key to later success. If not for the artificially narrow gate, that would basically be the case, especially since compulsory education is free. However, if in addition it is necessary to attend a good kindergarten, to have private tutoring and cram courses, perhaps to go to a senior high school that "guarantees" its graduates will be accepted into universities, then families with money will be in a much better position to promote their children's schooling. All surveys show that the University of Tokyo, as well as the other public ones, have a disproportionate number of children from upper-middle class families. The private colleges, where tuition is often expensive, obviously have even greater percentages. For the family concerned, the cost can be extremely high, and pressure on the child to make good such investments is correspondingly great.

What is even worse is that often devious tricks are used to get around the narrow gate. For entrance is not exclusively a question of passing a test. The colleges are very interested in knowing about the student's personality and receive reports from high school. Thus many parents tend to give their children's teachers expensive gifts during gift-giving season, which few teachers fail to accept. Some also use personal relations, or even a direct bribe, to get letters of recommendation. Apparently, the Japanese legislators are also kept busy during the examination season helping children into colleges, especially state or provincial ones where they have connections. In return, a handsome "gift" in cash is not unusual. But, the system has spread even further, especially for the private colleges whose endowment is insufficient to cover expenses and eagerly accept "donations" from parents not only of students, but also of potential students. This has come to be particularly wide-spread for private (and some state) medical and dental colleges. Tokyo Dental College was reported to be receiving donations of ¥6 million for students in 1972, and ¥14 million only four years later.[7] And Nihon University, one of the biggest in Japan, which announced in 1977 that it was going to stop (although it failed to admit it had ever started) accepting contributions to let in students who failed the extrance exam, was forced to dismiss several professors only two years later for getting students in through "backdoor channels" in return for large cash payments.[8]

Thus, the idea that the entrance examinations rule out any possibility of cheating must be taken with a grain of salt. There is reason to believe that the University of Tokyo (Todai), Kyoto (Kyodai), and other top schools are particularly strict. Yet, Keio University, one of the leading private schools, was rocked by a scandal when it turned out that copies of entrance examinations had been sold by several professors. Then came the turn of Waseda University when answers to the test of the School of Commerce were leaked by the staff. The case of Nara Medical College is even more instructive, for this practice of letting in substandard students had been going on for ten years and involved fully one-third of the student body. In exchange for "donations," students who scored at the bottom in examinations were accepted, while some with passing marks were dropped. Involved in the scandal were not only the professors and dean, but also Diet members and the Governor. The Governor regularly wrote letters of recommendation to the school, run by the prefectural government, on the assumption that the students were substandard, "otherwise they did not have to come to me." And the government seemed less concerned by the fate of the students who had passed the tests and been rejected, or those who had a right to study there, than that of the "backdoor" students who might be disgraced.[9]

* * *

Examination heaven and hell: winners and losers checking their results at University of Tokyo.

Photo credit: Foreign Press Center-Japan.

So, the student has gotten into the university of his choice, or some other. (Let us ignore, for the moment, those who did not make the grade and had to look for a job after high school or take a professional course.) Up to this point, education has indeed been hell for many of them. But, they have learned, or at least memorized, quite a lot. It would be assumed that this process will continue at college until it reaches its culmination with some of the most highly educated students in the world. Is this so?

In Japan, the emphasis has systematically been on getting into a good university. So far, there has been no reference whatsoever to getting into a good profession. Indeed, on the whole, the colleges are rather general institutes of learning in which the students tend to pick courses in keeping with some personal taste, or that of their parents, or the fads, but not on a clearly determined scale of values such as exists regarding the status of the university they hope to attend. And most students, no matter what subject they choose, end up as generalists of one sort or another.

It may therefore surprise the outsider, who hears so much of Japan's technical capabilities, to learn that the number of students of science and engineering is far lower than Europe, the United States, or the Socialist countries. Many more study history, sociology, psychology, or Japanese, English or other literature (this in a country with such poor foreign language speakers). Law is the favorite for students hoping to climb high.

Yet, each one of these fields involves only the shallowest of knowledge, the first two years being much the same for all students, and a bare minimum of specialization occurs during the latter two years. Then, all these subjects, and many more, are used as a foundation for young people going into business, the administration, politics or almost any field of endeavor. One will be amazed to learn that there are no law schools, aside from a small government institute to train lawyers, not enough teachers' colleges to train teachers, few schools of business administration to train potential managers, or even many secretarial schools of value to train secretaries. Only for medicine, dentistry, engineering, and a few other professions or specific trades, are there specialized institutes. But, they are still undergraduate schools. In most of the world, college level training is widely regarded as just a foundation to build on in graduate school. In Japan, it is the culmination of study.

Thus, a mere B.A. or B.S. diploma is the end of the road. But, if that diploma were as hardly won as entrance to college . . . Alas, it is not. For, unlike just about any other educational system in the world, a student who enters the university is almost guaranteed to leave with a diploma. Elsewhere, when one compares the number of entrants with the number of graduates, one finds a considerable drop-out rate. Not in Japan! The statistics of the Ministry of Education do not even have any such category as "drop-outs." They indicate rather that, if you take all the students who were admitted to four year colleges in April 1969, those who graduated in March 1973 were 79.1%. If you add to that the ones who managed to graduate a year later, the figure rises to 87.9%. The remainder were not dropped; no, they were permitted to repeat another, and perhaps yet another year . . . until just about all of them made it. Thus, although it is not really known, the graduation rate is estimated at something like 95% of all students. This can be compared to the situation in other countries, with a rate of 70% in the United States and 88% in the United Kingdom, both relatively lax, and 44% in France and 52% in Germany, where internal barriers in the university block all but the best.[10] This can only mean that the number of diplomas granted by Japanese colleges has little real significance.

If the students were pushed so hard in high school, why this automatic granting of diplomas in college? That is not easy to tell. It may be that in the private colleges, usually overcrowded, understaffed and underfinanced, it is essential to collect as much tuition fees as possible. But that could also be done by having larger entry classes and smaller graduating ones. And, the public universities, including even Todai, also more or less automatically pass their students. It is more likely that once again social constraints put the school administration, and faculty, in a position where they feel obliged to permit graduation of students (supported by their parents) who worked so hard to get into college, even if they slacked off considerably thereafter. What has this done to the university? That question is much easier to answer. Perhaps in the days of reconstruction, with discipline and patriotism driving students on for success and a chance to pull ahead due to one's own efforts, this meant little. More recently, knowing they will ultimately graduate, the trend among the students has been to relax and take it easy after "examination hell" and to turn the universities into centers where social, sports and political activities often overshadow the academic ones.

It is true, the students arrive at the university relatively broken in body and soul. Some are shattered. They have spun themselves out and have no taste whatsoever for learning. And, they are not forced to learn. Lectures are held, but attendance is sparse; there are tests, but not particularly difficult ones. The students who had to fight hard to get into the university can just float with the tide, since almost everyone eventually gets a diploma. Indeed, the university goes out of its way to help the students graduate. The professors call the rolls for compulsory attendance at classes—but close their eyes to the fact that many are missing and some are answering for several friends as well. Lecture notes are copied from one another and, for professors who rarely change, even printed and sold. After the tests, there are make-up tests, and re-make-up tests until nearly everyone passes. If some course or professor is too tough, the students take another to get their credits. And so on . . .

During the whole period, the social aspects receive top priority. Everyone joins a club, and most of the clubs are purely social or sports-oriented, although a few have academic concerns. There are also regional associations for students from out of town. Small outings are arranged, picnics, or ski trips. Some of the more dynamic *sensei* attract groups of students for informal study or social circles. The slouches, for whom commitment to a club is too much, chew the rag in nearby coffee houses or frequent mah-jong parlors. Girls from "good" families, all too numerous in elite private colleges, may wander into town to go shopping. Those less well off are often earning pocket money in part-time jobs (*arubaito*). Indeed, every possible attraction is usually within easy access of the students since most of the campuses are located in larger cities and towns, Tokyo alone having one million students. And, all these things seem to be adequate reasons to cut classes, not show up for or even fail tests, and expect the professor to accept any excuse that can be based on a social commitment. More and more, either because they realize the needs of socialization or because they do not have the courage to go against the trend, this is accepted by the professors.

Of course, radicalism on campus, riots and pitched battles are something else. The university administration and faculty could not ignore this, not because they would not have preferred to keep out of the whole thing, but because most of the battles were on campus and the student movements disrupted the normal college functions. Moreover, some of the disturbances were specifically directed against the colleges the students had studied so hard to get into: inadequate housing, poor service facilities, crowded classrooms, professors who gave lectures with little care as to whether the students followed, and so on. There were sufficient gripes about the university for them not to be forgotten despite the existence of broader issues like Japan's domestic policies and government, or its tolerance, and support, of American policy in Vietnam.

The student movement, Zengakuren, like every movement Japan has seen, split into factions after 1960, and as per usual the factions broke up into even smaller groups and bands, all of which were convinced that they alone knew the right way. Thus, they formed sides, and the battles were engaged as often as not between the student factions controlling one university, or faculty, and the others, rather than against the "establishment" as such. The methods the students used were often brutal, attacking one another with steel pipes and clubs and protecting themselves with helmets. Much of this was doubtlessly politically inspired, and some movements had Communist or Socialist backing and control, although the most radical escaped any of the recognized parties. But the roots went much deeper, and part came from the disorientation of the students' earlier lives and the atomization of society.

By the end of the 1960s, many of the universities were disrupted, some suspended operations, and even the University of Tokyo, the heart of the system and breeding ground for government officials, was closed. At this point, something had to be done. But, by whom? To be fair to the professors and administrators, they hesitated to call in the police because there had been earlier periods of unwanted intervention and they hoped to avoid interference from the government and public authorities. Yet this is not enough to explain it. The professors, like everyone else, were taken by surprise, and did not know how to react. They had also bottled themselves up in their prestigious role of *sensei* too much to have many contacts or any particular influence over the students. Also, like all good Japanese, they hesitated to take any action the results of which were uncertain, and preferred to let things ride. The government was not much more dynamic, but apparently became increasingly nervous. Thus, it was ultimately the police that intervened, protecting the universities and the public from the students, and protecting the students from one another. Finally, in August 1969, a law was adopted placing the onus on the university administration to keep order or face temporary closure and perhaps worse.

Now that pressure was put on the universities to keep order, and the government had the necessary means of repression to back them up, while the police was quite expert at putting down riots efficiently, the trouble quieted down. This may have been fortunate for the students in particular, more of whom had been maimed or killed than any other participant—without accomplishing anything of note as concerns a change of society or of Japanese foreign policy. Indeed, they promptly became calm and almost apathetic. Sports, social clubs, visits to nearby coffee houses, sex in rather modest doses, replaced the more vigorous political activities. The radical factions continued to exist, to proclaim the sole truth, and to periodically attack one another, but the masses of students were busier philosophizing about the future than acting to shape it. Everyone was relieved. And well they might be! Such turbulence was not completely new to Japan, but this time it tended to perplex the general public more than persuading them to make changes, and led to unpleasantness for all concerned.

Thus, we find somewhat greater success, if that is the word, on the socialization than the academic side. For, after the university, the students are indeed socialized and integrated. But, not in society as a whole. Far from it. What they have done is to enter a group, the university, and a subgroup, the club or circle of closer friends. The same applies to any "political" affiliations. And this is the mark they will bear for many years to come. It even helps determine their reactions in completely different contexts such as work or family. This style distinguishes them from other groups and is clearly shown by their approach, language and behavior. They also have a network of personal relations which will work for them. This is more precious, or so it would seem, than any odd bits of knowledge they picked up. Unfortunately, this does not mean that they have acquired the skills they need to accomplish something of value for society. Again, this ignores the specialist, who follows a narrower path into his chosen profession. But, it is the generalist, with his personal relations, rather than the specialist, with his know-how, who on the whole tends to rise in Japan.

* * *

At this point it would seem appropriate to describe the efforts students make to get a job. For, the primary purpose of university, or even high school, was less even to learn or socialize than to prepare for a "good" job. If one is interested in the prime motivation for attending college, "love of education" is not the place to look. Rather, it derives from a simple calculation that every school child knows, and their parents and friends drum into their heads from a very tender age. Yes, education means success. But, in much more concrete terms it means the following. Over the past decades, the lifetime wages of a university grad-

(unit: ¥ thousand)

Male: Average starting salary (9 8 7 6 5)	Male: Schooling differential	Final schooling	Age	Female: Schooling differential	Female: Average starting salary (5 6 7 8 9)
72.8	100	Middle school	15	100	67.2
85.9	118	High school	18	122	82.0
93.0	128	Junior college	20	135	90.7
105.5	145	University	22	149	99.9

Source: *Rodo hakusho* (White Paper on Labor), Ministry of Labor, 1979.

Lesson No. 1 on why it pays to study. Average nationwide starting salary by level of education (June 1978).

Credit: *Facts and Figures of Japan 1980*, Foreign Press Center-Japan, p. 85.

uate averaged as much as 30% to 70% more than those of a junior high school graduate, and even the wages of a senior high school graduate were as much as 20% to 30% higher for the three extra years of study.[11] Even if one were to include the costs involved, namely the university expenses and the loss of wages for three or even seven years, a senior high school, and especially a university graduate, could expect to do considerably better. In recent years, there has been a trend for the return on this educational investment to fall off.[12] But cetainly not enough for students to stop trying for college. The reasons here are equally simple. It is usually the parents or the state who foot the bill and even "examination hell" is nothing compared to the promise of four years relaxation in college followed by a better life in a bigger company. For, along with higher wages, there are also better working conditions and chances of promotion, more generous pensions and retirement possibilities, and especially enhanced prestige at stake.

Moreover, this activity, more than academic or social life, takes up much of the senior year, and already extends into the junior year as the students start thinking about what kind of a job they want, begin dressing better and adopt more positive attitudes about adult life. They often resume communications with their parents. Indeed, the selection of a job is frequently a joint decision, when it is not simply laid down by the parents or results from their connections. The pressure is tremendous, for it is traditionally assumed that a person will already know his future job well before graduation, so that when he leaves the university in March, he can immediately enter his employment in April.

Thus, another rat race is unleashed to get through another "narrow gate." This one is also exceptionally tough to get through because it was artificially narrowed. There is no absolute lack of jobs to go around, not even in times of recession, and in the earlier days, when the students were actively courted by potential employers, there was already tremendous competition. The problem is that all the students want to get into the same "good" companies, rather than just any company, and the "good" companies are not in a position to absorb more than a rather small percentage of them. Thus, for some of the more favored companies there may well be ten, twenty, or more students competing for each job opening, while in less popular ones a mere five, and others jobs just go begging. Nowhere is the competition as fierce as for the upper bureaucracy. In 1974, for example, there were 35,042 candidates vying for only 1,496 jobs.

What the students regard as a "good" job may change. Each year, among themselves, and then with the help of certain polls and surveys, a listing of the top thirty companies or so is drawn up, and they are besieged with applicants. The trends have been for business to rise high

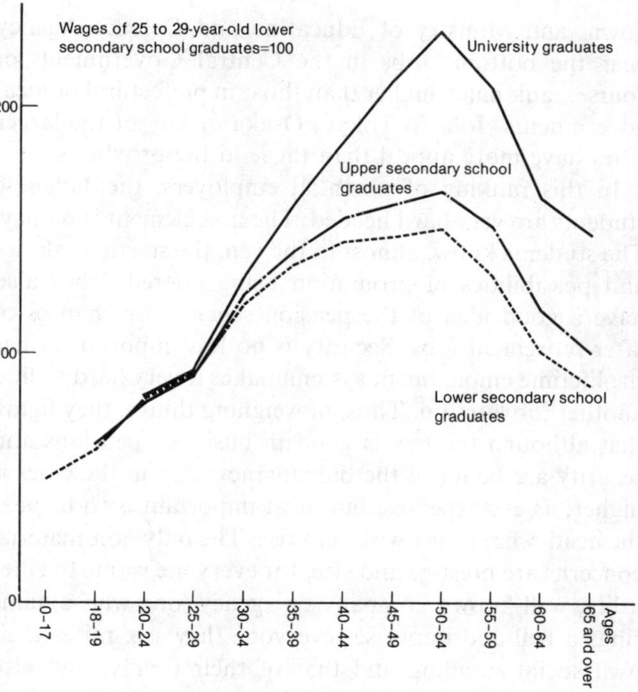

Lesson No. 2 on why it pays to study. Wage differentials between educational categories by age (1978).

Credit: Ministry of Labor, "Basic Survey on Wage Structure."

in their esteem during the boom when possibilities of promotion were particularly great, only to fall during the radical mood of the late 1960s, when business was deemed evil, as well as the late 1970s, when a job in the bureaucracy offered more security. Now, in the business world, nothing is more popular than banks and insurance companies, dull work but little chance of losing your job. In the bureaucracy, the favorites are the Finance Ministry and MITI, with Construction and Home Affairs further down, and Ministry of Education and Defence Agency near the bottom. Jobs in the Central Government, of course, rank much higher than those in prefectural or local governments. Jobs in Tokyo, Osaka or any of the larger cities have more appeal than those in the provinces.

In this ranking of potential employers, the Japanese students are very hard headed. The first element is money. The students know, almost to the yen, the starting salaries and possibilities of promotion being offered. They also have a good idea of the pension schemes or chances of after-retirement jobs. Security is no less important, since the lifetime employment system makes it very hard to find another job later on. Thus, in weighing things, they figure that although the pay is good in business, pensions and security are better in the bureaucracy. Pay in the cities is higher, as are expenses, but most important is to be near the head office if one wishes to rise. The only non-material concerns are prestige and size, for everyone wants to enter a big, well-known company or agency, one whose name rings a bell and impresses everyone they see, raises their own social standing and that of their family, and also presumes sufficient solidity of the employer to carry them through lifetime employment and retirement. For both males and females, the larger the company, the greater the chance of finding more people of their own age, educational and social background with whom to relate less formally. For the girls, size is important for another reason, namely to have a broader choice of young men as potential mates. Missing in much of this is any wish to join smaller companies, even if more friendly or potentially up-and-coming, or people who are trying to fulfill dreams, vocations or enter specializations because that is what they like and makes them happier.

However, to get a "good" job, it is very helpful to graduate from a "good" university. What does "good" mean in this context? As we saw, with the very clear and strict ranking of schools, merely graduating from a top school (what one did there is another matter) gives one a certain status. It also gives one access to the old boy network, which may have ramifications throughout the business world or government, and one of the first things a candidate for any company does is to get the names of the old boys (*sempai*) there. Or, the other way around, the company may send its staff members to their *alma mata* to pick up the best *kohai* there. Most colleges also have placement services, often with huge staffs, which try their utmost to get good jobs for their graduates, and are rated strictly on that account by the students. Often the connections from a given school to a given company or agency are so strong that it is an open secret that graduation opens the side door, or even the front door, to certain jobs. Each college has its own traditional clientele which it has been feeding with staff for years or sometimes decades. In this brokerage, not all school are equally effective and those that succeed, which happen often to be the "elite" schools, are no less elite for having hoisted their students to high postions in the nation.

Thus, although they represent a definite minority in the total number of universities and also the total number of graduates, some few state and private universities have a disproportionately large number of alumni in big business or bureaucracy. The leader is, of course, Todai, followed by Kyodai and Hitotsubashi among the public schools, while Keio and Waseda stand out among the private colleges. All the findings support this contention. Yanaga's figures for 3,000 top corporation executives showed Todai with 21%, Kyodai with 7%, Hitotsubashi with 6%, Keio with 7% and Waseda with 4%, nearly half the total. Mannari's study indicated that as late as 1970 Todai had 32% of his business elite and all the elite universities 70% of the total. And just recently a much broader survey of nearly 25,000 section chiefs still gave the top five schools (Waseda, Todai, Keio, Chuo, and Kyodai) about a third of the total.[13] In the higher bureaucracy, the state universities, and especially Todai, have an even more prominent position. Among the successful applicants for the 1,496 select jobs in 1974, 435 came from Todai and 191 from Kyodai. In certain other professions, a given school has often been in the forefront such as Waseda for journalism. In their respective geographical regions, the national public and prefectural colleges equally hog the jobs.

In earlier days, the rushing of companies already began in the junior year, and as often as not the rushing came from the companies, which would eagerly receive the potential graduates and sometimes entertain them quite lavishly. With the recession, things were reversed, with the students hoping to find a job as soon as possible and the companies cooler. This led the businesses, the universities, and the Labor Ministry to try to institutionalize the process by making October 1 (i.e. roughly six months before graduation) the official opening day for visits to firms. Yet, well before this, already in the summer vacation, the job-hunting season actually began, with senior students dropping into big companies to do "research" and especially going out to meet friends or former schoolmates working at these companies who might serve as useful contacts. Some of them were even tentatively employed. This meant that, for all practical purposes, part of the junior and senior years were still disrupted as the students sought jobs rather than studying, and, when they found a job, their academic efforts tended to drop to the minimum necessary to graduate.

So, finally comes the big day, October 1. Even for those from good colleges and with good marks, there is no time for complacency, for just about everyone is trying to get into the same few companies. They often get up early in the morning and rush to the company head office only to find that there is already a long line of applicants waiting to get in for an interview. And this goes on for weeks. To get some idea of what it all involves, let's take a look at the diary of a Waseda student who visited no less than thirty companies: after all, as he explained, "quantity is the name of the game; if I visit a lot of them, I should be able to hit one."

"Got up at 5:00 in the morning. Left home. Sleepy. Reached Marubeni Head Office at 6:30. Already three people there. We were made to discuss the topic 'How Should Japan Carry On in the Future?' After that, visited Suntory, Nissho-Iwai, and Mitsui. Forgot to take lunch. . . . 10: 30 Marubeni for the second time. A group discussion again on 'Japan's Future.' The fellow from Tokyo Institute of Foreign Studies tried to make international relations—probably his field—the main topic. However, I took the leadership advocating various art theories. I think I overdid it when I went so far as advocating the liberalization of pornography. . . . To NCR for the second time. Was told that they do not need someone with as much vitality as I have. To Mitsuhoshi Bussan via Kataoka Bussan. They were impressed by my coming, saying that it was the first time a university graduate visited them. . . . Ohsawa Shokai. Was told 'you're late in coming.' But, it's only a week since the official opening of company visits! . . . Postal and Telecomuuunications Bureau, Nikka Whiskey, and Japan Victor. Japan Victor tells me openly: 'We more or less already know who we want. We are meeting people like this just for formality's sake.' Impermissible attitude! Then went to Shochiku, and came home earlier than usual. Don't feel well."

Goodness knows what happened to that particular young man, who in addition to being energetic and dynamic was a very bright and successful student. Hopefully, these attainments, which in other societies are admired, were not held against him. It would be a pity. After all, as he said in summing up: "Yes, I visited a lot of them, and energetically. If I don't get into any of them, I'll really curse Japan."[14]

Then, on November 1, the company entrance examinations begin. These tests are open to all students, from any college, and the results do play some role in the choice of future employees. There is no doubt that an extremely high score will be helpful. There is also no doubt that the companies are looking for much more than just smart employees. They are looking for compatible staff, their kind of men (and maybe women). This means that there is a definite tendency to pick their future employees from a given university quite simply because the students have a suitable approach or style. Personality also plays an important role. The company wants a compliant person who will fit in with its structure and policies, not someone with too much vitality or who is too dynamic and may rock the boat. A good employee is one who is a blank page on which the company can write what it wants. That is why many of them prefer generalists to specialists, and they particularly like a "well-rounded personality." Far from complaining, they seem quite happy that the students have been relaxing and socializing for four years or more in college and are all the easier to shape.

More unpleasant is that there is increasingly little doubt that the job entry procedures are not quite as fair and open as they are supposed to be. First of all, it is a bit odd to hold the interviews first, meet the candidates, and only test them later. In addition, it is well known that long before the official interviews many student have begun making contacts in the companies through the old school tie. Here, especially, a good connection can go a long way. The company does not really object much either, since it will be stuck with the employee for another thirty years. There is no better way of getting inside information about the candidate's *real* personality. Due to the personal intervention, the personnel officer also has someone to shift the blame to if the employee does not turn out to be good. And, the new employee will tend to mind his manners so as not to offend the party that recommended him. All this relegates the examination, the only objective barrier, to a minor role. Indeed, one personnel officer went so far as to state: "The game is already over in October. Kind of a ceremony this, I mean the tests."[15]

One might even be so coarse as to say that connections are really the name of the game. This, at any rate, seems quite clear to the students themselves, and their parents, who put in a lot of effort to find the right *koné*. There are plenty of samples of grieving by those who do not quite make it. One job-hunter writes: "Since I have no connections in bureaus of education in any of the prefectures, my employment cannot be guaranteed even if I pass the exams, so I must keep on taking tests." Or a letter by a younger sister who was worried about her older sister, a girl graduating from a well-known first rate university, but whose father unfortunately had no connections. But what rejoicing in the family when, by "extracting a connection from my father's connectionless connections," they found her a job.[16] Of course, it is not expected that parents who have gotten their children into jobs through pull should go around writing letters to the editor to brag about it, although they won't hesitate to tell their intimates over a glass of whiskey. Instead, we have to refer back to one of the few Japanese who has committed the unpardonable sin of telling the truth about the situation to foreigners,

Japan's ex-Ambassador Ichiro Kawasaki in *Japan Unmasked*.

"If my son graduated from a university but failed to secure a good job, I would go to a good friend of mine who happens to be chief exective of a well-known business firm and ask him if he could use his influence to have my son employed in the firm. The chances are that my son would be accepted in preference to other candidates who applied for the job through regular channels, provided he was not a hopeless imbecile. In a case like this the executive would drop one candidate out of the few slated for employment. In the Japanese parlance my executive friend 'honored my face' by not refusing my request, simply because I was a good friend of his and he was therefore duty-bound to accede to my request."[17]

Nevertheless, judging by the pushing and jostling to get through the "narrow gate" one would assume that there were simply no jobs available. This is very far from the truth. Even after the oil shock, there were an estimated 2.1 job openings for each candidate in 1975, and as unemployment reached a peak there were still an estimated 1.5 job openings per candidate in 1977. In a survey by the Ministry of Labor then, it turned out that the number of situations open exceeded the number of candidates for eleven famous private colleges. Why? Quite simply because 80% of the job seekers wished to join a first class firm (i.e. one with over 500 employees), while these firms could take on at best a quarter of the new graduates. The problem was thus that all too many students would only settle for a job "befitting" them (calculated roughly on the basis of how their university ranked and what their schoolmates got). Thus, those whose parents could afford it, arranged to fail a few courses and stay on until something better turned up, reinforcing a rather purposeless class of students called *shushoku ryunen* ("staying on an extra year at the university for employment reasons"). Others, who failed to find the job they wanted, became a second category of *ronin*, this time masterless employees, looking for the big chance next year. Some, however, did accept lesser jobs. The unfortunate thing was that many of them left the job as soon as they found a better one or when it clearly did not match their desiderata.

This rejection of smaller companies is not even a question of money, for many of them are doing as well or better than larger companies, and can offer more interesting or challenging work. But the students, and their parents, have so thoroughly brainwashed themselves with the idea of entering a top company that they accept nothing but the best. Anything less is a loss of face and even caste. But, this haughty behavior is certainly not going to help. In the future, like it or not, more and more of the college graduates are going to end up in smaller companies and even in jobs that in no way call for a college education, such as taxi drivers, mailmen, or salesmen. According to a study by the Japan Economic Research Center, by 1990 only 30 to 40% of the university graduates will be employed in managerial positions as opposed to nearly 70% today. The others will have to go into professional, clerical, blue collar, and lesser posts.[18]

This study indicated that there was a definite surplus in college graduates, and one that was going to keep on growing. Whereas in 1965, college graduates only represented 10% of all those seeking employment, by 1975, the figure had risen to 30%, and could be expected to hit 43% by 1990. There would then be far more college graduates than needed to fill posts suited to them and far too few high school graduates. There would also be a shortage of professional, technical, and clerical workers. Even now, there is a serious imbalance and employers only offer 1.5 positions for each college graduate while the more lowly categories are wildly sought after: 1.7 openings for each senior high school graduate and 4.2 openings for each junior high school graduate.[19] Thus, one manager complained:

"Many of the medium and small companies want junior high and high school graduates. However, since the number is limited, some companies reluctantly hire college grads. But the good people are already taken by the good companies and the left-overs are usually very good at quibbling. Their salaries are higher than the high school grads so human relations within the company, between the college grads and high school grads, don't go smoothly. . . . I think that a normal employment or job seeking situation can be obtained only when three or four universities collapse each year and there are less surplus college graduates."[20]

Even the students, who complain roundly and bitterly about the quality of facilities, the teaching, the costs, and the outside world in general, sometimes complain about themselves. As one female university grad wrote:

"I feel that under the present circumstances, it is rather natural that university graduate girls find it difficult to obtain good jobs. Not only is the average length of service to the company shorter than junior college graduates, most of these girls have spent four years pursuing leisure and fashion and the fact is that their academic level is not much higher than that of the junior college graduates. Nevertheless, they go around claiming that the companies should open the doors for them. This is indeed an *amaé*."[21]

* * *

Japan has undergone a tremendous expansion in the educational sector over the past century, since the country was opened up, and also just within the last few decades.

Primary education for all, which was just a goal a century ago, has been attained, and secondary education for all is nearly achieved. Growth beyond high school level has come more recently, but at an incredible pace. The number of high school graduates going on to higher education was only about 17% in 1966, rose to 24% by 1970, and passed 39% in 1980. At the other end of the system, the number of first graders who attended kindergarten rose from 29% in 1960 to 64% in 1978.[22]

Obviously, in order to keep up with this expansion, Japan kept on building new schools and facilities and hiring new personnel. Since this effort was made at the same time as its general economic expansion, it was probably hard pressed to guarantee the same quality it desired at a time when manpower and material goods were under such strong demand from other sectors. Although there is reason to believe that a school system can expand reasonably well even if the physical plant is not quite perfect, there is also reason to fear that if the human element is not up to the task the whole system will collapse (if not physically, then perhaps academically or morally). And, it is on this side that Japan has encountered a lot of difficulties, most of which are hardly known outside, or even inside, the country. Evidently, during the rapid expansion of the economy, it was not easy to draw away personnel to fill the increasing number of schools and classrooms. There were periods when the expansion resulted in the same number of teachers handling much larger numbers of students. Over time, however, this was improved somewhat and, if not yet satisfactory, the student-teacher ratios in Japan are not much better or worse than any advanced country. One problem, however, is that Japan has both a public and private sector, and the public schools have far more teachers per student, thus skewing upward the "average" rate.

However, the real problem is probably of a different nature. In the early days, education was regarded as one of the nation's supreme missions and it attracted some of Japan's greatest thinkers and doers at the highest level. The prestige attached to the *sensei* was so great, and even the remuneration so attractive, that many outstanding people came to teach the rising generations. After the war, economics prevailed, and both the prestige of the teacher and the remuneration of educators were greatly devalued as compared to those of the businessman or bureaucrat. Teaching was rarely taken as a first choice by university graduates, and many grads simply sat for the teaching exam in case nothing else turned up. This is doubly unfortunate, since what was most needed was a vocation, and these "just in case" candidates sometimes got marks higher than other people who might have made devoted teachers. In addition, potential teachers did not have to go through a teachers' college but took only a few hours of teaching courses and an exam. So, often without vocation or previous training, and with some anger at being relegated to such a lowly position, a very mixed batch of personnel filled the schools. All this could have been made up for if there was some further training, but many teachers ended up facing students without having learned a thing about pedagogics, or public speaking, or having taken more than a few trial classes (and this often with very little supervision).

The teachers who were thrust into classrooms after the war were certainly not in as enviable a position as their prewar predecessors, backed by society and tradition, endowed with authority by the emperor, and bearing the glorious title of *sensei*. Once, they could expect the utmost attention and discipline from their students and support from the parents. They read from books duly authorized by the Ministry of Education and taught a widsom that was rarely contested. After the war, the sources of knowledge, the contents of textbooks, the choice of ruling virtues, and the very role of the *sensei* were all questioned. There were bitter quarrels between the political parties as to what children should be taught, ending in such a deadlock that "moral education" was watered down and imposing discipline in the classroom not really seen as good. The more concrete subjects, mathematics, geography, and so on posed no real problems as to their contents, but certainly as to the method of teaching. The learned *sensei* holding forth in front of a classroom that obediently copied his every word could no longer succeed, and some students dutifully learned without understanding while others simply paid no attention.

With the years, the old-fashioned teaching methods and the tremendous generation and mentality gaps between the teachers and the students undermined the system. The more spectacular events in the universities were obviously better known, oscillating from student radicalism and violence to more recent indifference and a very tame "hedonism." What was happening at the lower levels was probably more serious in the long run. There, the generation gap was even greater and the pressure to succeed such that many personalities were shattered in one way or another. The most striking concerns recently included an alarming trend toward absenteeism and dropping out among those who felt they would never make the grade. Some of them merely ceased learning, others struck out against the schools, the teachers, the parents, and society in general. Smoking at school, once unheard of was now occurring in many high schools; away from school, some endulged in glue sniffing and drugs. There was increasing use of violence against the teachers—and the good students—that left those in authority perplexed. The reactions of acceptance and "this too shall pass" were usually more highly regarded than imposing discipline, but utterly ineffective. However, the most general solution really wasn't one at all, namely to dump the bad elements from the high schools into vocational schools and, if they still created trouble, to drop them from the vocational schools and dump them on society.

Some of the fault, both for the present situation and the failure to overcome it, was due to the teachers themselves. They had become so touchy about discipline, which was a very delicate matter since the war, that their first reaction was to limit it, at least as far as they were concerned. Aside from pay raises, the Japan Teachers' Union (Nikkyoso) showed particular energy in protecting "academic freedom" by, among other things, keeping the police off the campuses as long as possible, trying to defeat the establishment of a chief teacher (*shunin*) system in the public schools and even avoiding a work efficiency rating system. Yet, they were not without blame in what had happened. At all levels, there was a tendency for the teaching to be rather dull and wooden, for them to make lectures (often repeated from year to year) with little attempt at communication, and some did not even come to class on time or bother checking how their students were doing. Informal relations were hardly better and few of the teachers knew as human beings the pupils and students they were directing. This atmosphere easily degenerated into rote learning and memorization for those who wished to succeed and utter disconcern and sometimes rebellion by the others. Moreover, how could they impose academic standards when so many teachers and professors were not really keeping up with things themselves? There were any number whose stock of knowledge was complete on graduation and simply stopped learning. There were teachers of English who hadn't spoken English in years and "experts" on socialist or developing countries who had never been there. Some became lazy once they received tenure and "lifetime employment." Worst of all they retreated to an "ivory tower" which was not only away from society but also remote from the students and from one another. Each group of teachers or professors, especially at the university level, formed its own clique and then engaged in factional struggles to get the plums of professorships or jobs for their acolytes. These cliques often traded academic barbs with one another but rarely engaged in anything like multidisciplinary study or cross-fertilization.

The administrators were largely concerned with making their establishment run, expanding it, modernizing its physical plant, and perhaps rising a notch in the rankings of schools. In the public school system, at least they had more or less adequate finances for the purpose. In the private sector, aside from a few elite schools, most of the others were constantly on the lookout for funds. They had to make extraordinary efforts to get even modest state subsidies. Otherwise, they turned repeatedly to their alumni, the students, and future or potential students. Very large sums were charged for taking entrance exams, those who tried out for several colleges had to pay a year's tuition in advance which they lost if they went to another college, the tuition fees were high at all levels and growing very rapidly. In addition, the students and their parents were often expected to make "voluntary" contributions to the school and donations were also accepted from those who failed the exam but were then let in through the back door. To keep up their finances, many of the schools hardly set limits on the number of students accepted, often going well beyond the official level, as they squeezed more and more students into less place, with fewer personnel, to keep on a sound commercial footing. This applied not only to a few institutes of learning but to many of Japan's schools, from the kindergartens, to the cram and prep schools, to the universities, representing a sector that was often larger than the public sector. (Fully 80% of the university students attend private colleges.)

As for the Ministry of Education, it is hard to understand exactly what its role is. True, it does lay down general guidelines regarding courses and curricula. But it stands by as they are distorted and replaced by cram courses for college. It establishes certain academic standards. But it permits schools to fall below them. It does not react to problems like suicide, or lack of discipline, and it allows the "examination hell" to invade its establishments. It authorizes private schools and colleges but does not impose academic standards or even limits to enrollment. It does not plan or implement projects so that the supply of graduates may meet the expected demands of the economy or society. It has permitted the return of the elite structure, and even encouraged it by overendowing Todai and Kyodai as compared with other schools. It does not provide a single national test (to the exclusion of all others) for entrance to all its universities. And it completely forgets the need for any examination to graduate from university. The Ministry of Education cannot be unaware of the problems, especially not given the number of excellent books written by leading scholars to criticize them. Indeed, one such critic, Michio Nagai, was Minister of Education for a while. But, the Ministry seems to live in a super-ivory tower impregnable to outside concerns.[23]

* * *

So, let us return to the more widely known views on Japanese schooling as propagated by official Japanese representatives and amplified by proponents of their educational system here and abroad. "European rigor, American scale, Japanese intensity—those words capsule education in Japan, possessor of one of the world's most

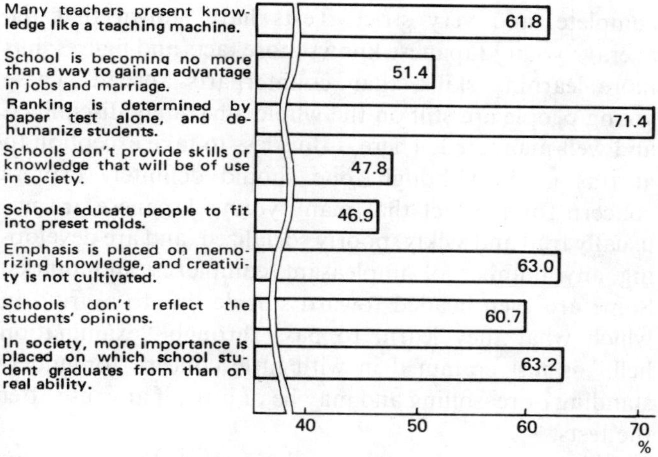

Source: *World Youth Survey,* Youth Bureau, Prime Minister's Office, 1972

What do Japanese students think of the world's best educational system?

Credit: *The Rising Younger Generation in Japan,* National Assembly for Youth Development, p. 53.

advanced and successful school systems." This comes from Bill Forbis' "inside" book on Japan. And Ezra Vogel, who would have America emulate Japan, claims of all things that "as a result of the examination system the nation acquires a large reservoir of well-trained people with a substantial core of common culture, people who are curious, teachable, disciplined, and sensitive to humanistic and civic concerns." These are typical of some of the stuff one reads. The only drawback is that they do not quite correspond to even the shallowest understanding of how the system actually functions and would make any Japanese student or teacher snicker, if they were not too polite to do so with foreigners, and "experts" to boot. [24]

It is true, and it has been proven, that primary and secondary education in Japan is very thorough, very complete, and very strict. Tests have shown that the average young Japanese knows more facts and figures, has more learning skills, than counterparts abroad. These young people are still on the whole amazingly disciplined and well-mannered. There is thus less to take exception to at this level. Although, one should definitely express concern for the fact that many young Japanese are unusually frail and sickly, poorly socialized, and are developing any number of unpleasant complexes and quirks. Some are even headed toward suicide due to a grind in which what they learn, to pass through "examination hell," is just crammed in with little concern for understanding or reasoning and may be of little, if any, use after the tests.

Still, even the staunchest admirers of Japanese education must admit that no matter how good the education is at lower levels, there is little point to that effort if the foundation is not built upon later on. Unfortunately, the university level is where the educational system really performs worst, and in many ways wipes out all the gains of earlier years. Nothing should be said about education in Japan without a very good look at the university. For, this is the apex of the system more than anywhere else in the world, with everyone striving from the very youngest age to get into college. Everything before is just preparation, a costly and painful one often, to which the students must sacrifice themselves. Unfortunately, it is also the apex because very few go on to graduate school. Yet, it is an increasingly pointless achievement as more and more students attend college, probably well over half the student population by the end of the century, in a society that is not quite certain what to do with them all.

The worst and most obvious failing of the colleges and universities is that they simply relax the pressure and make graduation so certain and easy that the students do not work hard nor learn much. Indeed, there is reason to fear that many students graduate from college knowing no more, and perhaps less, than when they entered. Of course, Japan has not held many comparative tests at this level so the standing of its students is largely a matter of conjecture. Nevertheless, observations by Japanese and foreign students and educators make it clear both that the Japanese have learned less than in most other countries and certainly also much less than they would have learned in a better system. The graduation rate, which is inordinately high, is probably the best objective proof of the system's laxity. Without having to study, the students engage in social and political activities, which partially make up for their earlier lacks . . . but can create other problems when they have to adjust to "real," i.e. professional life.

There is little love of learning or academic calling in all this. Indeed, the people who suffer most are the rather bookish students who are regarded as "eggheads" or "bookworms" (*gariben*) and at best tolerated. If they cannot be drawn into the social circles, they are simply left on their own, outcasts in the institution theoretically built for them. The same applies to any professors or teachers who want to bring learning of some sort to their students and find them unreceptive at best, aside from a few, while many simply cut classes and cram for the periodic tests. If they insist too much on study, the students will simply cease taking their courses. Unpopular teachers fare little better than unpopular students. How anyone can expect much "love" of learning, however, is a bit incomprehensible, since primary and secondary education was such a grueling experience that, if anything, hatred and anguish was aroused toward the "learning" process. Moreover, most of the facts and figures crammed in throughout the educational system were for very specific reasons: first, to get into a good college, then, to get a good job. The girls, who could conceivably devote themselves to subjects they are really interested in, are kept busy learning the necessary accomplishments for marriage.

Even without "love" of learning, the sytem could have encouraged professionalism and specialization. But, it does not do that. For, the students are allowed to study pretty much what they want to with little consideration of the needs of the labor market. Moreover, the companies and bureaucracies make the leeway greater by taking in generalists to reach their highest positions. Then, after getting a job, people are traditionally shifted around from one division to another, one task to another, so that anything specific one would have learnt would have little overall relevance or purpose. Moreover, according to recent surveys, the liberal arts majors are finding it easier to get jobs than the science and engineering students. Worse, the specialists are limiting their possibilities and labelling themselves by getting into a technician slot that does not lead very far. Why then should anyone work harder to obtain a technical or specialized education or attend post-graduate courses?

This lack of professionalism is clearly seen in the Japanese companies and bureaucracies and even their teaching establishments. It is amazingly enough found also in the field of research, where purely commercial, product-oriented work is excellent, while basic research that does not promise an early pay-off is highly limited. There are relatively few institutes to carry on such work, since the companies are not interested, the government does not have the money, and the universities do not regard that as a major task or have the graduate-level personnel to do the work. Research in the social sciences or economics is that much more limited. Naturally, such intangibles as inquisitiveness or imagination, vision or creativity, receptiveness or sensitivity, things that have often transformed the world, fare even less well.

There is one other negative aspect, elitarian hierarchy among all colleges, ranking them and through them their graduates for life. Despite the efforts of the occupation authorities, the prewar system of "elite" schools was recreated. What is more, the earlier system of "elite" high schools leading into the "elite" universities is also developing nicely. The University of Tokyo used to draw most of its students from certain public high schools. Now it has tests that should offer equality to all candidates. Yet, somehow it lets in far more from the expensive high schools and prep schools whose whole teaching program is slanted toward preparing for Todai tests. (Indeed, the high schools are ranked by how many of their graduates get into Todai.) But the pyramid extends much further. For example, the old Peers School, created to train the Imperial family and former peers, since turned into Gakushuin High School and University, is still attended by the Imperial family. Some of the private colleges also have their own high schools and even junior high schools, each given a quota for entry to the next higher level. This includes such top schools as Keio, Waseda, Aoyama Gakuin, as well as many lesser ones. And primary schools are serving as feeders to these junior high schools, and kindergartens as feeders to them.

But, what is the academic value of, say, a Todai diploma? To be perfectly frank, no one, neither the students, nor the parents, nor the teachers, nor the state actually knows. Since membership in the Todai or other "elite" club almost guarantees that one will get a good job, this is no way to compare and evaluate students. There are, however, reasons to doubt that these top schools are always that good. It is true that the state colleges do have a lower teacher-student ratio, as do some of the better private schools. They generally also have a better faculty and facilities. Finally, they take in the "best" high school graduates. On the other hand, all these students know from the day they enter that they do not really have to work hard to make good. Meanwhile, those from smaller, less well known or provincial colleges are keenly aware that they can only succeed by working particularly hard showing greater drive, and certainly some of them do. Others may give in to despair at knowing they can never quite make up for this initial handicap, and a few simply develop a "second-rate" mentality. Since there are no uniform nationwide tests to compare all graduates, one has to fall back on personal observation. Yet, one rarely hears that the "elite" school graduates are systematically outstanding or different in any way except for their feelings of belonging to an "elite."

Unfortunately, no one really seems to care. For, in Japan, a person is judged far more than necessary by the school he came from, whether top or second-rate, and not nearly as much as he should be on his own personal merits. This categorization is deceptive, but simple, and has been adopted far too much by not only employers but the public in general. It is not only easier to get a good job if one comes from a top school. It is easier to enter better society. It is easier to obtain a good match if the prospective bride or bridegroom attended a well-known college. And, even the children may get off to a better start. "Meritocracy" is often given as a major principle of Japanese society. Yet, this has nothing to do with merit. It even goes beyond a mere question of academic background (*gakureki*). For that reason, it is perhaps better to speak of a "schoolocracy" and "schoolism," one that separates the "successes" from the "failures" at college entrance time and marks the path they shall follow for life.

Oddly enough, although the system is overwhelmingly

accepted in the sense that it perpetuates itself with little change, it is not really desired or even praised by many of those most intimately concerned. Neither the students nor the teachers like the position they are in and they try to revolt in one way or another. Although criticized as a breeding grounds for "salarymen," the potential employers have recently had to be prodded into hiring college grads, especially female ones, yet gladly accept high school leavers. Former Minister of Labor Ishida complained about the distortion of the educational system and the tendency of students to "aim for something higher than what one deserves." In particular, he characterized this as an age of "low academic level—high educational background society."[25] There have been complaints by leading educators like former Minister of Education Nagai, who felt that the schools in Japan "came to be characterized by the easy adaptation to the practical needs of society rather than by their long-term contribution to the formation of culture through the detached pursuit of truth. Education designed to develop men who think for themselves has already been abandoned."[26]

Nevertheless, nothing much has been done to carry out a complete or partial reform of the educational system. Most changes are a bit superficial and not always complied with. Thus, the machine has kept following the same old ruts for over thirty years now and, where it has veered from that course, it has tended more often to go back to discredited prewar models than to move ahead to something new. By now it would seem reasonably clear that there is some need for change. But, there is no reason to assume that it is on the way.

Notes

1. Herman Kahn, *The Emerging Japanese Superstate*, p. 119.
2. William H. Forbis, *Japan Today*, p. 112.

3. See the informative prize-winning essay by Barbara Fujiwara, "Some Concerns About the Entrance Exam System in Japan," *Japan Times*, December 29, 1978, p. 10.
4. *Japan Times,* September 27, 1977.
5. Ibid.
6. *Japan Times*, February 27, 1979.
7. "Inside the Weeklies," *Japan Times*, March 29, 1976.
8. *Shukan Shincho*, December 8, 1977, p. 136, and *Japan Times*, July 3 & 4, 1979.
9. *Japan Times*, November 10 & 12, 1977.
10. *Educational Standards in Japan 1975*, Ministry of Education, Science & Culture, p. 56 & 58.
11. Ministry of Education, op. cit., p. 22.
12. *Sunday Mainichi*, November 13, 1977, p. 37.
13. Chitoshi Yanaga, *Big Business in Japanese Politics*, p. 32, Hiroshi Mannari, *The Japanese Business Leaders*, and *Japan Times*, October 24, 1979.
14. *Shukan Asahi*, October 28, 1977, p. 36.
15. *Asahi Shimbun*, November 11, 1977.
16. "Readers' Corner," *Asahi Shimbun*, October 6, 1977.
17. Ichiro Kawasaki, *Japan Unmasked*, p. 149.
18. *Japan Times*, April 12, 1978.
19. *Japan Times*, November 31, 1977.
20. *Shukan Shincho*, September 29, 1978, p. 23.
21. "Readers' Corner," *Asahi Shimbun*, October 6, 1977.
22. *Facts and Figures of Japan 1980*, pp. 91–97.
23. See Michio Nagai, *Higher Education in Japan*, 1970.
24. Forbis, op, cit., p. 112, and Ezra Vogel, *Japan as Number One*, p. 167.
25. *Mainichi Shimbun*, December 3, 1977.
26. Nagai, op. cit.

5

Strange Ways of the "Economic Animal"

Japan has risen in a bare three decades from a defeated country with a devastated economy to the third greatest economic power in the world. It has done all this with the most meager of natural endowments since the country has few raw materials, limited farm land, and high population densities. It obviously could only have reached its present level through hard work: importing raw materials, processing them, and then exporting them, seeking out new processes, technologies, and products, manufacturing them, and sending out more agents to sell them. Thus, in explaining Japan's economic miracle, just about every writer has referred to its strong work will and ability to cooperate for economic goals. Herman Kahn, one of the first to proclaim the rising economic sun, insisted: "The first and foremost cause of Japanese economic growth was the general energy and dedication of the Japanese and their capacity for purposive communal action which, when it was finally reactivated and focused on the problem of recovery, performed with its usual skill and dynamism."[1] Edwin O. Reischauer repeatedly praised it's "protestant ethic," far stronger in Japan than in the West. This work ethic, he explained:

" . . . may be basically associated with climate, but it has probably been strengthened rather than weakened by the group orientation of the Japanese. A good group cooperator is also a good worker, and the camaraderie of group work can be a positive pleasure, even when the artisan's pride in individual work has been replaced by more routine machine production in modern times. Diligence (*kimbensei*) is generally recognized by the Japanese themselves as one of their most outstanding characteristics. Certainly the primary identification of the individual Japanese with his work group and his enthusiastic, ever joyous, participation in its activities are reasons why the Japanese work ethic even today seems little eroded."[2]

Of course, a lot of this praise is exaggerated, and some of it is highly imaginative, expressed by people who have observed but never actually worked with Japanese or by foreigners who criticize the workers back home by making invidious comparisons. Still, there is no doubt that the Japanese once worked terribly hard, today still work relatively hard, at least as compared to the West, and have pulled the economy up by the boot-straps. Whether they did this out of love of work, or under pressure of one sort or another, is an entirely different matter, usually overlooked by those who gush over the work ethic. And whether this same ethic will continue indefinitely into the future is an even more crucial question. There is never any guarantee that a given social characteristic will remain unaltered by changes in circumstances and hold steady over time. If the work ethic were to be lost, Japan would doubtlessly suffer, given its poor natural endowments. But this does not exclude the possibility.

*　　　*　　　*

The Japanese have been referred to by some as "economic animals." They are supposedly different from everyone else in that, far from regarding work as an unpleasant necessity, it is to them a source of pride and joy, an expression of their personality, a means of fulfillment. That such people should exist anywhere seems a bit strange. Yet, over the decades before Japan's modernization the moral and social foundation was laid. Neither Shinto nor Buddhism placed particular stress on hard work, and the latter suggested that material rewards were vanities. Zen put stress on self-discipline, but since its disciples were largely *samurai*, this did not take the expression of economic pursuits. Confucianism had to be introduced during the long Tokugawa rule to make the Japanese accept discipline, obedience, and hard work as prevailing virtues. After being opened by the West and the Meiji Restoration, constructing a strong economy became a joint, and then subsidiary, goal to creating a strong army. And every means of a late feudal and early modern polity were applied to make the Japanese work hard. After the defeat in World War II, the Japanese were prohibited from waging war and could only express their national pride and ambitions in the form of economic progress.

This was the ideological framework. But no less important was the material context. In Japan, the land is quite mountainous, the climate often harsh, and the peasants had to work harder than elsewhere merely to grow enough rice to pay their taxes and feed themselves. A rigid discipline was imposed by the weather. Planting poorly or too late might mean that there was no harvest, and there were rarely enough reserves to make up for a shortfall. Starvation periodically ravaged the population. Adverse natural phenomena, storms, typhoons, earthquakes, and fires, to say nothing of periodic wars and uprisings, made things terribly perishable and forced each new generation to recreate wealth rather than just preserve it. After the war, with the economy shattered, much of the housing destroyed, and the administration disorganized, the Japanese had a very good reason for working hard— survival.

Physical hunger and the need to purchase basic necessities, reinforced by the moral goad of having to regain their self-respect as a people, was a strong enough "stick" to get the Japanese working again. But it certainly was not enough to keep any nation busy working forever. Moreover, even if they did work hard, unless it were suitably organized the work would never have been accomplished efficiently or well.

In the countryside, the farmers were still influenced by the elements, but were using much more modern methods. After the postwar land reform, they began working for themselves rather than for large owners, as many had done previously, and communal efforts were channelled through cooperatives. Productivity and production kept rising for those who remained farmers, but a gradual migration to the towns and cities cut the full-time farming population to a small minority.

In the modern factories, highly rationalized and well-organized, the workers could be integrated in the process with rare efficiency. Foreign experts who visited Japanese factories were amazed to see how a smaller staff could run a larger unit than elsewhere with greater outputs. The plant layout experts managed to put the person exactly where he, and increasingly she, should be. The staff was further trained in quality control, so that they would not only perform better but have some idea of what their role was. The foremen, rather than drive their subordinates on from a distance or from above, joined them in simulated campaigns and actions to get the work done. In Japan's factories, already highly efficient to start with, the productivity kept on rising at extremely high rates for two full decades, only slowing down recently.

The two sectors best known are the productive agricultural and manufacturing ones, and in manufacturing most acquaintance is with the modern efficient plants and the

Reminder of the past: hard, physical, menial labor.

Photo credit: Foreign Press Center-Japan

large companies. In much smaller factories, the methods were often backward, and the machinery somewhat outdated, but the workers were no less, and probably much more, hardworking. In the small companies, which were often just subcontractors for the larger ones, the employees had to keep their nose to the grindstone if they were to make do. Their pay was much lower, quite often merely half of that for workers in the major companies, and their equipment less efficient. Nevertheless, by dint of hard work and longer hours, they managed to reach satisfactory levels of production in most cases and get by.

Where people tended to get bogged down and accomplish less, especially in the big companies, was in the administrative offices, where personnel were not hired for specific jobs or tasks but had to create their own work. There was often too much staff, too poorly trained or specialized to be effective, and many of the choice posts were reserved as a plum or sinecure for those who had served the company well and not those who could direct it best. Unlike the factories, where nothing but the latest technologies and machinery had been adopted, management failed to reflect the modern managerial techniques and tools used in the West. Indeed, it put up a fierce resistance to this, preferring to follow precedent, resort to endless meetings to coordinate policy, and making often optimistic projections rather than careful plans. No one bothered with time-and-motion studies of the white collar worker and an amazing amount of the energy was expended to little avail.

In the distribution and services sectors, the employees and their bosses were working very hard, putting in long hours, and also showing due humility. But, they were making a rather marginal contribution to the economy. For, unlike farming and industry, which had been strictly rationalized and the work force cut to the bone, distribution passed through a lengthy chain of agencies, subagencies, and sub-sub-agencies, each taking the product a bit further or doing part of the work, whereas in most other "modern" countries fewer intermediaries would have been necessary. In services, also due to reasons deriving more from tradition than common sense, there was no end to the superfluous personnel. The more bowing salesmen to receive one in a shop, the more technicians coming out for after-sales service, the more smiling girls to receive one in a bar, the higher the prestige—and supposedly reputability—of the establishment and the happier the Japanese were to do business with it. That much of this was superfluous and also costly did not cut down on such practices perceptibly. In fact, these relatively inefficient sectors were steadily growing while the more productive sectors shrank.[3]

* * *

Even when the Japanese are using the same machinery and plants, even when they make the same articles with the same processes, they usually organize their work force in very different ways. The Japanese employment system so often referred to, and often seen as the true key to success, consists of various elements, among the best known being "lifetime employment" and the "career escalator," the in-house training of personnel and recruitment of workers in age or graduation classes, as well as the forms of paternalism associated with the "company family." Many observers become quite lyrical when describing this wonderful system and the unwary reader would indeed have a hard time understanding what could possibly be wrong or how anyone—including non-Japanese—could forgo these advantages.

"Why, indeed, should one want to leave a job with a good company, where one's future is secure and one's happiness is guaranteed? The employee has the security of belonging to a great family, a modern embodiment of the feudal clan. His membership satisfies this need for group living. In his conversation, he will say 'my' company. He will always wear his company button in his buttonhole, even while on vacation. He is very proud of his affiliation and considers himself at all times as a kind of public relations representative for his company. To safeguard his company's reputation, he will watch his behavior carefully, as much during his non-professional moments as during his working hours."[4]

This company "family," its supporters insist, arose out of the close and harmonious family relations that are supposedly traditional to Japan. Its detractors regard it as feudal. In practice, it draws on all of these customs and traditions and has formed an overall "system" which is generally accepted in the country, although fully practiced in perhaps a third of the cases, since only rather large and reasonably prosperous companies can afford the added frills, personnel and organization that is necessary to keep any family going in style. In smaller companies, more backward sectors, or depressed branches, this is just acknowledged as an ideal. In addition, not everyone who works in the firm is a member of the family, the benefits do not usually spread to part-time and temporary workers, nor do they accrue to those—like women—who leave the firm early. And the subcontractors have to look after their own employees in more primitive ways.

The Japanese "system" is certainly one of the smarter methods for utilizing personnel for given purposes, under given conditions, and obtaining as much of the commitment voluntarily rather than by constraint. But, it was neither inherited nor invented. It arose out of trial and error in seeking to overcome a number of extremely serious problems. One of them was that Japan, entering the industrial age on a large scale and at a late date, had to hire inexperienced and often uneducated workers, and train them on the spot. Later on, when the educational system evolved and graduates could be recruited, they still had to be trained in specific skills and the ways of the company. Drawing, in some industries like textiles, on young female personnel often from remote areas, the staff had to be housed by the company and looked after at least well enough to keep them strong and healthy for work. The men, frequently organized into work gangs under control of their own leaders, were kept in line by much tougher methods. These two faces of the employer could create both a positive and negative paternalism, the former of which was eventually judged the more effective. The other major problem was the turnover of workers, which the employers could ill afford since they were expanding and needed more staff, could hardly organize and plan ahead with constant changes, and did not like to train workers only to lose them soon after. By giving greater benefits for longer service, it proved easier to hold on to the labor force.[5]

Some of the companies became huge organizational structures which not only paid a salary but also offered housing, medical facilities, canteens and cafeterias, social centers and vacation homes, as well as loans or access to credit. Top executives also got chauffeur-driven cars and perhaps a golf club membership. In addition to monthly wages, the companies granted their personnel a bonus, originally at the company's discretion and only in good times, but since become institutionalized. If a person was taken on for life, this meant that the company would protect him against unemployment. The company was also responsible largely for old age, via severance payments, pensions, and often the grant of a second job on retirement. These were considerable benefits for any employee and each one drew the personnel more tightly into the company's embrace. The extensive lack of such benefits outside of the company, either provided on a private basis or through the government, meant that most

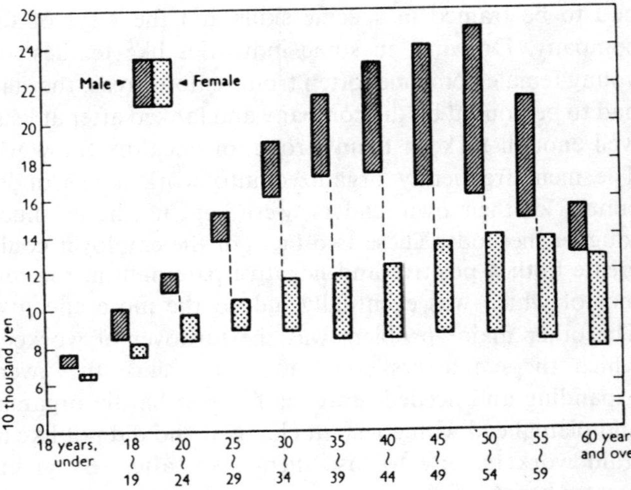

The range refers to size of enterprise.

Salary profile of the career escalators: a rapid one for men; gentler for the ladies! The range of earnings by age (1976)

Credit: *Statistical Handbook of Japan 1978*, Bureau of Statistics, Office of the Prime Minister, p. 105.

people had nowhere else to turn. Up to very recent times, a person could not really count on the state for unemployment benefits, health plans, old age insurance, or social security. Employers were the only source of salvation.

Many people praise the "loyalty" of Japanese employees. This loyalty is hardly surprising under the circumstances, and it does not spring solely or spontaneously from people's better nature. It results from perhaps the cleverest means ever devised for holding on to personnel. It grew out of the tendency to take in employees as groups, have them undergo much the same training, and then letting them rise gradually with the years. This created the "career escalator" which many Japanese ride until the end. Of course, not everyone wants to get on. Many young people balk at this. But, once on, the carrots replace the sticks. From year to year, their salary rises. From year to year, their status rises. Gradually, their position rises. In some cases, the increments with seniority are disproportionately large and at any rate the older employees, without necessarily being harder, better, or more valuable workers, always get a substantial reward for "loyalty." Losing a job, aside from the moral blow, would also mean the loss of accumulated wage increases, benefits, allowances, and retirement possibilities, and a return to the bottom of some other escalator. Switching jobs to get ahead is difficult since one company rarely regards experience in another as relevent, distrusts "disloyal" personnel, and has too compact an internal structure to assimilate outsiders. No wonder people are wedded to the company family for life!

Still, if everyone was fated to remain together, it was just as well to create a happy family. Since personal relations were so important to its smooth running, the company encouraged people to mix and get to know one another. The company offered sports and social facilities, helped support teams and clubs, rewarded workers with trips to hot springs or junkets abroad. The foreman was expected to know and look after his workers, the section and department heads to care for their personnel, and the company president periodically appeared as the "father" figure. The links that were ultimately forged were much stronger than the purely contractual ones in a Western-style company. Knowing one another better, they were often also better able to bear with one another. People were not placed under undue pressure as to how the work should be done as long as it got done. In return, if the company was in a tight spot because of a rush order, the staff was expected to sacrifice their private interests to meet the deadline. In return for tying its employees to the company, the company itself would not, in principle at least, dismiss them, even if they were a bit slipshod or inefficient, and continue to carry them in hard times as long as they did not do something dreadfully wrong.

*   *   *

All of this was supposed to engender harmony or *wa*. This *wa* was often seen in rather idealistic terms. Come what may, the interests of the group were always expected to prevail. To determine them, *ringisho* were circulated up and down and endless rounds of meetings were held. There might be differences of opinion about how to do something, or what to do, but once the decision was taken, everyone was expected to fall into line to achieve the goal. There might be conflicts about how the fruits of the company's labor should be shared, but none of this was in any way to harm the company or prejudice its success.

In one respect, things did seem to work out quite well. Although the Japanese were unionized to a rather great extent, with about 33% being union members, trade unionism never became a serious problem for the company "fathers." Since the workers were organized along enterprise and not craft or industry lines, they all had a vested interest in their particular company succeeding no matter what happened to anyone else. Since they all worked in the same plants or offices and were shifted from job to job, there were no jurisdictional quarrels. For employees who were hired for life, there was little fear of redundancy and technological change. Moreover, since management rose largely out of the ranks of the employees and workers, there was an understanding among the younger managers (those usually in charge of union matters) of the union's demands and among the union leaders (older workers, perhaps on their way to managerial posts) of the company's limitations. This did indeed create a reasonably cozy situation which made it possible for Japanese companies to progress with rather few strikes, not much work stoppage, and scant resistance to modernization and rationalization. At peace with their employees, they could forge ahead of the foreign competitors, especially those that were bickering with their unions.

Many critics have thus regarded the unions in Japan as weak and ineffectual, labor as being under the thumb of management, and unionism as a facade or sham. In practice, the unions and workers have not done all that poorly for themselves. The enterprise unions are recognized by management, they are reasonably well organized and amazingly well financed, and they do engage in collective bargaining systematically, two times a year, for the spring and winter offensives. Admittedly, they did not get as big a share of the pie as the more aggressive British unions.[6] But, they did keep wages progressing about as fast as the growth rate, and on a par with profits. They also did beautifully as concerns fringe benefits. However, by allowing their companies to concentrate on production, the pie itself has grown tremendously from year to year. To this is added the annual premium for "loyalty." When everything is put together, the Japanese workers did considerably better than their tough British counterparts, and better than workers anywhere, to become some of the best paid employees in the world.

Harmony between management and labor may result partially from the high recognition accorded to *wa* and a dislike for open conflicts. But it does not in any way prevent workers from expressing their grievances or making excessive demands, especially where the employer is the government. Many strikes are brief and sometimes the workers do not even leave their posts, simply wearing a red armband to signify their displeasure. This, however, is quite enough for management to get the message. And it is not spoiling for a fight either. Rather, to avoid confrontations, the company is busy conferring with the union leaders all year round, seeking the good grace of the employees by granting little favors, and trying to head off any potential crisis at a very early stage. A tremendous amount of time is devoted to keeping the employees happy and the supervisory staff are expected to make every effort to maintain amicable relations with their subordinates in utter disregard of the Western dictum that "time means money." Massive sums, tax deductable, of course, are spent on keeping the personnel sweet. Thus, keeping the work flowing smoothly is not gratuitous; it may even cost the company as much or more than a confrontation in material, if not moral, terms.[7]

Where harmony has failed to prevail, although this is not very widely reported, is at the highest levels, within the ranks of management itself. Both workers and junior managers rise from year to year on the career escalator . . . but only to a certain level. Beyond that, for most supervisory and managerial posts, there are more candidates than can be accomodated and it is necessary to stop some and let others move ahead. This could be done by merit. Yet, the machinery for judging merit is very inadequate, and Japanese companies are very "human" institutions. The real path to the top is one paved with connections and pull, well-placed *oyabun* pulling their *kobun* up, the *kobun* organizing to hoist the *oyabun* yet higher. Factionalism is rife, and the biggest or best organized faction, or the one with the most pull (*hiki*), is liable to claim the choice posts and enjoy *shussé*. This is not only a question of pride or hunger for status. The winners get largely honorary jobs, with little work and substantial stipends, while the losers may well be retired out early.

Factionalism is the plague in the otherwise calm life of the salaryman. Already in preparation for a conflict that may not take place for another twenty years, the young employee, fresh out of the university, looks for a protector. This may involve a lot of boot licking in order to ingratiate himself with the boss and perhaps become his "bag-carrier." All the while, he works his way further into a faction and joins sides in the many squirmishes of an unending civil war. If his protector rises to the top, no hope is too high; if he falls, then the whole faction may come tumbling down. This phenomenon is likened to a popular tongue-twister that goes: "a child turtle was on the back of a parent turtle, and a grandchild turtle was on the back of the child turtle, and a great-grandchild turtle was on the back of the grandchild turtle, and when the parent turtle fell flat on his face, the child turtle, and the grandchild turtle, and the great-grandchild turtle all fell flat on their faces." How a person feels when the whole family falls flat on its collective face can be seen from endless letters to the salaryman's advice columns in the business magazines. Here is one:

"I am the regional manager of a branch office of a certain company. It is a third-class branch with a small budget and personnel. There are various reasons for me to be located here, but the words of a company director I respect 'perseverance brings success' always gave me hope. However, this director passed away suddenly this spring, and thus it is pretty definite that my hope of returning to the head office in Tokyo is completely gone. The personnel structure of the company is nothing but an outright battle between factions. Thus, when the head of a faction dies, the people in the faction, unless they shift themselves to another faction very tactfully, end up eating cold rice . . . Should I manipulate things very carefully in an effort to be sent back to Tokyo or should I accept this as my life's fate and seek an easy life in this local town? My feelings are still uncertain and this makes my days grey and heavy."[8]

*   *   *

When foreigners refer to the Japanese as "economic animals," they are almost always thinking in terms of their own experience, namely a depersonalized automaton, a human machine to tend the steel machine, a shapeless and spineless robot to be used any which way, or wretches with no outside concerns and interests, no loves or passions, to keep them away from a dull routine. At best, the Japanese are put in the same category as the Germans. Much to the surprise of anyone who has worked with them, the Japanese, even the most dedicated and disciplined, are not "cold-blooded" animals but very "warm-blooded" ones. If anything, they are closer to Italians. Personal life, passions, higher aspirations have not disappeared from their existence. Instead, much of this has been brought into the work place or been attached to the company's aims. Rejection of sentiments, single-minded pursuit of lucre, sacrifice of all personal concerns . . . none of this applies to Japan. It is all the opposite. Sentiments, generosity, personal desires and quirks have all gotten into the system.

The West's experiences with paternalism, let alone feudalism, go very far back and are but dimly perceived. Having once rejected them as reactionary, a Westerner has trouble remembering that there ever was a positive side, without which such structures would never have existed as long as they did. Japan had only just come out of the feudal period and close relations among patron and client, master and apprentice, father and son, were very real. In addition to the functions, Japanese business leaders have inherited some of the emotional roles. Today, it is not at all exceptional for a department chief to propose possible marriageable partners to the men or women in his department or for the plant supervisor to officiate at the wedding of a worker on his team. After working together all day, there is nothing unusual in the men going out for a friendly drink and then helping one another stagger to the subway. These relations become particularly intimate after company-arranged parties and vacations. A foreman who sees a distracted worker would not hesitate to enquire whether there is something wrong in the family, an illness or perhaps trouble with the wife or kids, and to suggest remedies. An employee who is expected to put in overtime for the company could also obtain the company's understanding if he has to take leave briefly to attend a funeral.

Most Westerners would find this sort of involvement a bit too much and reject it as interference in their private life. To the Japanese, privacy, of which they have pitifully little at any rate, is not so sacred. It is far better to feel understood and supported. When asked whether they would prefer working for a firm that paid very well but didn't look after them when sick or in similar circumstances and a firm that paid lower wages but was more human in its approach, the Japanese workers, unlike their British counterparts, were overwhelmingly in favor of being looked after.[9] Even the younger workers, who dislike paternalism and invasion of privacy in theory, tend to seek out an older colleague as a vicarious father figure or their *oyabun* for factional purposes. Those who try to keep out of company politics just end up in tight little peer groups, since griping together with colleagues, or fighting for their rights, is much easier than going it alone.

The personal relations that unite the company—and divide it—extend further into the working world. Foreigners who refer to *zaibatsu* tend to think of them in terms of impersonal trusts or conglomerates, playing with people like pawns and ignoring individual needs. Originally, many of the old companies grew out of very intimate, family-like relations between a master and an apprentice or say Mitsui proper and a former executive, who, rather than breaking away, preferred to stay closely related as a subsidiary branch. Indeed, often the person concerned actually became a family member through marriage or adoption. Nowadays, although the managers of a big company and their small subcontractors fulfill stricter economic functions, the personal relations remain and the length of service for the patron is not forgotten. Conglomerates in Japan are not run ruthlessly from the center. Instead, each branch is given very considerable freedom to organize its own activities. The links that hold them together include some supervision by the bank and cross-ownership. But the real cooperation grows out of repeated personal contacts between the heads of the various subunits.

In the distribution and service sectors, personal relations play a far greater role. A distribution network is built on many such relations accumulated over a long time, and sometimes passed on from father to son. The links are not purely through business. A successful distributor knows the retailer's family and his problems, may well have helped send the son through college or made a loan when the retailer was in a pinch. The retailer would not fail to send the distributor gifts on suitable occasions. Doing business at the lower level implies running a reputable looking establishment and creating a proper atmosphere. This may well involve more floor space than necessary and often excess personnel to serve a client courteously. The sales personnel must absolutely know how to play up to the potential customers and feed their ego. Without that, the finest products would be hard to sell at even the cheapest prices.

Sales between companies, and even within the same group, are made only after both parties know much more about one another than in most "modern" economies, and this includes not only credit references but the personality and tastes of the people concerned. It is hard to do business at all without a personal introduction, since mutual contacts are the best recommendation and trust must exist for any relationship to flourish. Then immeasurable time is spent simply discussing, feeling one another out, trying to get on the same wave length. In this process, things like similar background, perhaps coming from the same prefecture or college, membership in the same groups, or common friends, can play the decisive role. Even prices between companies are not simply the going rate where supply and demand meet; they result from painstaking negotiations influenced by the situation of each side, favors asked or granted in the past, the personality of the negotiators, and so on. A prime contractor may squeeze the subcontractors in hard times and then show unexpected generosity when the going gets good.

Many readers will find it hard to believe that such premodern practices are standard in Japan's apparently sophisticated economy. The role of personal relations and special contacts comes as no surprise to those who know it more intimately. The only thing that can amaze the businessman is the extent to which the basic rules of a market economy are overshadowed by earlier patterns. Thus, the discovery that the huge Nippon Telegraph & Telephone Public Corporation only drew material from within the "NTT family" of suppliers, which did not even include many major Japanese companies and certainly no foreign ones, was no real surprise. What was less defensible was that not even 4% of its purchases were obtained through competitive bidding, while the rest resulted from friendly consultations.[10]

"Japan, Inc."—for all its power and despite the parallel with a limited corporation—is nothing of the sort. It is simply a much broader network of contacts. This time the contacts are between higher civil servants in certain key ministries, middle and top management of the companies, and certain politicians in a position to provide backing. There is no legislation creating this particular institution nor any regulations that are followed half as often as they are flaunted. Everything is worked out in private or among small groups, frequently in tea houses, hotel rooms, on the golf course, or behind the scenes somewhere else. In this battle for government protection and aid, business interests pull no punches and the friendly relations can be oiled with palpable material benefits, both for the politicians and civil servants. The winner is the party which has the best connections and can get the most leverage, and only coincidentally, if at all, the company which would have won in a more strictly regulated system of competitive bidding or decisions based purely on economic rationales.

* * *

By now, more than three decades have passed since the Japanese threw themselves into the tasks of reconstruction. In that time, they have built up an incredibly strong economy and even made good on their old dream of passing the West. Only the United States perhaps has as powerful an economy and not even the Americans are as well paid as some Japanese. This transformation in their material world was so sweeping and decisive that it could not avoid affecting social attitudes as well. The old virtues of discipline, hard work, ambition became a bit passé and

Foreign visitors duly impressed by Japanese ingenuity.

Photo credit: Japan National Tourist Organization.

there was no guarantee that the creators of this success, the farmers, workers, and salarymen, would be followed by others with equal ability and dedication.

Once the farmers had to put in long hours just to get by, and much of this was back-breaking physical labor. Now they have mini-tractors to help them. Indeed, farming is increasingly passed on to the women while the men work in nearby factories. Some have been particularly lucky in selling land and just moved to the city. Most farm households are now relatively well off. They also have modern conveniences, cars, and a standard of living similar to that of the city dweller. There is hardly a cooperative member who has not been to Paris or at least gotten as far as Manila. Their main struggle now is less to grow a large crop than to talk the politicians into subsidizing their produce, such as rice, or keeping out foreign competitors, as in cattle-raising and fruit and vegetable growing.

In the factories, some workers still perform unpleasant, strenuous or dangerous tasks, although this is outnumbered by the jobs which are merely routine or tedious. For such work, the wages have been rising steadily for years. No one works any more just to keep alive and most blue collar workers feel more middle class than proletarian. They, too, have a home, car, and the modern conveniences, even if a bit smaller. To get more, they would certainly think twice about working much longer hours. Rather, for a constantly falling work week they try to bring home a steadily growing pay check. The salarymen, whose standard of living was usually above average anyway, often made that extra effort in order to rise to the top. Nowadays, it is harder to get promotions, so some don't try, and others don't care, and ambitions tend to flag.

What is more serious is that the old division between white collar and blue collar workers, based on graduation from college or only high school, has led to a situation where the number of people who will become mere laborers is shrinking rapidly. It is increasingly hard to find country dwellers, uneducated or unskilled workers willing to take on the harder tasks. The women have become increasingly genteel and also seek office work. Even when the wages are bid up above white collar wages, it is extremely difficult to find people for the construction trades or sailors to man Japanese ships. There are plenty of "help wanted" ads for sales, delivery, or clerical staff, for security guards or drivers for men, and for shop attendants, waitresses, switchboard operators, or nurses, for women. But there are very few takers . . . even in the midst of a recession.

The school leavers are not willing to start at the bottom. Indeed, why should they? They were told that by studying hard and getting diplomas society would guarantee a good job, and now they want one. They are quite willing to turn up their nose at second best. Many demand "job suitability"—not that they should suit the requirements of the job, no, the job should meet their expectations. Such comments come from the National Working Youths' Hall in Tokyo, visited by over three hundred young workers a month. They come to complain "I don't understand the meaning of work" or "the present job doesn't suit me, please find a job suited to me." One job advisor who heard more than enough of these griefs stated:

"The young people seem to have a strong belief in 'job suitability.' Many of them over-evaluate their abilities, or, without putting in any effort to speak of, they come and complain that they find their job uninteresting or that they are tired of human relations in the company. They seem to think that somewhere there is a job that will suit them, as if they were looking for the 'bluebird of happiness.' "[11]

Perhaps these youngsters had trouble fitting into the work situation because the school situation they just left was about the worst conceivable introduction to work life. The problem does not seem to reside with the high school graduates. After all, they have just come through a period of serious study, when school discipline was relatively strict, and tests had to be passed. If they tried to get into college and failed, or simply realized they would not make it, they do not enter the company with undue feelings of pride or superiority. Those who do pass the exams, almost automatically feel part of an elite. They then proceed to spend four years or so pretty much at their own pace. They take whatever courses they want, and skip them if they desire, putting in more time with the club or in radical activities. When they graduate, many do not have any professional training, worse, they find any discipline unpalatable. How then are they to be inserted in the company system which requires a completely different behavior?

There is one more element which undermines the work will, this time within the company itself. Although the happy founders of the employment system may not have noticed, those applying it today could scarcely fail to. The career escalator can boomerang very seriously. It was assumed that the carrot of annual promotions would keep people busy working. This, of course, had no effect if the career men did not really care if they rose to the top, which is often the case now. After all, if you are going to be promoted every year anyway, why kill yourself? On the other hand, the go-getters who might have shown special initiative and drive, quickly saw that trying to press ahead only got them into trouble with the others but did not result in much professional progress. Once again, what was the point in killing yourself?

* * *

As a result of the very different material context and education of each successive generation, the whole attitude to work and society underwent considerable changes. This was not always perceptible from year to year, since each age class moved just a shade further in a given direction and it took a number of years to see the trends. By now, however, the direction has become amply clear to anyone who knows Japan.

After the war, pushed on by poverty or pride, it was not hard to convince the Japanese that they had to show unusual dedication and ability . . . and they rose to the challenge. Wages were still low, so people got along on less. Working conditions were anything but good, yet no one complained. They pitched in to build new factories, import more raw materials and machinery, and then export the finished products so that the cycle could resume again at a higher level. Growth was the goal, so rather

Luxury buying is also a time-honored tradition.

Photo credit: Japan National Tourist Organization

than consume people saved, and the savings went into further expansion. Work was a virtue. Employees put in six or seven days a week, and skipped holidays or vacations if necessary. Managers showed no less dedication, and often accepted even greater sacrifices. Eventually, this generation was given the nickname *moretsu-gata* or super-dynamic type.

Not long after the early booms, many Japanese started thinking about what they could do with their growing wages. They still put some of it aside. But there remained an increasing share left over for consumption. The population passed through various phases. First their expectations were quite modest. Everyone wanted the 3Cs—car, color TV and cooler (air conditioner). Some then moved on to the 3Ds—dish washer, (garbage) disposer, and (clothes) drier. But there was nothing like the urge for a home. Then, along with money, they also had an increasing amount of free time and began to wonder how to fill their leisure, through sports, travel, or just relaxation. Of course, all these material goods could not avoid creating a different type of Japanese. There was considerable talk about getting back to that home more often (my-home-ism) and seeing more of one's family. There was increasingly little willingness to accept overtime or work on weekends. What was holding people in their jobs and making them perform reasonably well was the fact that they had to keep earning money to pay for everything they bought. They would do the work, but there was some doubt as to whether their heart was in it.

The children of these people, already mellowed and bourgeois as compared to their rough-hewn ancestors and the all-for-work generation, were surrounded by a comfortable shield of material goods. They were often given little gifts to bribe them into working for school, rather than being simply ordered to do so. When they went to college, some revolted against the established order, at least for a few years. The student radicals had it in for the big companies and the government and they frightened them enough to be barred from entry quite often. However, once inside the companies or bureaucracies, they seemed to calm down externally at least and to work at a reasonable pace. If they did not show the dedication of earlier classes, at least they had stopped rebelling openly and did what they were told. The only noticeable effect was a bit more toughness in some unions. Thus, the radical generations were coopted if not fully digested.

The next generation, so the employers thought, would be ideal. These were reasonably polite and meek youngsters, interested in home and family, television and car, good food and clothing, and certainly not likely to put up a row. But they were not bloody likely to immerse themselves in work, worry about what happened to the company, or take on additional responsibilities if they could avoid it either. They had little ambition but to earn their salary and get away. They would stand patiently on the career escalator rather than push and shove to make it to some titular post. Management had a generation on its hands that had escaped the contagion of radicalism and the Marxist virus but had come down with something akin to the "British disease." Under certain conditions, especially those of Japan where hard work and dedication are a prerequisite for economic viability, this ailment might be more disastrous than it appeared.

The Japanese economic miracle arose not only out of certain virtues that were broadly accepted, it also resulted from the tremendous force of conformity in Japanese society. In the early days, not everyone wanted to work all that hard, but no one was willing to stand up to the leaders or masses of coworkers and admit to this failing. However, as has now become clear, conformity can work in both directions. The *moretsu* type from the early days is in a dwindling minority. The my-home and new family types are increasingly numerous. Already, a decade ago, they revolted aginst being forced to conform to such an uninspiring life style with the slogan of "from *moretsu* to beautiful," this last word in English. They did not overturn society or close down the factories, but society was no longer going to determine how they would live to anywhere near the same extent. Now, they are joined by people with little discipline, little taste for work, and sometimes who don't even mind whether they earn much or not (either because they can fall back on their parents or they will live with less).

With this, the work ethic tipped seriously. The beautiful people were winning out. This was very simple. It has always been hard to urge people on to greater efforts. Now, the rallying call was to take life easy. It may have been resisted by those trained in the old school or with a liking for their work. But, it was terribly hard to keep plugging away when other colleagues were doing less and earning the same pay. This explains the rather strange dichotomy encountered in many companies, where some are busy working in their corner, others are engaged in a more or less pointless meeting, and those who have opted out may simply be having tea or reading a newspaper. If you were to recite some of the paeans to Japanese work ethic quoted earlier on, they would probably laugh.

* * *

These comments may seem as loose and hard to substantiate as the earlier comments on a nation of hardworking, dedicated, cooperative employees. Still, they are based on observations made time and again by a large number of people living and working in Japan. They fill the columns of the businessmen's magazines. And they find their reflection in the polls and surveys. Thus, when asked whether he regarded himself as a "workaholic" for joining a Japanese company, one young American had to explain: "Japanese people work long hours, but the density of work done during those hours is considerably less than in an American company. You often see businessmen in pachinko parlors and movie theaters during the day when you know they should really be out visiting clients and drumming up business. Also in the office people are more relaxed, chatting with other people, going off for a cup of tea and so on."[12]

The archetypical figure of the Japanese business world, and the backbone of the companies, has been the salaryman. Five hundred of these young salarymen in leading companies were surveyed and asked "What will you be like in the year 2000?" The result was that only 25% expected to remain salarymen. As for the others, 24% hoped to have become either entrepreneurs (11%), shop owners (8%), or taken over the family business (5%), and no less than 40% wanted to be independent freelancers. What about company loyalty? About 37% thought they would have quit their present company. Work ethic seems to have fared no better. Only 21.4% gave answers showing anything like it: Will be living for work only (4%); Will be working hard for promotion (1.4%); Will be up to my neck in work (16%). For the others, work would have become rather secondary: A good my-home husband, family first! (17%); Easy-going days at 'my pace' (29%); and will probably be finding the significance of life (10%).[13]

Observations made by employers of the new generations of workers bear this out. The men, who will still have to spend a long time in the same enterprise, make some effort to fit in snuggly. Referring to some of the first university graduates who deigned to work as mailmen, one supervisor said: "At first, we were worried that these people might be ex-radical students or that they might agitate things in the union. However, in our office, all of them are thoroughly the my-home type and they are all so quiet. They probably have their future *shussé* in mind, because instead of joining the radical trade union they joined the moderate one. They don't complain, they don't grouch. Although they are never late for work or absent, they always stop their work at the prescribed time. Right on the dot!"[14]

The remarks about female college graduates, an increasingly large contingent, are far less kindly. Literally millions of them, who graduate with no specialization or skills, end up working as "office ladies," glorified secretaries or so-called "assistants." One of their supervisors griped:

"When I am receiving a guest, it is the high school graduate girl who brings tea immediately. There are even those who cannot use the simple phrase 'I'm sorry' when it is necessary. Does 'cultural education' hinder such desired attitudes? In work itself, high school graduate girls are faster and more serious. They do not quibble either. They are cultivated. When a meeting is held, the college graduate girls usually have something to say in the beginning, but there is a great imbalance betwen what they say and their working abilities. As a fighting force, too, they (and I'm sorry I have to be so curt) are inferior. What's more, the college graduates lose their temper easily and complain. They take days off without giving it a thought. In other words, there is nothing good about them!"[15]

However, since most Japanese are rather good at disguising their feelings, particularly if they fear they may not appear sufficiently noble, it is worthwhile seeing how they speak of themselves in unsigned letters to the editor.

"I am kept so busy going around from one customer to another that I hardly spend any time sitting at my desk. Since I am out most of the time all of the paper work has to be processed during overtime. There is no overtime pay. And each day is nothing but work, work, work. I am constantly dissatisfied and frustrated . . . Could you tell me whether it is stupid to just work earnestly and nothing else and whether it is not better to goof-off whenever I feel like it?"

"My life as a salaryman has become suffocating ever since our company went into a capital tie-up and my share of the responsibilitities has gotten heavier and heavier. Moreover, when I am yelled at and told 'you can't call yourself a professional unless you go around finding work by yourself,' I can't help asking myself—what in the world is 'work' anyway? As far as I am concerned, I am happy as long as I can properly process the work I am given and earn a stable income. If possible, I don't want to work overtime because I'd rather enjoy a relaxing personal life outside of work. Fortunately, there is a division where the pressure of the parent company is rather low. Should I work things out cleverly to find refuge there or should I bear the present situation since such a step may be disadvantageous? Which is safer?"

The answers to these letters are even more revealing for, by and large, they show that the whole attitude to work has tipped. Rather than urging the young salarymen to persevere for the good of the company and society, they tend to agree with them about taking things easy and often go a step further. The first is comforted. "Don't burden yourself with elitism and, when you are tired, be honest and say you are tired and goof off not 'whenever you feel like it' but 'within reasonable limits.' It is only during the first two or three years that one is truly busy in the physical sense. After the moss grows a little, many people just move around idly more than just 'within reasonable limits.' You, too, should take advantage of this." The second is actually praised. "Until a decade or so ago, people like you were hard to find and even if there were some they kept quiet. Today, the number of such people is increasing and they are sometimes referred to as the 'beautiful-ists' and they have succeeded in obtaining a place in society. This diversification of the life styles of salarymen is really a wonderful thing." The advice: if the boss has an appealing personality, go along with the tide. If not, "if the boss is nothing but a peasantish old *moretsu* bastard, it is safer to thumb your nose at him and escape as soon as possible. Don't you think it is a question of who will shed extra sweat for the earnings of the parent company?"[16]

* * *

There seems to be little doubt that the depth, and especially the permanence, of Japan's work ethic have been greatly overestimated. The rise in the economy has been paralleled by a fall in the willingness to make sacrifices to keep it going. Generations of hardworking parents have created wealth that new generations of easy-going children show little willingness to replenish or preserve. Although the increase in individualism can be a positive sign, it does not help if this only means taking things easy rather than seizing initiatives. It is not very encouraging for the economy at any rate. If things continue this way, the future can follow along two paths . . . with very different destinations.

It is possible that the recession will do some good in moral terms by reminding the Japanese that they are in a difficult spot, more so than most other countries, and that they can prosper only through dedication and hard work. For some time now, management has been talking about tying wages not only to seniority but also to ability, productivity, or merit. A certain degree of merit payment has been worked into wages, but the unions have kept it from going too far. Nevertheless, the principle is accepted and, under certain circumstances, could be advanced to provide a material carrot when moral pleas fail to get results. Equally important is the announcement by several major firms that they will not promote people into managerial positions purely on the basis of seniority. If a person is not good enough, he may be given the choice between a special bonus for retiring early or a chance to stay on with lesser wage increments. The real problem here will be to introduce an objective evaluation machinery rather than factional in-fighting. The appearance of unemployment has also given a less noble support to the company family, one it lost during prosperity when people could pick and choose a bit more. Employees will be considerably more hesitant about leaving the company when the alternative may be unemployment.

The other possibility is that Japan's economy will slowly dip or even come crashing down at some point. This is not really that farfetched, and the list of once impressive economies that have been humbled is rather long and steadily growing. Indeed, one may well wonder whether the present recession is not in some ways the result of the excessive fat in the economy, the personalization of economic decisions and processes, and doubtlessly also the smaller doses of work put in for ever bigger transfusions of money. Japan never had this much trouble coming out of a recession and certainly not in conceding that there was a crisis and something had to be done. Both government and private business still refuse to admit the extent and depth of the problems and thus to take serious measures to counteract them. The people are still in a spending mood and refuse to let the "new affluence" slip through their fingers without leaving something behind. Of course, a dedicated communal population could pull in its belt and get down to work again. But, who can say that Japan is still such a society?[17]

NOTES

1. Herman Kahn, *The Emerging Japanese Superstate*, p. 87.
2. Edwin O. Reischauer, *The Japanese*, p. 154.
3. See Jon Woronoff, *Japan: The Coming Economic Crisis*, pp. 139–170.
4. Jean-Francois Delassus, *The Japanese: A Critical Evaluation of the Character and Culture of a People*, New York, Hart Publishing Co., pp. 143–4.
5. See Ronald Dore, *British Factory, Japanese Factory*, pp. 375–403.
6. Dore, op. cit., p. 267.
7. See Thomas P. Rohlen, *For Harmony and Strength.*
8. *Shukan Yomiuri*, September 24, 1977.

9. Dore, op. cit., p. 215.
10. *Japan Times*, February 22 & 26, 1979.
11. *Mainichi Shimbun*, December 3, 1977, p. 7.
12. *Focus Japan,* October 1979, p. 21.
13. *Sunday Mainichi*, November 13, 1977, p. 37.
14. *Shukan Shincho*, February 2, 1978, pp. 120–7.
15. "Readers' Corner," *Asahi Shimbun*, October 6, 1977, p. 14.
16. *Shukan Yomiuri*, January 22, 1978, p. 116 & August 20, 1977, p. 207.
17. See Woronoff, op. cit., pp. 198–227.

6
The All-Powerful State, and Who Runs It?

Many people, on thinking of Japan, assume the existence of powerful, massive, ruthlessly efficient institutions. Of course, none could be assumed to be more constraining than the Japanese state, given the extreme stability of leadership, the regularity of the electoral process and lack of upsets, and the relatively smooth flow of economic and social life. There have been periodic troubles, but none have kept up very long or seemed at all able to overthrow the superstructure. They were annoyances, nothing more. Indeed, there was even a spate of books, reaching back into the dark prewar period for parallels, that claimed that Japan was a fascist or militaristic state and that the government was crushing any opposition and regimenting daily life.

This sort of behavior, if it were true, would seem to be completely out of keeping with what has been observed in every other sphere of activity. In each institution so far, to the contrary, there have been clear signs of group formation and fragmentation rather than unity, factionalism and friction rather than harmony, much uncertainty and confusion as to policy, and rather little follow-through. Some of this must also apply to government and the state, although how much remains to be seen. After all, when you try to point a finger at this state, it is extremely hard to know in which direction to point: is it the political parties or just the LDP? Is it the bureaucracy? Or, is it business? This sort of question has been asked repeatedly and there are few quotations on Japanese politics as well known as Chitoshi Yanaga's reference to the game *janken* in which paper is stronger than stone, because it can wrap the stone; stone is stronger than scissors, because it can break the scissors; and scissors is stronger than paper because it can cut the paper.

"There seems to be general agreement among students of Japanese politics that the nation is governed jointly by organized business, the party government, and the administrative bureaucracy. As to which of the three groups is more powerful, there is no agreement. . . . Professional politicians believe that the administrators are running the country. Businessmen are quick to assert that the party politicians determine national policies. Administrators are convinced that organized business, working through the party in power, is in control of national policies."[1]

Already, by having to ask such a question and then having to look for the prevailing partner, it becomes obvious that the state is anything but monolithic and those running it anything but all-powerful and dominating. In addition, the three institutions named actually make up a big chunk of the Japanese leadership, as this club consists of numerous Diet members and local officials, even more top administrators, and far more business leaders. And some of them are very busy people, concerned with more than just running the state, although by cooperating they tend to share the burden and spread the responsibility thin . . . perhaps too thin.

Looking at them, no one really seems to be grasping power ruthlessly. The Diet? If one heard the debates, or noticed the lack thereof, and saw the members at work (or asleep), one would have serious doubts. The ruling party? It hardly has a popular backing or regular structure, although it wins elections. The Prime Minister and his faction? Aside from the fact that the Prime Minister is repeatedly changed, he is kept busy getting agreement and consensus rather than imposing it ruthlessly. The bureaucracy? Certainly, to some extent, the bureaucrats do have to direct people. But, they do it according to the rules and more likely than push, the average bureaucrat would try to remain safely within bounds. Businessmen? They are too involved with business to keep a close watch on general policy.

Strange as it may seem, perhaps the state in Japan is even more amorphous than elsewhere. After all, the country is kept in by a body of water and a common body of philosophy. People are going about their lives in a well-regulated society, doing more or less what they should. New laws and rules are gradually adopted, following some urge coming from somewhere—but also ignored if not particularly palatable. Japan's neighbors are far enough away for it to require relatively little foreign policy, and most of this economic. Protection by the American nuclear umbrella considerably simplifies any defence policy. It is relatively rare that issues crop up that inflame passions. And much of domestic policy is economic or business-related. The conservatives have been in power for over thirty years, some Diet members were in politics for almost as many, and the top businessmen and bureaucrats have reached such positions after untold years of apprenticeship at the task. With such a routine and apparent lack of challenges, one really doesn't need much of a government.

* * *

Japan is a democratic state and its Constitution, based on some of the finest models in existence, lays down the framework for democratic government. It provides for a bicameral Diet, with an upper house or House of Councillors and a lower house or House of Representatives. The upper house is more than just ceremonial and is supposed to balance the more political lower house through its wisdom and perhaps age. The upper house helps adopt legislation and it can also block measures, unless this is overridden by a second adoption in the lower house. The lower house, however, takes the lead in initiating legislation and alone appoints and removes the Prime Minister. The majority party puts forward the Prime Minister, who freely appoints his Ministers, and is responsible to the lower house. The Ministers then present legislation which is debated and adopted or rejected.

The theory, as all so often, does not seem to have carried over too well in practice. Theoretically, there is a balance of power between the two houses. However, since both are elected in much the same proportions and for not very different reasons by the same parties, they do not really balance policies much or expand the range of useful opinions. There is, in theory, also the balance inherent in freely elected representatives, in principle coming from a number of opposing parties. Japan is in fact a multi-party state. However, in practice, the conservatives, now established in the Liberal Democratic Party, have been in power with a brief interruption since 1945. And the largest opposition party, the Japan Socialist Party, has been so splintered internally and weak in terms of number of seats in the Diet, that what has evolved is known as a one-and-a-half party system. Other parties exist, including a Japan Communist Party on the left, and a Democratic Socialist Party, United Social Democratic Party, Komeito, and New Liberal Club in the center. Only recently, with the dwindling support for the LDP, have they been able to play much of a role.

Thus, observing the Diet in action does little to explain

how legislation is passed or worked out. For, the LDP manages to have its legislation adopted come what may. There have been two basic styles until now. When it had a powerful majority, and the socialists were weak, while ideological passions burned high after the war, there was a tendency for the LDP to use strong tactics in imposing its will. In return, the socialists often engaged in bitter opposition, usually verbal, but including on occasion actual fighting in the Diet and obstruction of the parliamentary process. This could be backed up by protests, strikes, or demonstrations in the streets. This background accompanied debates on the Self-Defence Force, the reversion of Okinawa, and especially the adoption of the Japan-U.S. Security Treaty. Still, in the end, the LDP had its way. More recently, as the LDP majority slipped, it has had to seek support from centrist parties like the NLC and Komeito, and there has even been talk of a coalition. In this atmosphere, discussions were usually engaged behind the scenes until some agreement could be reached to ensure adoption of the legislation, not always on its intrinsic merits, but as a result of a swop of legislation desired by the various parties. Once agreed, this could be slipped through the Diet with little difficulty.

So, it is far more interesting to watch the ruling party to find out how decisions are reached and what policy is likely to be. For, most issues are first discussed among major political leaders and party elders until their views can be harmonized or taken into account one way or the other. With first a majority and later a still impressive block, LDP agreement was essential to having its proposals adopted. Agreement was also necessary to hold the party together. Since it was far from monolithic and rather consisted of a grouping of factions united in the common desire of staying in power, internal divergencies could be quite sharp. The party had been formed in 1955 by a merger of the old Liberal Party and Democratic Party and the differences took some time to subside. Ideologically, membership ran from old guard nationalists to some very liberal thinkers; as regards personality, from dynamic young men to cautious old ones. Another line of cleavage was between the "politicians" who had worked their way up the party hierarchy and "bureaucrats" who had used a bureaucratic post to catapult themselves into politics, and frequently prevailed. More important, there were some half-dozen leaders at any time who regarded themselves as potential prime ministers, formed clienteles that hardened into factions, and struggled for power. It was between these factions that some middle-ground had to be reached. Democracy was thus due perhaps less to the multi-party system in some ways than the intra-party factionalism in the LDP. Unfortunately, even its internal decisions did not always come about democratically either, by counting those in favor or against a measure, but rather by balancing issues to give each faction some satisfaction on what interested it most.

In practice, legislation has taken up relatively little time of the Diet members. It is usually drawn up for the government by the bureaucracy and with only marginal input from the legislators. Since votes take place largely along party lines the debates have often been perfunctory. If the LDP knew that it had a majority, it would proceed to have the legislation adopted while the opposition, which could not really prevent this, engaged in delay tactics. The interpellations were made more to embarrass the ruling party, and replies to defend it, rather than representing an attempt at discussing the merits and demerits of a proposal, bringing about greater understanding, or conceivably reaching a compromise. Despite the large number of committees, relatively little legislation was adopted at any session, the Diet often had to be reconvened, and some bills were carried over from year to year. Even if the Diet members had wished to make their body more effective and efficient they were stymied by a lack of expertise and research staff to work out proposals and counter-proposals on their own. Although far from a rubber stamp, the Diet was not a decisive and dynamic body either.

One reason was that the Diet members more often kept busy with other matters. For professional politicians who live off the trade, the primary concern was obviously to get re-elected. Although lower house elections only have to be held every four years, often when a prime minister feels that he is in a particularly strong position he will call for an early dissolution in order to reconvene the Diet with a more favorable membership. Thus, elections to the House of Representatives have occurred roughly every two-and-a-half years. If the regular elections for upper house members (half every three years) are added, then Japan has had an election about every sixteen months.[2] Thus, rather than worry about parliamentary business, the Diet members have to spend an amazing amount of time waging electoral campaigns.

In the case of the LDP, electioneering has been very broadly studied and excellent works on the subject exist.[3] The process is not necessarily "ideal" from the philosophical or ethical viewpoint, but the candidate's main concern is one of effectiveness. In earlier days, in the rural districts (which then predominated), he might proceed to obtain a block of voters through the status or connections or wealth/land he possessed; and this has not quite ceased. Both Hayato Ikeda and Eisaku Sato, former Prime Ministers, as well as dozens of lesser lights, have traditionally held a bastion which re-elects them periodically and almost automatically. With modernization the politicians have also put together support groups or plugged into existing groups with similar interests. Business or professional associations, trade unions, even religious sects have provided such foundations. A person going into politics without this backing is far more dependent on the party, or a faction in the party, which proceeds to endorse him and throw some political weight behind him. It does sometimes happen that an independent will go in without the endorsement of a party or faction, but hardly any remain such.

Even after having gotten elected, the politicians are still campaigning. For a mere seat in the Diet does not get them as much prestige and patronage as a post as Minister. Within whatever faction they belong to, they jockey for position or to form part of an inner circle that chooses ministers. Within their faction, they do whatever is necessary to rise. This rarely consists of making themselves noticeable due to superior drive or ability, something more likely to arouse suspicion and concern. They rather tend to give unstinting support, very visibly so, to whoever can aid in their rise. They support him and his plans. They keep their nose clean and get elected time and again. Upon reaching a certain age, i.e. having accumulated enough seniority, they are in a position where one may consider them as ministerial material. Of course, they also have to be lucky, as they may be passed over if their faction head is too weak or too many others have the same qualifications.

The faction leaders, with the obvious hope of becoming Prime Minister—if they last that long—are constantly rivaling one another and intriguing for position. They form loose coalitions to hoist one of them into power, hoping to get aided later on in return. If not, or if they sense any weakness, they try to undermine the Prime Minister and have him ousted . . . not necessarily for personal or ideological reasons, but just to leave room for themselves. This has led to an amazing turnover in Japanese politics as faction leader replaces faction leader. In recent years, only Eisaku Sato managed to stay on top long. That was because he had two strong lieutenants, Takeo Fukuda and Kakuei Tanaka, he could depend on (and play off against one another). When he stepped down, Fukuda, as the senior man, expected to be elected Prime Minister. Instead, Tanaka jumped the gun, won over a number of factions, and got into the number one position himself. Fukuda did not forget this, and when Tanaka was in difficulty due to dubious business dealings enough pressure was brought in the party to drop him. Fukuda again expected to come in. This time, however, in order to prove the party was clean and because the rivals couldn't agree among themselves, Takeo Miki was chosen. No sooner in place, and busily making good on his promise to clean up politics, he started digging into the Lockheed scandal and thus worrying some of his colleagues. Tanaka, down but not for good, worked with his former opponents to get Miki dropped and replaced by Fukuda. No sooner in, of course, than those who had supported him were forming combinations to oust the Prime Minister, who, like all his predecessors, was never free from concern as to what his own colleages were doing to undermine him.

By this point, factionalism was becoming a bit disreputable again and hurting the LDP's public image. Theoretically, the Prime Minister should in some way be responsible to the people and a result of their choice as expressed through elections. Instead, the highest position in the land seemed to be the joint possession of a handful of faction leaders and the party "elders" who periodically had to calm their rivalries or decide among them. Once this tiny coterie had decided, the LDP fell into line and elected the man party president, proposed him as Prime

Minister, and the Diet approved the choice. Occasionally, when the electoral situation looked right, the nation's leader would have himself ratified by the populace. Fukuda thus felt the time had come for a new image. He proposed that the factions be disbanded, accepted more dues-paying party members and friends, and gave them a role in electing the party president. The factions, however, rather than disappear were disguised as study groups or clubs. And Fukuda himself was the first victim of the reforms when the primaries gave Ohira an upset victory, but one clearly based on a combination of his own and Tanaka's supporters. Despite bitter complaints of vote buying and other abuses, Fukuda stepped down. But he demanded the same sacrifice when the 1979 elections called by Ohira failed to give the party a "stable majority" and the incumbent was blamed for this "defeat." Ohira was willing to apologize, but resigning as Fukuda, Miki and Nakasone wanted was another matter. This set off one of the bitterest factional struggles the LDP had ever seen, completely ignoring the supposed democratization of the party and the national interest.

The politicians were also kept busy with other chores, which were far more important for their survival in politics but kept them away from legislative matters. Having once gotten into power, it was necessary for them to thank those who had helpd. First of all, there was the general constituency. A school, road, or project of some sort had to be gifted to the home region. "Pork barrel" politics thus became an art, few being more accomplished than Tanaka, who won his hometown of Irihirose a railroad, paved highway and modern school building.[4] But he was far from the only one. Such things were run-of-the-mill, and whoever failed to show his beneficence might fail to be re-elected. There were other things that had to be obtained. For example, for a politician from a farming

LDP leaders putting on a show for the public.
All together now: long live harmony!

Photo Credit: Foreign Press Center-Japan

area, it was necessary to get quotas as protection against imports; for a manufacturing area, perhaps some aid to exports. Through the companies that supported him, it might be possible to have a factory built in his region. Then, to thank the business interests that filled his campaign chest, the grant of a public works contract, research funds, financial backing, tariff protection and so on.

But, the return of patronage often goes somewhat further. Those in the support organization, the power brokers and suppliers of votes, are given a traditional petty sum of money in gratitude, but also perhaps attend a "seminar" at a nice hot springs resort. They may also get some other gifts and a share of the patronage. In fact, the poor politician is constantly kept busy trying to repay his voters for their kindness. He must receive an unending stream of supporters and "friends," each coming to his office with some request or favor needed. He helps out with sundry matters, many of them really none of his concern, such as getting people's children into schools they didn't qualify for, helping find a job for some relative, obtaining contracts for a businessman in difficulty, arranging introductions to influential people, acting as mediator in disputes, fixing traffic tickets, and so on. He then has to spend his time gracing every conceivable sort of gathering. In the personal contact society of Japan, a politician even has to officiate at weddings or send wreaths to funerals.

All of this, namely the election campaigns and the patronage he is expected to provide, costs a tremendous amount of money. The Dietman is not poorly paid by Japanese standards, a monthly remuneration of ¥810,000, another ¥650,000 for transport and correspondence costs, and a semi-annual bonus of ¥3,847,500, or over ¥21 million all in all. But, this was obviously not enough. Rumor has it that Dietmen must spend at least ¥3 million a month to remain popular in their constituency. They were partly funded by the party, each LDP member getting about ¥1 million as a year-end bonus, while the faction leader may have added another bonus (and none was grander in such things than Tanaka). The party also provided much of the campaign expenses within the officially allowed limit of ¥10 to ¥27 million. Unfortunately, although the limit was fixed by law, everyone knew that you could not win an election on that sort of money. It was commonly felt that at least ¥50 to ¥100 million was needed to win a seat. This got the politicians onto two rather slippery tracks: they had to rake in tremendous amounts of money to get the wherewithall for campaign and other expenses; they had to evade the laws on electoral expenses if they wanted to win.

So raising campaign funds became a major task of all of the politicians and parties, not only the LDP. For this, the LDP could expect pitifully little from the rather small "popular" membership it first had. But, it could count on big business. In 1974, the LDP collected a treasure chest of ¥18,879 million and untold millions more went into the campaign funds of the factions and the individual candidates. Indeed, the use of money was so scandalous that something had to be done. In July 1975, a Political Funds Control Law was adopted—although narrowly so, by a one vote margin—to replace the old law, manifestly ineffective. The new law provided for public disclosure of funding and put limits on amounts that could be granted to parties, factions, and individual politicians by specific sources. The next year, the LDP had fallen to ¥10,081 million and was in tough financial straits. It went through a period of soul searching or simply seeking a means to round out its financial resources. Among other things, it decided to form a "grass roots" organization of dues-paying members. But, big business still had to come to the rescue at election time.

The real problem, again for all the parties, was how to disguise the sources that exceeded the limits and how to spend far greater amounts than permitted by the law. This situation has doubtlessly led to abuses. By forcing the politicians to bend the law, and most Japanese seem to feel that the restrictions are too tight, an opening is provided that can be pushed any desired distance since they are behaving unlawfully anyway. The insistence on frequent electoral campaigns, which is really not desired by the LDP's backers in business, leads to a situation where the politicians are not only kept from fulfilling their responsibility as legislators but become a heavy burden on those who support them. Thus, Ichiro Kawasaki complained:

"Generally speaking, the political parties have hardly made a positive contribution to the development of postwar Japan—their existence is largely parasitical. In present-day Japan the business world bears the chief burden of supporting these parasites . . . But this interdependence in postwar years has resulted in the deviation from the proper functions of government and has hurt the legitimate interest of big business . . . The result is often political atrophy and poverty of leadership. The fact remains, however, that if a Diet member merely had lofty national interests uppermost in his mind, he would most likely not survive in the complicated scenes of political struggle."[5]

If that were all, it might just be excusable. Unfortunately, even that tenuous line between right and wrong is ignored by some politicians who engage in outright graft, bribery or more serious crimes. Reischauer claims that "political corruption is not widespread in Japan;" Tetsuro Murobushi, author of *Postwar Scandals* and *How to Become Corrupt*, speaks of "structural corruption."[6] The impression one gets is that there certainly is a fair degree of impropriety going on. One reads occasionally of a mayor who took bribes to have a factory or nuclear power plant built in an area where objections had been raised by the populace, a Governor who arranged major contracts for local builders, or a Dietman thanked palpably for an introduction. Those involved were not always small fry and it almost appeared as if the higher one went the larger the sums involved. In the old days, it was not rare to hear of someone who refused to go into politics because the cost of running for office might eat up the family fortune. Nowadays, many people have gone from rags to riches thanks to the perquisites of the profession and did not enhance the reputation of politicians in so doing.

The only reason so little is known of corruption is the extraordinary finesse and discretion of those concerned which leads one often to feel that each act uncovered is only symbolic of many others and at most the tip of the iceberg. The Japanese term for such phenomena shows just how unseizable they are: "black mist." "Black mist" already began rising over Japan noticeably in 1954 during the shipbuilding scandal. Despite serious suspicions of bribery, Prime Minister Yoshida prevented a proper investigation by keeping the prosecutor from arresting Eisaku Sato, then Liberal Party Secretary General. There were repeated complaints about company donations to political parties exceeding the legal limits and providing funds unnecessarily large given the restricted campaign expenditures allowed. But nothing much was done to clamp down on abuses and those arrested were usually low-level campaign workers but not the politicians they worked for. Only one case was prosecuted involving Nippon Express and 47 Diet members, including Prime Minister Sato, of which only 2 were found guilty.

Thus, Japan must have been more embarrassed than otherwise when the Securities and Exchange Commission began showing unexpected zeal in investigating American companies for engaging in bribery to sell goods in Japan and began uncovering one case after another: Lockheed, Grumman, McDonnell Douglas and Boeing. The biggest shock came with the Lockheed scandal which involved former Prime Minister Tanaka, the then Transport Minister and LDP Secretary General Tomisaburo Hashimoto, the Parliamentary Vice-Transport Minister, and several other "grey officials" as well as fixers Osano and Kodama. The affair, which was promptly dealt with under Prime Minister Miki, has since dragged on. It resulted in serious allegations of a ¥500 million kickback to Tanaka for helping Marubeni sell Lockheed aircraft to a major airline. Somewhat later, Raizo Matsuno, former Director General of the Defense Agency, was accused of accepting—or rather demanding—¥500 million for his good offices in selling (via Nissho-Iwai) Phantom jet fighters to the Defense Agency. Other findings can be expected in the future, but very few penalties, for most of the events have passed the statute of limitations. Any hope that the voters would react by turning on those suspected, accused or even proven guilty, dissipated as fast as the mist. Aside from Matsuno, most of those involved in the various scandals retained positions of prestige or power.

None of this casts a very good light on the present political class. Compared to politicians of the Meiji era, or politicians in other democratic countries, they cut a rather sorry figure. Few seem to know or care much about legislation or the nation's needs. Few rise to the height of statesmen, and some are outright incompetents or hacks. They have simply learned the profession of politician, and learned it well. Once elected, they become experts at winning elections, often winning five, ten, or more times in a row to stay on to a very ripe old age. They are also part of a professional clique that looks after its own interests, mixes with its own kind, and has little to do with the people.

* * *

With the politicians so caught up and engrossed in the demanding career of politics, there is not much time for them to run the country. This task, by and large, is left to a body not mentioned for the purpose in the Constitution, the civil service. Without its civil service, Japan could not have survived either in pre- or postwar days. Since the government's employees have indeed such an important role, and maintain such close relations with politicians and business, they should really be called—as usually does happen—bureaucrats. These people are among the best educated and most disciplined in Japan, they are among the few who rise to fill the political vacuum left by the elected leadership. The degree of guidance they receive from the government is minimal compared to the amount of advice they give it, indirectly and discreetly. This, of course, enhances their prestige and permits a certain degree of efficiency. But it can have its drawbacks in practice and also as concerns the goal of a democratic society.

As we saw, the ministers are chosen by the prime minister, giving a certain share to his own faction and the rest to supporting factions, with less concern for specific ability than a proper political balance and to pay back favors. It rarely happens that non-party men or independent experts are chosen. Those selected usually fit into three types. Some have significant interests in the field, like a businessman running MITI or a farm spokesman at Agriculture, who thus wield power in support of a specific constituency or grant favors to obtain patronage. Others, former bureaucrats themselves, know the administrative machinery inside out and can use it effectively. But the majority do not know enough about the field or the machinery to shape policy to any great extent. Thus, the minister and parliamentary vice-minister are likely to depend heavily for advice on the administrative vice-minister, the highest bureaucrat in the ministry. He and his staff usually draw up the budget which serves as the basis for the various programs. They also draft specific bills and plan the tactics for getting them through the Diet. They repeatedly go beyond the line of passive onlooker to guide the law-making process. Then, once a program has been adopted or a budget voted, it is again up to the bureaucracy to work out the ways and means of attaining the goals. The degree of latitude given regarding implementation of policy is rather large and even quite low level bureaucrats have a reasonably free hand. Judging by Vogel's paean to the bureaucracy, it is definitely running the show.

"Politicians respect the ability of bureaucrats and recognize that they need their good will. Diet members have no independent research staff and rely on bureaucrats for specialized staff work. Politicians who try to work around a bureaucrat are likely to have the whole bureaucracy poised to retaliate by embarrassing the politician at the first opportunity. A Diet member may, for example, be given incomplete briefings by bureaucrats so that he can easily be made to appear foolish and ill-informed in Diet interpellation. It rarely comes to such a showdown, however, because politicians realize the advantage of maintaining the cooperation of the bureaucrat. They will want the bureaucracy to support construction projects in their locality or stand up for rice price supports . . . When it comes to the balancing of interests between farmers and small and big business, the politicians have considerable say if it does not greatly affect the budget. However, when it comes to the basic administrative work of the ministry, politicians know they must defer to the administrative vice-minister and the bureaucrats beneath him."[7]

With all this responsibility entrusted in the bureaucrats, it is vital for Japan to get the best possible people. And, in a Japanese sense, they do. Very strict examinations must be passed to enter any administration, and especially the central government. The tests are so hard indeed that the chance of getting into the higher grades of the national civil service at all is only about 1 in 40, that of getting into the administration (as opposed to say fisheries or the tobacco monopoly) is about 1 in 150, and for the law category almost 1 in 300. Many of the candidates start preparing for the exams years in advance. After a strict written examination, the candidates are interviewed by juries until they are accepted in one of the open positions. They come, in amazingly high percentages, from certain "elite" schools that have traditionally supplied bureaucrats, University of Tokyo first, and somewhat less the University of Kyoto, with Keio and a few others trailing behind. The best point of entry is the law faculty of these schools. The percentage of Todai graduates in the ministries, from section chief up, has been out of all proportion to the number of entrants: some 53% for Transport, 58% for Construction, 62% for Finance, 63% for MITI, 66% for Education, and 73% for Local Government already in 1963.[8] However, there is some reason to wonder why so many get in from certain schools and whether the old-school tie did not play a role. More serious, in local and even prefectural administrations, there has been a clear trend toward getting jobs through connections with some politician or ranking civil servant or even through relatives, this both in conservative and "progressive" strongholds.

Without really checking on the quality of the bureaucrats, some observers assume that they must be highly efficient and competent since they are chosen by such strict examinations and come from the best schools. But, even then, the entrants have only had a general education in many cases and a brief acquaintance with law at best. Generalists are still preferred to specialists. And none were trained specifically as civil servants in a school such as the Ecole Nationale d'Administration in France. Like every other branch, the young bureaucrats come in pretty much unprepared and need on-the-job training before they are of any use. Rather than put them in a given field, where they may stay for a rather long time until they know it thoroughly, they are often moved about as much as twice a year, obtaining at best a superficial knowledge of many areas, but also a broad, overall view of the ministry as an apparatus and plenty of personal contacts. Although familiarity rather than specialization has its virtues, there are some former bureaucrats who dispute the merits. According to Shigeru Sabashi, former MITI Vice-Minister: "If you are transferred from one post to another every six or twelve months, you can't organize your job productively." Hajime Iwao, a former Director General of the Ministry of Finance also felt this did not permit a person to show his ability. "It seems to me that posts are not created for productive work but are there so that they can be filled when transfer time comes around."[9]

Another reason why bureaucrats might have trouble showing their ability, aside from repeated transfers and lack of in-depth knowledge, is that it is far more important to fit into the human relations context of the section, department, and ministry. They seek out a friendly older bureaucrat, and help hoist him into a leading position, while hoping to be carried along. They attend the interminable decision-making meetings, being careful to keep on good terms with all concerned rather than put forward proposals or take initiatives. Ultimately, they may join a faction that hopes to appoint one of the department heads or vice-chiefs. And, finally, they may push their man up to the position of vice-minister. In this jungle, however, the old school tie seems to be even more important than elsewhere. For Todai and Kyodai graduates, who were the first to inhabit the ministries at the turn of the century, have often gotten such a strangle-hold over the apparatus that others have trouble rising. The democratization achieved by letting in graduates from other schools is somehow nullified over the years as those from the select few move into key positions. For example, in 1959, only 63% of those entering the higher civil service came from Todai, but those reaching the highest level were 95% Todai products.[10] Even if the figures have fallen somewhat, there is still a great handicap for non-Todai or Kyodai graduates.

However, although the bureaucrats run the administration and almost the country pretty much on their own, this does not mean that they go about recklessly taking initiatives. To the contrary, they tend to follow customs or precedents where possible and shun taking really new decisions. When that must be done, the responsibility is made as collective as possible. The bureaucrats are certainly not, in most cases, a dynamic element, but rather a conservative one. They are trained to follow orders, do what they are told, and work their way up slowly. They would be loath to risk their accumulated status and privileges by going out on a limb. If anything, in carrying out decisions, they stay on the safe side. And they avoid anything that might conceivably hurt or indispose any interests, especially those close to the LDP or business. As Dr. Shintaro Hayashi, then being ousted in a factional struggle, pointed out: "In today's MITI it is the young men who are earnest, patriotic and who seek justice who are in disfavor. Only 'yes-men' are appreciated."[11] Comprehensive studies of the foreign office and diplomatic corps came up with much the same results. Bureaucrats who did take initiatives often paid dearly for it, as happened with Takakichi Yanase, a high official of the Environmental Agency, squeezed out after angering MITI and Construction by promoting the crucial law for any ecology program, one requiring an environmental impact assessment *before* beginning large-scale development projects in order to prevent pollution.[12]

Fortunately for Japan, there have always been very competent and dedicated people in government service, and they have done a tremendous amount to rebuild Japan after the war. The only question is whether such people will still appear in the future or be able to play a dynamic role. Recent trends seem to indicate that those entering the bureaucracy are not necessarily doing it for the best reasons. The turn away from business by young graduates was not due to patriotism or a feeling that business was dirty but rather that the recession made the bureaucracy a safer place to be. Wages were not as high, although not so low, but job security was unusually great, retirement benefits good, hours regular, and the career not all that demanding. According to Saburo Shiroyama, who wrote a best selling novel on Japan's bureaucracy, this trend "also shows a lack of spirit." The young people "aspire to a career that is directly opposite to one in venture business. They are secure jobs that do not require creativity."[13]

Just how "good" or "efficient" the bureaucrats really are is hard to tell. Many of the older generation were indeed very dedicated and hardworking. Dr. Hayashi, referred to above, took the ailing Japanese sewing machine industry, revived it, and made it an export industry. Similar little miracles were worked by any number of other MITI officials. Government officials carried out a monetary reform and land reform. Extension workers helped revolutionize agricultural production while various research institutes promoted new products. Diplomats strove to restore Japan's good name after the war and smooth over complaints of economic imperialism later on. Yet, if the successes were widely heralded, the failures are kept a secret, unless latched onto by some opposition politician or newspaper. (And even the opposition and newspapers do not lightly pick a quarrel with the bureaucracy.) For example, the Transport Ministry, which was involved with the Narita Airport, rather than admit it was well behind schedule actually claimed that the rail and road constructions had been completed by 1976, when in fact none existed aside from whatever general facilities were there to begin with. The Livestock Promotion Public Corporation, which siphoned off tremendous sums of money by selling imported beef expensively, was supposed to use that money to raise the level of self-sufficiency. Yet, from 1960 to 1974, the number of stock farms dropped by three-quarters and the number of cattle by 20%. Japan National Railways, famous for its bullet train, is infamous for its incredible deficits. The Japan Housing Corporation has been criticized for substandard workmanship on its buildings. Defects in public housing projects, some of which are unsuitable for living and lie empty, include bad designing, inferior materials, cracks in walls or wooden panels falling off. Even in the Foreign Ministry, where errors should least be expected, it was amazing that Prime Minister Tanaka had not been warned of the ugly mood in Thailand and Indonesia before his ill-fated trip in 1974 or that the oil crisis, and the fact that Japan had few friends in the Arab world, should come as such a surprise.

The bureaucracy also tends to treat its employees, i.e. itself, too well on occasion. The work load for some at any rate is quite modest and in many offices one can see, with little attempt to hide it, civil servants goofing off, reading newspapers, chatting, or having tea. This is most flagrant at the municipal level where the pay is often 10% higher than the national level . . . for people with far less qualifications. One sometimes wonders if the bureaucrats are hired to do a job or one is just created for them. This may be the cause of the tremendous amount of red tape which officials impose on the private sector. Often the "workers" are treated even better. JNR, despite its disastrous financial situation, has become the pace-setter for railway strikes and wage offensives and the amount of feather-bedding is very impressive. Boondoggles do exist, a more flagrant example coming to light in the Forestry Agency. As many as 3,000 out of 5,000 lumbermen employed by it were paid, at public expense, ¥1.4 billion for not working plus ¥4.1 billion in medical and welfare measures as they were allegedly suffering from "vibration disease" due to use of chain saws. Workers were diagnosed by "progressive" doctors and won the right to work only 10 minutes every 2 hours. Lumbermen in the private sector had to prove illness and got benefits much lower than in the public sector.[14]

The biggest question, however, is whether so many bureaucrats are needed to accomplish the work. There has been a trend for the numbers to grow over the years and to keep on growing even when no new tasks were found. By 1979, there were 1,190,000 central government employees, 3,010,000 local government employees and 940,000 government-affiliated corporation employees.[15] Already a lot for Japan, their ranks expanded even in the recession. Ultimately, there seemed to be a consensus that the number of civil servants had to be cut back. Various Cabinets spoke of administrative reform but this always got bogged down. Finally, the ex-bureaucrat Fukuda worked out an ambitious plan to reduce the administration. But it, too, had to be watered down tremendously due to opposition from the bureaucrats who also managed to obtain support from many LDP politicians. In the end, a certain number of branch and field offices, very few public corporations, and some chauffeurs were eliminated . . . a drop in the bucket. Ohira, also a former bureaucrat, promised to streamline the bureaucracy as of

1980. It remained to be seen how he would fare.

Along with its competence, which appears somewhat mitigated, the bureaucracy is admired for its honesty and incorruptability. According to ex-Ambassador Reischauer, "the national bureaucracy has been entirely untarnished by scandal."[16] In the Japanese situation, and especially compared with the politicians and businessmen, the bureaucrats are indeed "pure." Yet, how can they rub elbows with such people day after day without becoming contaminated? After all, it is the bureaucrats who draw up decisive plans determining which industries, branches, or companies will receive what, and how much, support from the government. They know where future projects will be built. To guarantee their freedom from temptation at least, one would assume that highly objective procedures would be used in making such decisions. For example, in the choice of a construction firm for a project, competitive bidding and strict inspection; in land purchases, preemptive buying and eminent domain; in picking suppliers, careful comparison of prices, delivery dates and so on. Instead, in deals involving fantastic sums, huge subsidies or chances to gain major competitive advantages, incredible leeway is left to the bureaucrats concerned. There is more than enough room for personal intervention, directly or via politicians, and so few records are kept that one would never know the sources of a tip or favor. Thus, companies and individuals will do anything to get on good terms with key bureaucrats.

How they do so may vary. With all due apologies to Reischauer, there are cases of corruption, especially in the national and local bodies that hand out public works contracts. They are worth an awful lot to the companies concerned and irregularities occur in granting the contracts as well as later on in inspecting the finished work or in imposing government building, antipollution, and other regulations. Anything involving land in Japan has become equally suspect, since the government always seems to get stuck with the highest prices, all too often for land that was purchased shortly before the announcement by the government to buy. The Ministry of Construction has a particularly bad record. One recent scandal involved a former JHC official, fired for taking bribes, who set up his own company. In only a few years, it managed to rise from nothing to the third biggest contractor. How? Thanks to the contacts he maintained in the Japan Housing Corporation. This went beyond receiving juicy contracts to using moonlighting JHC architects to draft the same plans they would have to approve later on. Other scandals involved the JHC's use of general contractors who then farmed out all the work at rates forcing the subcontractors to pay minimal wages and leave behind substandard work . . . which was then approved by the inspectors.[17] But, the Lockheed affair and some land deals were such massive rip-offs, involving much collusion at different levels, that it is hard to believe no one in the bureaucracy knew about them.

However, a scandal that surfaced in late 1979 involved the bureaucracy very directly. It concerned primarily the Japan Railway Construction Corp. responsible for building Japan National Railway's infrastructure and endowed with a massive budget of ¥355 billion. Through a number of tricks like padding the work force with nonexistent staff, collecting for social insurance premiums never paid out and billing for travel and missions never undertaken, it was able to lay aside a ¥1 billion slush fund in 1978 alone. This money was used to pay its workers higher bonuses than allowed by its regulations, offer tax-exempt allowances for overtime work or business trips that had never been accomplished, and to entertain senior government officials and politicians lavishly. This included contributions to LDP fund-raising affairs and wining and dining of Transport and Finance Ministry officials, especially those from the latter's Budget Bureau which controlled its budget and the Financial Bureau that regulates loans to public corporations. The dimensions of this scandal were most impressive as concerns the amount of money involved, the number of high officials and probably also average employees who must have known about it but participated in the cover-up and the obvious ramifications in JNR, the Transport and Finance Ministries, and the ruling party. That anything this big could occur, and be kept hidden for years, led to strong suspicions that other cases existed in similar public corporations. And, indeed, further investigation uncovered similar practices in the Environmental Agency, Defence Agency, Prime Minister's Office, and Tokyo Metropolitan Government.

This came not long after another scandal involving relatively modest sums, but touching upon very essential principles. It concerned the Board of Audit, supposedly the government's "watchdog" to avoid waste, inefficiency, and corruption throughout the administration. Yet, when checking on works being undertaken for the Ministries of Construction and Transport, as well as the Defense Agency and perhaps some others, the watchdogs were apparently treated to lavish meals, entertainment and gifts. This was strictly against the rules, and one might also wonder why the officials had to buy the favor of the inspectors. This was picked up by the JSP, whose members sharply attacked the practices (until it realized that some of the wrong-doers belonged to the leftist trade union Sohyo). But this was not the worst, for it later turned out that, when the inspectors found wrong-doings, they merely reported this to the Ministries which were left free to follow up and usually did nothing. Moreover, in this particular scandal, those involved were merely given admonitions and warnings but no disciplinary action was taken.

Even when things do not reach this dimension, it would seem incompatible for civil servants to accept gifts of any sort. Nevertheless, according to Ichiro Kawasaki, who wrote it, and untold millions who know it: "Often a high-ranking government official of the Finance or Trade Ministries ends up filling an entire room with presents received from numerous associates or business contacts. Some of these officials cannot possibly hope to use these goods themselves and so dispose of the items and realize a handsome fortune."[18] However, even when no money or gift changes hands, business interests are in a position to buy the favor of bureaucrats. There is such a thing as postponed rewards, and the Japanese are unusually good at waiting. All the little gifts, free trips and vacations, as well as good paying sinecures can be collected after retirement, when there is no danger for anyone, and when this ceases being a crime and becomes not only acceptable but almost "honorable".

For, the biggest plum for any bureaucrat, and the way the top bureaucracy in particular rewards itself, is by moving into excellent "retirement jobs." This is known as *amakudari* or "celestial descent." Although civil servants can stay on in their jobs until 55 or more, the average retirement age is 50. Thereupon, they take up positions in business, public corporations, or other government functions like ambassador, judge, etc. The most improper form in a way is not even work in the private sector but rather in one of the many semi-governmental corporations that were set up under the ministries, often by the very people who later retired into them. It might be noted that the Audit Bureau often employs its retired staff in the very same corporations it is supposed to audit. There are about a hundred of these bodies and they cost the government over ¥9.5 trillion in subsidies in 1977, their contribution to the economy or the nation often being highly dubious. The contribution to superannuated civil servants, however, is clear, since salaries in these sinecures are often higher than in the original jobs, most presidents and managing directors getting an average salary of over ¥1 million a month (or more than a minister). Meanwhile, they collect their retirement benefits as well, and some retire again and again, passing through as many as five jobs. The same things occur at the lower level where local governments, otherwise short of money, set up superfluous and loosely organized bodies as a "retirement home" for municipal employees. No matter how well known to the Japanese, nor how much attacked, even the government hesitated to diminish or control this source of privileges.[19]

So, it would appear that without being overly demanding or self-seeking, but also without being unduly patriotic or self-sacrificing, the bureaucrats have carved out a very nice little niche for themselves in the nation. They enjoy a reasonable salary and regular raises, often doing better than the private sector in bad years, although now toned down a bit. They also get bonuses which, unlike the private sector, are not tied to productivity or profits. They have tremendous security, it being rare that a civil servant loses his job for any reason, including those laid down in the regulations, if he keeps his nose clean. More important, however, is the knowledge that when they retire they will be receiving good severance pay and/or a pension that dwarfs those of the average citizen. Nor do they have to retire early, many staying on in some government job to 65 or 70, far longer than is usual in the private sector.

This is all most unfortunate for Japan, because it still does have a reasonably competent and honest bureaucracy. Ignoring problems, failing to apply penalties provided for by law, accepting gifts and bribes as just part of the game could ruin this. Instead, strong laws are needed to encourage the bureaucracy to keep its standards up. Strict competitive bidding should be the rule. The whole process of "administrative guidance" should be carefully reviewed and guarantees provided for all, especially the taxpayers who foot the bill and the firms that were not fortunate enough to be selected for promotion. Any corruption must be stamped out by the most severe measures. Not doing so is tantamount to notifying the bureaucrats they can carry on as in the past . . . as long as they are more discreet. The final step would have to be to prevent conflict of interest not only on the job but between the official position and one taken up later on in the public or private sector. In addition, of course, it would seem appropriate for the elected officials some day to assume the function of direction and supervision rather than leaving the bureaucracy on its own.

*   *   *

The third in the troika pulling Japan's state machinery is business. Business circles are obviously very interested in what the government is doing, all the more so since in Japan government seems to concentrate more than elsewhere on economic matters of vital importance for them. If business mixes in politics, one simple reason is that it has to since politics is mixing so much in business. Things have been that way ever since Meiji days. It was often the state that decided which projects should be launched, purchased or subsidized factories, and directed the whole economy. During the reconstruction of Japan after the war, it was again the state that directed the economy to a very large extent. It did not control or dominate, but it did guide and manipulate. Thus businessmen were soon establishing relations with politicians and bureaucrats who could help them.

There was no end to the forms this aid could take. To get things started again, it was obviously necessary to obtain financing, which often passed through the government. The state, via MITI, decided which technologies and equipment could be imported and by whom. The state then subsidized production if it wished. Otherwise, it could create a protective market by raising tariff barriers against imports. When Japan began exporting, it could offer subsidies for exports and guarantee loans to purchasers. In bad days, it decided which companies to bail out and which to let collapse. The role of Finance and the Bank of Japan was very important here. For other branches of business, other ministries could be decisive. Public works passed through the government and were essential to construction and other companies. Producers of pharmaceuticals got various assistances from Ministry of Health. Ministry of Agriculture could offer extension work or also protect domestic farmers from imports, or even subsidize them. Finally, and more generally, it was the state which laid down a general framework for business which was capitalistic without being truly laissez-faire.

It was thus normal that business organized to protect its interests through bodies such as the Japan Federation of Economic Organizations (Keidanren), the representative of big business, the Japan Federation of Employers' Associations (Nikkeiren), bringing in middle-sized companies, the more general Japan Chamber of Commerce and Industry, and the "think tank" Japan Committee for Economic Development. Their heads or representatives would advise government on business concerns and use some pressure to obtain positive treatment. But, along with them were any number of other bodies. There were all sorts of trade associations to protect manufacturers of items ranging from optical goods to sugar refining. The farmers, through the various cooperatives and associations also brought pressure to bear. As did the doctors and dentists through the Japan Medical Association and Japan Dental Association. In addition to proposing, or opposing, legislation, they often had their representatives elected to the Diet or lower level bodies to see to it that they received a favorable hearing. Toshio Komoto, former head of a shipping line, and Tokusaburo Kosaka, former head of a chemical company, were thought of as pro-business even in the pro-business LDP. The farmers, indeed, had as many as 100 Dietmen in their pocket and could put up as stubborn a fight as any big business lobby.[20]

This, of course, is the surface. What went on below that level was often more active and persuasive. This is the realm of "tea house" politics where key politicians and business leaders get together for a chat to discuss matters often more important than are ever brought up in the Diet. Reaching still further, it happened that individual businessmen would strike up relations of a very particular and practical nature. Here we are entering a field that often not only bordered on the illegal but crossed the boundary-line. Many cases exist of businessmen who rose by hanging on to the coattails of politicians.[21] There are also fixers and arrangers who work out deals that ordinary businessmen could not pull off, by using their contacts in the political world. The best known are Yoshio Kodama, a rightist and former agent for Lockheed among others, and Kenji Osano, director of all three major airlines and many other companies and a close friend of Tanaka.

The situation can be even worse when there is not only collusion between a politician and a businessman but the politician is a businessman himself, or uses a front. One typical scandal arose over a land deal made by a real estate firm associated with former Prime Minister Kakuei

Tanaka. It purchased a piece of relatively worthless dry-riverbed land for ¥55 million in 1965. In 1966, after the government announced it was going to build a highway bypass there, the value skyrocketed 200-fold to ¥10 billion.[22] This case is an exception only in that it was uncovered. The vast majority are covered up or poorly documented, but not enough to avoid the appearance of more "black mist." One would assume that particular care would be taken to avoid such things, but apparently not in Japan. No amount of "black mist" kept the Construction Ministry from dealing with Tanaka's companies or other bodies from dealing with companies backed by key politicians, and if anything dealing more favorably with them.

Relations with the bureaucracy could also take on this special flavor. It was standard procedure to get on very good terms with the bureaucrats taking decisions in the company's field. Given the importance of personal relations, these were cultivated as much as possible. One trick was to use the old school tie by sending salesmen from the same *alma mata*, often Todai. Small gifts and favors might follow. Nor were bribes unknown. But, even when there was no impropriety about relations with the bureaucrats during their career, other means could be used to obtain their loyalty, none more powerful than the offer of a good job after retirement. Since bureaucrats had excellent connections in their own administration, they could be most useful in using these connections for the company while being rewarded with a high paying sinecure. There were rules to prevent this conflict of interest for some time, usually a very brief one, after which they could go back to work in the same field, but on the other side of the fence. The ministries whose personnel was most desirable for such tasks were MITI, Transport, and Construction, where a good connection went a particularly long way.

Although occurring in the government-supervised international telephone and telecommunications monopoly, Kokusai Denshin Denwa (KDD), investigations as of 1979 uncovered irregularities that most clearly illustrate the dark underside of Japan, Inc. The criminal aspects of the case, such as illicit use of assets, massive unreported purchases and entertainment, kick-backs to company personnel, and the systematic smuggling of valuable articles through customs, were enough to create a scandal. Far more insidious, and significant, was the discovery that most of the purchases were intended as gifts for some hundred politicians in most political parties, albeit predominantly the LDP, who expressed their gratitude by supporting KDD's interests. These politicians included several ministers, especially Posts and Telecommunications Ministers, and well-placed members of the Diet and LDP bodies dealing with telecommunications. KDD also lavishly wined and dined high-ranking officials in the Posts and Telecommunications Ministry, some of whom received suspiciously large gifts. They were supposed to supervise its operations and examine its accounts. However, since KDD's President Itano and most top staff of KDD were former Ministry personnel, and KDD was a traditional pasturing ground for retired officials, they may not have been as zealous as intended. The reason for all this largesse and manipulation was that KDD sought to maintain the old exchange rate of ¥360 to the dollar in its billings even after the dollar fell to ¥300 and then about ¥230. This brought KDD huge windfall earnings and profits of some 20% at a time when other non-manufacturing businesses only averaged 1.5%. Even if they could not benefit directly from these huge profits, KDD's top brass managed to get extraordinary bonuses and retirement provisions. But they also had to please all those whose favor was necessary to maintain the artificially high rates in the face of growing public criticism. This they were able to do until an unexpected slip-up at customs exposed the whole web of relations and connections carefully spun over past years.

So there are clearly two sides to the business-government nexus. One is a perfectly fair and above-board effort to build up the Japanese economy, make it strong, and have it prevail over foreign competitors. This is well known and lauded in the form of "Japan, Inc.," with businessman, bureaucrat and politician cooperating for the common good, or through "administrative guidance," often seen as the clue to Japan's economic success. However, there is also the underside, namely when the relations become too particular and sometimes illegal. This side has gotten Japan a bad reputation among some, at home and abroad. At home, it is not only labor and the left that complain about this sort of overly close relations, complaints also come from the right. There are plenty of businessmen without quite as good connections or who lost out against competitors due to intervention and others who think that the Japanese economy would be much sounder if it were left alone and market forces decided which company should come out on top. One might also remember that dirty politics and dirty business were seen as the cause for the militarists coming to power in earlier days. Thus, it was an ultrarightist group that raided the Keidanren Building in March 1977 to protest about such relations. Abroad, in the advanced countries, Japan got a reputation for excessive protection and trickery in dealing with foreign competitors; in the developing countries, a reputation for bribery and corruption of local officials.

However, in addition to these more specific pro-business actions, there is also a global concern. For, it is obvious that business has a vested interest in maintaining the overall system of a liberal economy. Business, and especially big business, is defending and promoting itself by funding and backing the LDP, its factions, and individual politicians. It has even been rumored on occasion that it finances opposition candidates just to play it safe. In the old days, Mitsui was known for bankrolling and controlling the Seiyukai party and Mitsubishi its opponent, Kenseikai. Nowadays, with only one party in power, all of business backs the LDP and any differences appear in the form of special support to specific candidates and factions as well as involvement in the campaign for Prime Minister. In many cases, business does not hesitate to let it be known that it disapproves of a candidate or even the incumbent, coming out strongly against Tanaka after the scandals, then Miki on the antimonopoly law, later Fukuda, for slowness in handling the recession, and finally Ohira for calling the unsuccessful 1979 elections.

In the good old days, business backing of the LDP was massive. When Jimpachiro Hanamura was running Keidanren, apparently it used to determine how much each corporation should contribute to the LDP on the basis of size, turnover, profits, and so on. Similarly, in 1974, LDP Secretary General Hashimoto farmed out candidates to the major corporations such as Mitsubishi, Sumitomo, Hitachi, Fuji Bank, Nippon Kokan, etc. When Mitsubishi launched a "total involvement" campaign to have Ken Saka elected, it set up a board of advisors with the chairmen and presidents of the major firms, and they were backed up by the second-line managers with 50,000 provincial office managers under them. Each one was assigned a quota of 20 adherents. Throughout the period, in general, considerable pressure was used by major companies to have not only their employees but anyone else related to them, and their families as well, vote LDP.[23]

However, after the complaints of "black mist" and with

the coming of Toshiwo Doko, a blunt and dour Buddhist, as president of Keidanren, there was a considerable change. To dispel the stench of "money politics" (*kinken*), the LDP's old People's Association (Kokumin Kyokai), which used to raise an average of ¥200 million a month in political contributions from companies, was replaced by the People's Political Association (Kokumin Seiji Kyokai), which at first only brought in about ¥200,000 a month, and rose slowly without hitting the previous levels. As we saw, the LDP campaign chest fell from ¥18,879 million in 1974 to ¥10,081 million in 1976. This was far less than the JCP, despite such major donations as ¥90 million from Nippon Kokan, ¥85 million from Mitsubishi Heavy Industries, ¥81 million from Nippon Steel Corporation, and large sums from many construction firms, banks, etc. Given its expenses, it was in a sorry state. The reason was that Doko and others had decided that Keidanren should stop acting as a direct pipeline for campaign funds. He pointed out: "I am a strong believer in a free economy. That is why I want to see a strong Liberal Democratic Party. What I object to is the recent trend toward money power."[24] Business leaders were tired of being milked by the politicians for unending electoral campaigns, many of them unnecessary as only to settle intra-party squabbles. They also objected to being expected automatically to fork out the money, in such large quantities, and in such hard economic times. Finally, business was also unhappy about some LDP policies. Thus, the reaction was both one of righteous indignation and a warning that, although the money would come, the politicians would have to perform to get it.

* * *

The record of the LDP as an election-winning party is almost unparalleled in the democratic world; the conservatives were only out of power once briefly ever since the war. Although its margin has been constantly shrinking, the LDP is likely to hang on for some time to come. The erosion of its power base was slow and erratic showing unexpected upsets as well as major comebacks. It managed to have its candidates elected as mayor or governor in some of the cities and prefectures that had been dominated by "reformist" coalitions and, although its Diet representation fell, its popular vote rose in the 1979 elections. The main threat was increasingly a centrist coalition growing out of relations between Komeito and the two socialist rivals JSP and DSP. This could be countered by an LDP coalition or coopting of individual members and by greater cohesion within the LDP. Its leaders usually remembered that unity was their real strength and managed to keep factional struggles from ending in a split. As long as they stuck together, no matter what they were worth individually, they stood a good chance of ruling Japan.

This, of course, has left the public a bit out in the cold.

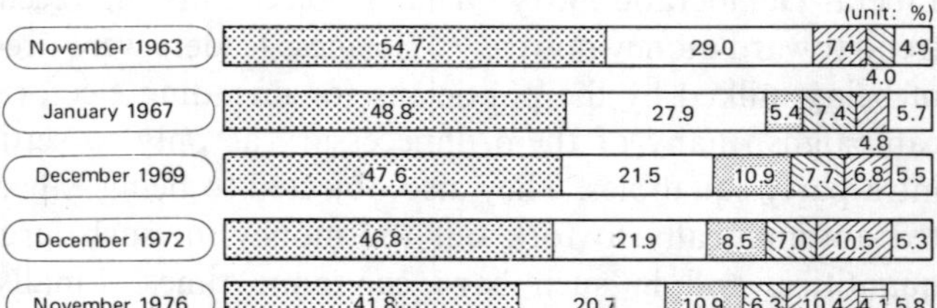

The political balance of power: erosion on the right, erosion on the left, expansion in the middle.

Credit: *Facts and Figures of Japan 1980*, Foreign Press Center-Japan, p. 85.

For some time, it did not really seem to disturb the LDP. As a concession to democracy and for practical reasons, many politicians set up small "modern" support organizations along with the old vote broker and contact network. This reinforced the cohesion of the party, got new blood into it, and helped get protégés elected. As long as they were bankrolled by the companies, there did not seem much need for more. When the funding sums went down, and there was criticism of unrepresentative parties, the LDP also decided to go "popular" by recruiting members. Much to everyone's surprise, the party soon managed to recruit over three million members. It also offered them a share in decisions via a primary system. Nevertheless, with "money politics" and "plutocracy," with scandals and corruption, many people did not like the LDP. Its success at elections kept on dwindling, and in polls between elections, it reached new depths.

However, did this mean that the public preferred the opposition? Apparently not. Although there had been few opposition politicians voted to positions of responsibility where they actually implemented policy, the results were not all that good. The effectiveness and efficiency of the reformist mayors and governors were questioned and even the issues they represented (ecology, welfare, etc.) paled during the recession. There was also considerable uncertainty about how the other parties were run. None of them was actually as open as the LDP. The socialist parties were closely linked to the trade unions, which provided the mass of their funds and much of their votes. In addition, the left was constantly quarelling internally and splintering (JSP, DSP, USDP). The more disciplined Komeito was originally an offshoot of the Soka Gakkai religion, not known for its liberalism or internal freedom, and even distancing itself from the religion left questions as to who took decisions or named leaders. The Japan

Communist Party, despite its repeated attempts to 'Japanize" and appear "lovable" was tightly controlled and appeared a bit suspicious both to voters on the right and left. Thus, although the LDP vote and popularity dropped, it was not really being taken up much by the opposition. Part of the LDP's loss went to the break-away NLC, the rest to medium-sized centrist parties, showing the trend was not really to the left, and the Japan Socialist Party was more than ever a weak opposition. As for popularity, no party seemed to be doing very well.

A more accurate conclusion would seem to be that the Japanese simply do not think very highly of politics. It is interesting to note that every Prime Minister managed to lose popular support and end up with amazingly low popularity figures: Ikeda —27%, Sato—22%, Tanaka—19%, Miki—30%, Fukuda—28%,Ohira—18%.[25] The general image of politics was very bad. From his own research, and many previous surveys, Bradley Richardson found unusually negative views of politics. "The day-to-day activities of public officials and the struggles between powerful figures and factions seems to attract little enthusiasm from the average Japanese. To some degree this is the result of the presence of a widespread pessimism and distrust regarding the behavior and responsibility of politicians. . . . Negative evaluations of politicians and politics are in fact the norm in Japan, a fact which is apparently related to a sensitivity to the gap between the conduct of politics and desirable levels of honesty, as well as to a distaste for the open competition characteristic particularly of national and partisan politics."[26]

This is the kind of attitude that had undermined the political system in earlier days and led to the rise of nationalism and fascism. Since the war, it has again aroused anger, although more diffuse and futile, as there was no longer any alternative to the parties. Moreover, more of the extremism was on the left than the right. During the 1950s, there were marches and *demos* against the Americans over military bases, Okinawa, the Security Treaty, and later Vietnam. During the 1960s, the main scene of radicalism moved to the university campuses. But one could hardly claim that this accomplished much more. The manifestations were often just sudden outbursts rather than continued action and often the reaction to violence was such a strong backlash that the body politic did not really move ahead. Whereas the earlier demonstrations often drew a broader backing, the student radicals, sometimes vying with one another in extremism, tended to form rather small and isolated pockets of resistance. They were very rarely joined by the workers, minorities, oppressed, or "people" in general. Worse, many of the students (although not all) returned to the straight-and-narrow as soon as this "phase" of their life was over.[27]

Thus, the far more prevalent expression of this dissatisfaction was apathy. What can we do? What can be done? Politics are like that! And the voters reacted by turning away from the parties, with few bothering to support any party in 1977.[28] Only two years later, polls by two leading newspapers showed that 31% and 35% of those questioned did not support any political party.[29] Thus, the rejection of politics continued. Unlike disaffected voters in many other countries, the Japanese gave up trying to influence their parties, but did not try to accomplish their goals by entering the political arena themselves or working on other means of obtaining reform. Passivism was more noticeable than activism. As Richardson noted: "When asked about the best way to express opinions or articulate wants at the level of prefectural or national politics, or 'politics' in general, Japanese voters were inclined to be especially passive in their attitudes."[30] Of course, if this is the general reaction, there was little reason for the politicians to change their own practices or fear for their careers.

So politics, like business, like education, like many other things, was regarded as its own sphere, left pretty much to the professionals there . . . even if not much was thought of their ability. It was not carried out openly in the Diet but in "back rooms" and more elegant "tea houses." Meetings were for the initiates. Only those who had some direct interest, namely the pressure groups or fixers, would go to the trouble of messing with politics. Since the average person acting as taxpayer, or consumer, or sufferer of pollution did nothing much to react and left the field free, it was not surprising that business or special interests should be so successful in having their needs tended to. The bureaucrats, there to serve the nation, were obviously not going to go out on a limb to keep rein on the politicians.

Like other groups, the politicians and the few dealing with them, as well as the bureaucrats, tended to form encapsulated units. Politicians were bred or trained for the profession, being coopted by the parties in most cases, and rarely rising to the top on their own or at popular demand. The LDP absorbed younger politicians and helped them move upward by providing the three *ban*: *jiban* (electoral support), *kaban* (bag loaded with money) and *kanban* (reputation). It coopted businessmen who had their own *kaban* and celebrities (with a sort of *kanban*) and supplied the *jiban*. It also absorbed considerable numbers of bureaucrats whose connections were solid. But the other parties, although less known for money politics, operated in similar modes since the biggest block of socialist Diet members and supporters came from the trade unions, the Communists used party officials and Komeito, Soka Gakkai adherents. More striking has been the rise in all parties, and especially the LDP, of the so-called "second generation" representatives. A Diet member who strongly controlled his constituency (*jiban*) would try to pass it on to a son, son-in-law or other relative. In fact, the number of such "juniors" has grown rapidly to well over a hundred. There has been a similar trend for secretaries of local support committees to inherit the seat. This makes the politicians an increasingly inbred class.

The bureaucrats were even more inbred, in that they were systematically taken from "good" colleges. They also lived in their ivory towers and only mixed with select people, specialized enough to know only a narrow range of citizens, and mainly just tried to do a satisfactory job as they rose through the rivalry and squirmishes of factionalism. The bureaucrats tended to take good care of their own interests, of one another, and thus of themselves . . . just like the politicians, although the methods they used were much more suave. No one saw the civil servants soul-searching about the fact that they had much better pensions than the average Japanese or that they were taking over top posts in big companies or public offices and thus squeezing out employees who had served there for years. The bureaucracy also tended toward elitism, already by origin from Todai, etc., but also by tradition. Despite the postwar reforms, high officials remained an "aristocracy" of sorts and there was some trend for the bureaucracy to be a bit proud or overbearing with the public, as in the old days, rather than embrace a more democratic approach.[31]

If the politicians were living in their own world, and the bureaucrats were even more in the shadows, how was the public to know about them? Despite all the examples elsewhere in the world, very few chose to go on radio or TV or speak to the people informally. Rather, they held court in small circles or private meetings and only those on the inside really knew how policy was being shaped. The one exception was the journalists, as each politician and each ministry had its own stable of newspaper reporters assigned to it. These reporters only knew their own contact, but at least an assembly of notes from different journalists handling different men and fields would give the newspaper reader some idea of what was going on. Indeed, it sometimes even gave the politicians, tied up in their own party or faction, an idea of what other politicians were doing or saying. It notified the bureaucrats at one ministry or level what was going on in the rest of the bureaucracy. Thus, some have claimed that the newspapers were a form of "press government." True, they did make things known, but one should not go that far. For they rarely criticized consistently or sharply. Oddly enough, when that did happen, it could be quite successful as when all the newspapers got together to attack Kishi's handling of the Japan-U.S. Security Treaty or Tanaka was brought down by the "Anatomy of Kakuei Tanaka" published in the *Bungei Shunju*.[32] That, however, was exceptional, since the newspapers and less so magazines seemed afraid of their own power and were worried about being kept away from sources of news. Muted or broad criticism, however, was often expressed, and in their own way the newspapers did manage to help express the popular will and shape policy.

Yet, the main reason politics were so unsatisfactory in Japan was not only the separateness of those engaged in it and the indifference or apathy of the common man. It went deeper. For that common man, the victim, was no more blameless than many politicians. Corruption was not only or really an aberration but part of the system. Japan was based on a society of personal relations, contacts and *koné*. Many people used contacts to get a job, to get children into college; factionalism was rife in all institutions and people hoped to rise that way and not through ability, merit or knowledge; personality regularly played a larger role than ideas or ideology; and so on. The politicians were not only corrupt because of their attitude but because society made it easy for them and in fact the voters, the very same ones who criticized them, also called for favors and wanted to know what the candidate could do for them. The voters were the ones who were still more concerned with personality than platform and let their representatives get away with what they did. As Ichiro Kawasaki pointed out:

"Much of the political corruption stems from the traditional reliance in Japanese communities on personal connections in all social activities. It is an attitude that expects special private favors in return for forming personal ties with others as distinguished from public or contractual relationships. This attitude is intense, and deeply rooted in Japan's rural communities, where, for instance, supporters of a national legislator seek tangible returns quite naturally when he is appointed to a high public office . . . Such an abnormal state of affairs can only be reproduced in a country where individualism tends to take a back seat to be replaced by the concept of obedience to authority—the authority of the family, the local community, and the state."[33]

There is no doubt that these reflexes and attitudes hidden behind the facade of democracy tend to sap its strength. It was assumed that with "modernization" they must disappear. And there is no doubt that there are trends, especially in the cities or among some educated groups, to put ideas before persons and shed some of the personal connections society. But this is far from a ground swell or revolution. It affects some people. But not enough by any means. Thus, any complaints by the public must be taken with a grain of salt as long as that public does not react to change the situation or, indeed, to change its own approach. And one can agree with Kawasaki that "while there is considerable disgust and discontent with the existing system, it is not likely that any big change will occur in the near future."[34]

The unlikelihood of basic change was shown by the June 1980 elections. They arose partly out of the growing factionalism in the Liberal Democratic Party which seemed to offer the opposition an unprecedented chance. But the other parties never managed to forge the necessary unity either. The broad coalition only resulted in loose links between the Japan Socialist Party, Komeito, and Democratic Socialist Party that were most sharply criticized by the Japan Communist Party. Faced with division on the right and the left, many electors preferred sticking to an unsatisfactory, but at least familiar, LDP. When the sudden demise of Prime Minister Ohira magically restored party unity and sparked a "sympathy vote," the LDP obtained what some called a landslide victory and returned to the Diet with a "stable majority."

However, the party showed that it had only learned a few lessons from this recent perilous episode. One was that it had to attain, or at least feign, unity to remain in power. For this reason, the factions were officially disbanded and the man selected as party president and then elected Prime Minister, was not one of the many strong figures vying for the post. Rather, it was Zenko Suzuki, known for his mediating role behind the scenes and chosen to restore "harmony and peace." But he was chosen by the party elders and faction heads instead of the formal "democratic" machinery and his cabinet was carefully balanced to please all factions and all contenders. With little experience of national policy-making, it did not seem likely that Suzuki would be an active leader. And that was probably what the party wanted.

Notes

1. Chitoshi Yanaga, *Japanese People and Politics*, p. 27.
2. Koichi Kishimoto, *Politics in Modern Japan*, p. 67.
3. See Gerald L. Curtis, *Election Campaigning Japanese Style*; Bradley M. Richardson, *The Political Culture of Japan*, and Robert A. Scalapino, *Parties and Politics in Contemporary Japan*.
4. *Japan Times*, "Inside the Weeklies," April 17, 1976.
5. Ichiro Kawasaki, *Japan Unmasked*, pp. 200–1.
6. Edwin O. Reischauer, *The Japanese*, p. 309, and *Japan Times*, April 15, 1979.
7. Ezra Vogel, *Japan as Number One*, pp. 60–61.
8. Yanaga, op. cit., p. 34.
9. *Japan Times*, "Inside the Weeklies," July 1, 1974.
10. Akira Kubota, *Higher Civil Servants in Postwar Japan*, p. 129.
11. *Japan Times*, "Inside the Weeklies," July 1, 1974.
12. *Japan Times*, September 16, 1977.
13. *Japan Times*, "Inside the Weeklies," July 5, 1976.
14. *Japan Times*, "Inside the Weeklies," April 12, 1976.
15. *Nihon Keizai Shimbun*, December 13, 1979.
16. Reischauer, op. cit., p. 309.
17. *Japan Times*, November 23 & December 26, 1977.
18. Kawasaki, op. cit., p. 167.
19. *Japan Times*, November 20, December 24 & 27, 1977.
20. Jon Woronoff, *Japan: The Coming Economic Crisis*, pp. 156–60.
21. *Japan Times*, "Inside the Weeklies," May 24, 1976.
22. *Japan Times*, November 2, 1977.
23. *Japan Times*, "Inside the Weeklies," June 9, 1975, August 27, 1974, & June 17, 1974.
24. *Japan Times*, "Inside the Weeklies," August 27, 1974.
25. *Japan Times*, April 6, 1978; *Mainichi Shimbun*, December 10, 1979.
26. Richardson, op. cit., p. 55.
27. See Ellis S. Kraus, *Japanese Radicals Revisited*.
28. *Japan Times*, December 12, 1977.
29. *The Diet, Election, and Political Parties*, Foreign Press Center, June 1979, p. 40.
30. Richardson, op. cit., p. 93.
31. See Kubota, op. cit.
32. *Bungei Shunju*, "Tanaka Kakuei Kenkyu," November 1974.
33. Kawasaki, op. cit., p. 201.
34. Ibid.

7

The Religious Totem Pole: Shintoism, Buddhism, Materialism

When it comes to Japan's religions and traditional virtues, we find some commentators engaging in mental gymnastics that would make the finest team of acrobats jealous. Yet, they always seem to land on their feet. According to them, the Japanese are basically a hard-headed, practical-minded, worldly people which has nonetheless adopted and adapted several major religions and philosophies and apparently manifests a great inborn religious sense (despite its secular action). That these religions have come from far off India, China, and the West to take root in a completely different indigenous worship does not faze them, for Japan's ability to blend and harmonize is fabled. That the same religions in Japan bear little similarity to their counterparts elsewhere, or to the precepts as originally taught or preached upsets no one, for we all know how good the Japanese are at transforming things. Even the fact that by now many Japanese have turned away from all these earlier faiths and show little active interest or even pay much lip-service, especially among the younger generation, does not detract from their interior religiosity. Thus, the myths persist and flourish:

"In the long history of Japanese religion, many concepts of heaven have been put forth: the 'other world,' the abode of the gods, the abode of ancestors. Simple people accept the idea of an afterlife in a place in the skies where water lilies grow and Buddha sits in a corner, and others believe that the spirit lives on after death; but many Japanese, in the Japanese way, 'harmonize' their afterlife. The syncretism of the Japanese is demonstrated over and over. People marry in a Shinto ceremony because it stresses purification, live by Confucian ethics, and go to the grave in a Buddhist rite because this guarantees that one will be remembered for a few generations. The edifices of Japanese religions are often built side by side. . . . . Buddhism and Shintoism have always been more compatible than competitive."[1]

Unfortunately, even the briefest and sketchiest of religious histories of Japan will show that none of these lovely metaphors corresponds much to reality. Japan is not the only source of native cults, which have sprung up all over the world, often also related to manifestations of nature. In early days, the various peoples inhabiting the islands developed many localized cults to worship perhaps a specially shaped rock, a tree, a spring, or waterfall. Soon enough a priestly class grew up around these places to direct the worship and play certain other social roles. There was a myriad of peoples living more or less isolated from one another, and a myriad of myriads of cults, all of which were lumped together much, much later as Shinto or "the way of the gods." This primitive Shintoism was very simple, with a few broad principles like a concern for purity and ritual washing or cleanliness and otherwise a tremendous range of variations and forms. There was no unity to speak of; indeed, certain Shinto gods were constantly disputing with others, involving the people worshiping them, or perhaps vice versa.

Later on, this religion was overshadowed by the far more sophisticated Buddhism which was introduced to the Japanese court from Korea in 552. Buddhism was not embraced by the Japanese then; rather, it confused them.

What was worse, the Shinto gods still being worshiped at the court were aggrieved and ominous phenomena led the Japanese to reject Buddhism twice. The only reason that it was ultimately adopted was a more propitious reaction of the elements on its return, and the fact that the religion was taken up by the Soga family, then at odds with two other leading families that controlled the court and its religion. Had the Soga lost, Buddhism might never have been heard of again, or had to await another attempt at a later date. But the Soga won out over their opponents, and so did Buddhism, which was made the state religion in 594, during the reign of Suiko. More important, the regent during the early seventh century, Prince Shotoku, was both a great secular and a great religious leader, one of the few Japan ever had. The court threw its weight behind the new religion, promoting the worship of it and the founding of monasteries. Monks were also sent off to China to study there. But the religion still spread very slowly in a rather backward country to which the power of the court did not reach, and where the local deities and their priests were still strongly rooted.

Buddhism spread gradually, but not as a oneness despite its precepts. For it was introduced from different parts of the mainland, by different people, at different times, and in different forms. Within a century, several basic sects were introduced, Ritsu, Tendai, Shingon, and Zen. Temples were built by these sects, monks proselytized and founded schools, and often these different schools began rivalling or even quarelling with one another. Later, to the sects introduced from China were added new ones established by local monks, such as Jodo and Jodo Shinshu, Ji, and also other branches of Zen. One of the most prominent was Nichiren, the first to be named after its founder, and one of the most aggressive. Nichiren was known not only for his fervor in making converts but also in condemning the other forms of Buddhism.

Buddha, like Christ, would have been amazed to see what was happening to the religion he founded. The increasing assimilation of Buddhism often verged on transformation and distortion. The oneness had long ago disappeared during the passage through China, but Japan added an incredible number of new variations, often integrating local deities and practices, and finally leading to a Buddhist-Shintoist dualism in which local gods were incorporated into the Buddhist hordes and many superstitions crept in, while Shinto shrines took on Buddhist characteristics. Meditation and simplification of rites to the point of mere repetition of words rather than a deeper understanding of the sutras could pass. But the worldliness of temple life, especially those near the capital, had nothing in common with the otherworldliness of the primitive religion. Japan not only permitted monks to marry, the monks sometimes had mistresses and frequented whore houses, they accumulated and spent wealth, much of it derived from the labor of peasants on monastery land or from public taxes, and they were far removed from what the bulk of the population expected of them. Worse, they dabbled in politics, taking sides with different leaders, disrupting court life in Kyoto, and ultimately tangling with the powerful *shoguns*.

It was the Tokugawa Shogunate that finally not only subdued but also channelled Buddhism into forms that appeared suitable for the state, its state. However, in so doing, it tended to weaken the religious fervor and morality. The number of members increased vastly; indeed, it was a duty to be a member of some temple. And the quarrels between sects were pacified or forbidden. Yet, in this easier life, only Zen, which was taken up increasingly by the *samurai,* prospered and showed any development. Meanwhile, Confucianism began to exert more influence

Traditional religion in modern times.

Photo credit: Japan National Tourist Organization

and even overshadow Buddhism. Many Chinese scholars came to teach respect for the state, loyalty to one's superiors, class and sex distinctions, whatever elements the Tokugawas thought would buttress their rule and provide calm in the nation. And, much of the social structure and philosophy of the Tokugawa period —and modern Japan— were derived from Confucianism, again as understood, assimilated and distorted.

Nevertheless, a number of subversive ideas did grow up during this period of tranquility. Rather than new ideas, actually there was a return to the old sources. At the same time that Japanese history was being re-examined, and rewritten, showing the unbroken line of emperors and their legitimacy as opposed to the Tokugawa *shoguns,* the early religion was also rediscovered. This time, however, Shinto was built up into a more united and a deeper religion than it had ever been, especially during the second half of the Tokugawa period. Attempts were also made at purifying it by throwing off the Buddhist veneer that had so actively been sought after during the vogue of dualism. The stronghold of these ideas was the Mito branch of the Tokugawas, within the *shogun's* own domains, and the more peripheral regions where Buddhism had never really penetrated in depth and where people still believed more in the old gods.

When the shogunate was overthrown, Buddhism, which had been too closely associated with it, was also attacked. These were not purely verbal attacks but actual acts of violence in which Shinto priests backed by anti-shogun/anti-Buddhist forces physically destroyed Buddhas and scriptures, burned down temples and sacked the property of monasteries. Then, in 1868, fully thirteen centuries after it was introduced to the country and made a state religion, Buddhism was disestablished, and two years later Shinto was made the state religion. This time it was Shintoism that was drawn upon as a source of legitimacy for the emperor and ideas and concepts for the new national doctrines. Ultimately, it was made an integral part of the growing nationalism. When this collapsed during the war, Shintoism was stunted as badly as Buddhism had been before.

One other religious strand must be mentioned, Christianity. This, too, was an imported religion. Just as the Chinese traders brought along buddhas and monks, the Portuguese came with crucifixes and missionaries, the most famous being St. Francis Xavier, who arrived in Kyushu in 1549. Although St. Francis, who was received at the court in Kyoto, left soon after, the movement was carried on for decades by missionaries who set about making converts with a dedication that was in sharp contrast to the passive and idle life of the monks in the surrounding monasteries. Due partly to a wish for trade with the Portuguese, but far more to the misery of the peasants, the flock grew and in 1562 had its first success in converting a local *daimyo*. Soon after, the center was moved to the port of Nagasaki, built for foreign trade at the missionaries' suggestion. In 1578, a more important *daimyo* of northern Kyushu was converted. Indeed, the religion kept on spreading at an incredible pace given its earlier setbacks and the tiny number of missionaries, reaching an estimated 300,000 Christians in half-a-century.

Any progress, however, was being made largely in the remote region of Kyushu. Moreover, as a foothold for dangerous and rapacious Western powers, this success was not politically desirable for Japan's rulers. At the same time, the Christians were creating trouble for one another. The Spanish Franciscans vied against the Portuguese Jesuits, and the Dutch and British by not mixing trade and religion offered a further alternative. In 1587, Hideyoshi ordered the expulsion of the Christian missionaries, but nothing was done until 1597, when the first executions of European missionaries and Japanese converts took place. The persecutions continued on into the early seventeenth century. The torture and punishment the converts accepted rather than betray their faith showed that it was deeper than their detractors could claim. Slowly but surely, they were forced to abjure or hide their religion and go underground. In 1873, when the ban on Christianity was lifted, it was amazing to see how many crypto-Christians had survived. But, despite new efforts at proselytism, and the many different branches of Protestantism and orders of Catholicism that tried, the number of Christians never rose above about 1%, although the influence of Christian ideas was in many ways quite substantial.

Hindsight is better than foresight, and looking back on it so many Western writers have now decided that the success of Buddhism was due to its inherent nature meshing with that of the Japanese. Christianity, they claim, was doomed to fail. What they seem to miss is the fact that presently neither Buddhism nor Shintoism in their traditional forms are doing well either. Only the "new religions" are flourishing and gaining converts. They include hundreds, indeed thousands, of sects, some with a handful of members, others with thousands, and a few claiming millions of adherents, such as Tenrikyo and Soka Gakkai (or "Value Creating Study Group"). All of them are very syncretistic and draw their precepts from all the earlier cults, although they may have a preference for one, such as Soka Gakkai as a branch of Nichiren. There is also a strong dose of personalism in their make-up, since many grew due to the magnetism or force of the founder's personality and may have remained under the control of his disciples or family. But none of them would seem to have the intellectual and spiritual depth of their predecessors. This can be seen from most of the observations and studies, such as *Buddhism in Japan* by Dale Saunders.

"First of all, it is interesting to note that almost one half of all the new religions began in one way or another with a revelation. . . . A second point in common to a number of new religions is the working of miracles. . . . Frequently this power can be transmitted to believers, and the transmission is a drawing card for new believers with hopes of gaining material assets: health, success, happiness, and so forth. . . . Thirdly, the new religions were all originally characterized by the simplicity of their doctrines, which appeal most to people of modest intellectual attainments. . . . The new religions are essentially lay organizations with no complex hierarchy and with extremely easy conditions for entry. The new believer, for example, is often neither requested nor expected to give up his traditional religion. The minimal financial requirements pose no problem for those of modest means, and indeed, new believers are encouraged to join the order by the frequent reference to material rewards in the propaganda."[2]

However, even if there has been a growth of sects, the overall tendency still seems to be toward an abandonment of religion or at least a reduction in its active practice. The Religious Affairs Section of the Cultural Affairs Agency reported that in 1975 Japan had no less than 178,573,950 adherents in some 181,000 registered religious corporations—this for a total population of about 110,000,000. The explanation was quite simple, namely that many persons were listed twice as believers of both Shinto and Buddhism, and perhaps yet again for a sect. Many had a little altar for the house god plus a Buddha in their homes. But the temples and shrines only regarded about half of their own parishioners as real members, and this real usually meant that they came for special personal occasions or briefly on major holidays.[3] The "new religions" usually had more asiduous members, although this was often because attendance was strongly encouraged . . . and not always with the gentlest means. Yet, when pressed to tell what their religious activities actually amounted to, of this vast number of adherents of so many religions only 3% said they were deeply engaged according to a Ministry of Education Study of the Japanese National Character.

It is not easy to reconcile the two sets of statistics unless one distinguishes between a rather nominal adhesion and a deeper commitment. This was already shown by Ronald Dore over a decade ago: "The question: 'What religion are you in your family?' produces in overwhelming proportions the reply 'Buddhism,' which refers to the fact that the family has a family temple on whose services it calls if need be. On the other hand, the question: 'Do you personally have any religious belief?' produces 88 noes out of 100."[4] Repeated polls have shown a turning away from religion after the war, and now a reversal of the trend. In 1973, only 8% of young people from 20–24 claimed to be religious-minded. By 1978, the figure had risen to 17%, and it hit 40% for those aged 55–59. But being religious-minded was not quite having a religious faith, and only 34% of all age groups professed one (up from 25% in 1973). But, when another survey tried to see how this was reflected in one's life, the main religious activities it found were an occasional visit to family graves or a New Year's visit to a shrine or temple.[5] Such acts were also accomplished by millions of people who felt no religious calling and have in fact become rather commonplace social —and even touristic— events. It will obviously take more for the return to religion to gain a deeper significance. However, those who find such distinctions tiresome may still prefer Bill Forbis' explanation: "the Japanese are strongly imbued with what has been called 'irreligious religiosity,' an abiding concern with that which transcends daily life."[6]

* * *

Unfortunately, what transcends daily life is not any "religiosity" but materialism. The Christian missionaries in Japan are people with very few illusions left, no matter how great their faith. They know they have been defeated. And they know it was not by the island climate or by a plethora of religions. Buddhism, Shintoism, Confucianism, Christianity, and perhaps ultimately the new religions are being defeated by the same enemy. After thirty years in Japan, the Baptist Moorheads recall their career: "Back in 1948, we started out with high hopes . . . Our first years here were wonderful ones. I remember Mario preaching on street corners in Kyushu. Thousands came to hear him. The Japanese were in the beginning of the postwar recovery at that point. You could sense an emotional vacuum. We had hoped to fill it with a spiritual belief. Instead, the people who were have-nots looked at the haves—the American occupation forces living well, in some cases luxuriously. They saw the imported American cars and food and clothes. And their pursuit became affluence. It was affiuence that eventually filled the vacuum."[7]

Thus, all the religions and the religiosity have been vanquished by secularism and materialism . . . the worship of things. This is nothing new in Japan. Its roots are the oldest of any religion and its resurgence is less surprising than that of Shinto after the Meiji Restoration. Unlike the statistics for the other religions, which show a nominal adhesion by many and actual practice by few, an estimate of the materialists in Japan could already place them close to 100%, with a steady increase in commitment.

It is interesting to note that even in olden times, Buddhism, which is essentially a religion of meditation and contemplation, of otherworldliness, repeatedly fell into a state of decadence in Japan in which the temples became worldly both economically and socially, and on occasion even powerful politically. Buddhist monks were attached to political missions to T'ang China and afterwards played an important role in the trade with China. They possessed great lands, inhabited by peasants who paid rent, and they also received donations and gifts from the imperial, shogunal or other courts. Today, when neither Buddhist temples nor Shinto shrines could conceivably live off charity from the people, their staffs and possessions have shrunk. But they have not ceased playing a semi-worldly role which permits them to survive. Thus, the first schools were created in temples with monks as teachers, and today many of the kindergartens and day-care centers are run by them . . . for a fee. Much of the land has been sold off at good prices or sometimes turned into parking lots. The revenue from visitors, mainly Japanese and foreign sightseers, is considerable. Handsome fees are collected for every ceremony from birth, to marriage, to burial. Some temples prosper by blessing cars so as to avoid accidents or bringing luck to students taking university entrance examinations. The most successful sects deal in faith healing of many sorts.

During the Tokugawa period, in certain ways, materialism was despised, and the more a class had to deal in actually earning money the less respect it obtained. Thus the artisans and merchants, who fashioned or sold goods and whose activities were the source of the era's prosperity, were looked down upon. The peasants, who worked hard in difficult climatic and geographical conditions, had to bow to the *samurai*. But, the upper classes, warriors, priests, and court, all lived off the fruit of these working classes. However, due to the increasing need for wealth to uphold status and power, the merchants were able to gain greater influence over the upper classes and infiltrated them both by personal relations or marriage and ideologically. Younger sons of warriors or landowners often took up similar occupations as they could not live off their stipends. Under the Meiji reforms, with the loss of most privileges, this linking of the two classes became ever stronger. Yet, men in business always had to defend their endeavors for all sorts of extraneous reasons, such as the need to build a strong nation, to ward off foreign influence, or promote prosperity, rather than just making money. Earning a profit even now is hardly seen as a proper "purpose."

In prewar days, the business elite rose to unprecedented heights. Rulers of Mitsui, Mitsubishi, and other commercial empires, had greater power than was wielded by the politicians or bureaucrats, who were supposedly running the country. For, they managed to manipulate these two elites very nicely, supplying the former with the wherewithall for their political rise and costly electoral campaigns and occasionally coopting, bribing, or simply helping the latter achieve their ambitions. The military alone, although not entirely or impeccably, seemed to remain free of these "money-grubbing" activities that were bringing prosperity and power but undermining what was regarded as older and nobler virtues. The schism between the materialists and purists did not cease growing over the years before the war, with some businessmen throwing in their lot with the nationalists, often for purely material reasons (even if cloaked in more presentable ones), until those who placed "spirit" before matter won out: the military and nationalistic youth, reinforced by the poorer and more backward peasants and many who did not participate adequately in the economic rise.

Defeat in World War II left a devastated Japan. It had lost its colonies, its factories and farms had been destroyed, many of the cities were bombed. Worse, Japan's faith in itself, the people's faith in their leaders, the military, the bureaucracy, often the emperor, had also collapsed. Still, the country had to be run and leaders did come to the fore. Some of them had been leaders before nationalism arose and a few were essentially postwar leaders. Some went into politics from business or the bureaucracy rather than being professional politicians. But it was the businessmen who seemed to have the highest calling in the early days when the country had to be reconstructed and economic development was made the primary goal. Never before had businessmen and business been looked up to so greatly. Not so many years later, however, business had already coopted many of the politicians and not all relations were above board. The bureaucrats also flitted into business and politics. Part of the old nexus was restored. Yet, even if the prestige of

Japan's leaders dipped, one could not claim that materialism was overshadowed. Status, respect, honor were tied up more than ever with wealth and power and the more material resources a person or group had the more likely it was to lead.

There were few to criticize materialism as a way of life. Certainly not the business interests, nor the bureaucracy, nor the LDP politicians, who represented business big and small, as well as the farmers and fishermen. The socialists and communists, after much talk of ideological goals also got down to practical needs. Trade unionism on the whole was a very "bread-and-butter" oriented one. The new religions engaged in all sorts of material tasks and assistance and promised their members material rewards as well. Asceticism found scant favor anywhere and few would listen to men of little substance. The masses of the people showed their keenest interest in making acquisitions and filling the void with material goods. And it became easier and easier to do this, all the while driving out more spiritual or disinterested aims. As Japan rose from a devastated country to an economic power and the per capita income grew rapidly, it was quite natural that the life styles should also change, often quite radically.

The generation that rebuilt Japan consisted largely of the very same men and women who had fought its wars and tenaciously maintained certain virtues that could be useful after defeat. Once organized, the Japanese threw themselves into this new venture in a manner which was by any standards hardworking, dedicated, and courageous. Indeed, it was the older ones who were the most stalwart. They had known the prewar Japan which, although rising, was far from a fat or affluent nation. Even in the best days many of them had suffered privation, and another few years of deprivation was not too much to accept. This early group provided most of the creators. They set up factories and offices, they recruited personnel, they began to manufacture new products and open up new markets. They also provided the ideals and much of the tone of the years of recovery.

Obviously, they could not do this alone. Due to the war, it turned out that their children were far less sturdy. This Taisho era generation consisted of young men and women who had been brought up in a very strident and nationalistic atmosphere, had swallowed their lessons and could repeat them by heart, but with less conviction than their elders . . . especially after the myths collapsed in the flames of war. They had also known privation, but a more inward one of doing without this and that to save for the war effort or hiding in bomb shelters during air raids, not storming fortresses or ruling over other nations. The thought police and the very atmosphere of their youth did nothing to encourage imagination or dynamic action, but it did provide for considerable discipline and sacrifice.

These two groups, each in its own way, formed the nation builders. They devoted all their time and energy to reconstruction. They did not hesitate to work late or on weekends, sacrifice personal and family life to make their companies flourish. In the factories, the workers were organized in units that most resembled military brigades, each man at his post and doing his share, waging production and export campaigns, uncovering defects in products or going abroad to reconnoiter the enemy and learn about its markets and technologies. Most lived on a rather Spartan regime, often removed from their families and the motherland for years. It was partially bearable since, unlike the old army, this one was amazingly egalitarian. In factories, the workers and foreman wore the same uniform, ate at the same canteens, and the former aspired (and actually expected) to be moving to the position of foreman sometime, while the foreman might become a supervisor, the sectional head, plant manager, and so on up. These people, who dominated the first decade of development, were the Japanese "economic animals" and work-horses so well known to the West. They were later called the *moretsu gata* (intense or dynamic type) by their juniors, a term that eventually connotated "workaholic."

Slowly but surely, then more rapidly as the growth rate rose, the economy was reconstructed and prosperity began blooming . . . like a miracle. But it was a hard-won miracle, something those who worked for it never forgot, nor grew tired of telling their children about, somehow expecting a moral return. Their children, however, would seem to have gotten tired of hearing these stories and following the same precepts. Even while the *moretsu gata* remained in charge, the younger men and women started thinking of their own lives more and that of the company and country less. They wanted to create their own type of world, an inward looking one, centered around the home. These were the *mai homu gata* ("my-home" types) of the second decade. With time, they began to outnumber the diligent types, whom they actually looked down upon in certain ways. When things were not running smoothly or sacrifices had to be made, it was the former and not the latter who accepted them.

But the *mai homu* type had to work, too. Breadth of vision or not, a home was a very expensive matter and usually beyond their reach without some sort of financing, often from the company or parents. Even if they liked work less and dreamt of retreat to the *homu*, they had to work hard to pay the installments. This was probably less desirable for the company than the loyalty of its first staff, but it did keep people busy at work. Then, before another decade had passed, the *mai homu* type was being absorbed in, or edged out by, the somewhat younger men who

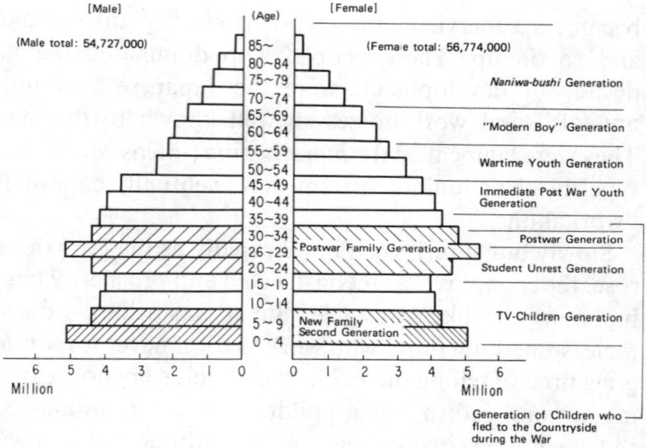

Source: "Estimates as of February '75" including "Estimates in the National Population by Age Categories," by the Statistics Bureau, Prime Minister's Office.

Generational stratification in Japan. Rise of the "New Family."

talked a lot about creating a "new family" and a different life style. The *nyu famirii* type was even less interested in working hard or sacrificing itself. But their fashionable "simple" life style was even more expensive, assuming a *homu* at any rate, and of course a car, as well as leisure activities, some sports, entertainment, and travel.

By the mid-1970s, Japan was more materialistic than ever in its love of things, but the attitude of its younger generations was moving away from that of the older ones. In the crucial group of those entering employment, the polls gave a very clear reflection of the dichotomy. In 1977, a survey of male freshman workers by Japan Recruit Center showed that the "my-home" and "new family" types accounted for 46.2% of the whole and that the "on-the-go work worm" type only represented 18.8%. This was a doubling of the former and a halving of the latter in only six years. Those who felt that "it is alright to sacrifice family life to some extent to put one's soul into his job" were rapidly being supplanted by those who say they "would like to work to create a rich and enjoyable family life." The idea that "it is stupid to work to an extent that calls for sacrificing one's everyday life" has become prevalent and spare time to engage in hobbies is regarded as more important than enthusiasm for one's work.[8]

But, this is not the end of the line. Japan now has a generation of young people, still in its schools, and others not yet of school age, who have never even heard of the privation of the war time or reconstruction period or felt the deprivation of very much in the material realm, although there seem to be great moral lacks. Surrounded by prosperity, nourished by illusions on TV and in popular magazines, they think that affluence is the natural way of life and assume some "right" to it. The duty side comes in grumbling from grandpa or preparing for entrance exams. In most little ways, however, they get their allowances and gifts in sufficient quantity to be rather well off. The models and ambitions have begun switching from anything associated with work to glamorous careers like TV personality, fashion model, or quite simply a pampered housewife (unlike their mothers) or sports heros and VIPs overnight (unlike their fathers). Ambitions, perhaps, is the wrong word, for the most striking characteristic seems to be a lack of ambition, drive, or vitality. TV-viewing is a major activity, dependence on mother (more often than father) a typical behavior, and disconcern with things implying work a way of life. They are called the *shirake sedai* or "reactionless generation" by their elders, who find that they show enthusiasm for nothing, neither work, nor family, nor home. This youth itself regards those who do get excited or carried away as not yet "enlightened," using the same Zen expression in a most different climate.

What sort of generations will Japan have tomorrow? That, of course, no one knows. There are positive trends among some young people who show concern for home and family, for certain human values, and reject the dehumanizing aspects of the materialistic world. They may choose their own careers and even prefer work in a small artisinal shop or open a restaurant rather than join a mammoth company. But they are few compared with the uncertain, confused, and listless ones. The most recent generation, the teeny-boppers of today and their younger brothers and sisters show little promise. A recent survey by the Tokyo Metropolitan Government on men and women between the ages of 15 and 29 found that they regard themselves as fitting into four groups: diligent 30.3%, easygoing 28.6%, independent 24.3%, and frustrated 16.8%.[9] Not exactly the traditional picture of Japan, but an increasingly familiar one.

So, in the few decades since the war, Japan was put back on its feet and built up by incredibly hardworking and dedicated people, only to be turned over to generations that apparently couldn't care less and were certainly not interested in killing themselves even to maintain what had been attained. Strangely enough, it is this very last —weak or reactionless— generation which is the most unique, indeed revolutionary phenomenon in Japanese history. In work or play, peace or war, for good or bad, the Japanese have always shown a will and/or discipline (even at times without a clear national goal or divided opinions on the goal). This is the first generation without these qualities and yet, on the whole, quite comfortable and pleased with itself.

* * *

In dealing with the Orient, for some reason, one tends to speak in terms of slightly more eternal values than one does in dealing with most other parts of the world. The Japanese, says Michiko Inukai, "are endowed by birth with a highly developed aesthetic sense."[10] "One of the outstanding features of the 'Japanese mind' throughout history has been its persistent inquisitiveness and flexibility in the face of new demonstrably superior intellectual systems," according to *Twelve Doors to Japan*.[11] "Japanese of all ages, in virtually any situation, have a powerful urge toward group formation," adds Robert J. Lifton.[12] "Self-discipline parallels obedience as a fundamental force shaping Japanese character," comments Reischauer.[13] "Thrift, industry, persistent struggles to success against heavy odds, and self-improvement in human skills and capabilities still continue to be regarded as virtues . . . Whatever the origin of the ideal, the modern Japanese 'naturally' wishes to succeed."[14] This last observation is from Norbeck. And Herman Kahn, like many others, devotes pages to Japanese characteristics and even draws up lists.[15]

The typical Japanese characteristics and virtues are usually proposed by rather astute observers and are certainly based on a reasonable number of valid observations. What is questionable about them is thus not the categorization that is made but rather the fact that they tend to be pervasive and are still regarded as valid and crucial even when they have disappeared, or at least been diluted or balanced by other characteristics which may not be noticed since the former ones are seen as so eternal, everlasting, innate, inherent, and natural. There are no characteristics that are maintained throughout history, either by grace of God or by genetic transmission, by any group of people, not even the Japanese. By doting on them endlessly and failing to update observations or seek a new understanding periodically, one is bound to commit many errors.

One of the most persistent myths has been the supposedly tight-knit, communal nature of society that permits Japanese to unite in harmony and accomplish veritable marvels. Herman Kahn lists as his No. 1 national characteristic a "great capacity for purposive communal action."[16] And many others would agree with him. Indeed, the dedication that the Japanese have shown to common causes and the nation was exceptional from Meiji days to the war period and did not slacken throughout the early years of reconstruction. Even today, among most adult Japanese, one can expect a reasonable commitment to social goals that extends well beyond lip-service. The only question is whether the younger generations will go along with that. As we have seen, and the Japanese have been repeatedly shocked to learn, younger people are very keen to profit from the good things of life that resulted from the earlier years of dedication by their elders but loathe to sacrifice their own lives for it. This may just be a reaction of youth, a very hasty and nervous reaction by youths who are often unfairly dominated by their elders, and the young people may become just as serious when they grow up. On the other hand, they may not!

One reason it is particularly hard to tell is that the differences between appearance and reality, thinking and doing, confuse the pattern. There has been a noticeable trend over the years towards individualism, especially among the younger groups.[17] This earlier entailed even a willingness to go against society. More recently, the trend has been towards conformity. A Ministry of Education survey showed that, while those who believed it is best to conform to the mores rose from 32% to 42% between 1973 and 1978, the number of those who would go against the mores while sticking to their own convictions fell from 36% to 30%. Yet, at the same time, more and more people wanted to develop their own life style, one completely out of tune with traditional mores. From 1953 to 1978, those who wished "to live according to one's own taste" rose from 20% to 39% and those wishing "to live a care-free life" rose from 10% to 22%. Life styles which implied a society-oriented career, such as "to live a clean and correct life," to acquire material wealth, or to seek fame, fared less well.[18] The two trends were only compatible if conformity applied to the public life and individualism ruled the private life. This may be more communal, but not particularly purposive or creating much action.

*　　　*　　　*

The Japanese have long been admired for their thrift. But, little effort has been made to define the exact nature of this virtue. There is no doubt that the savings levels are unusually high in Japan, and this was a major proof offered. A recent poll showed that, no matter what their age group, the average Japanese saved about 16–17% of his monthly salary and 34–39% of the bonuses, acquiring savings amounts that reached the equivalent of about one year's salary by the forties and two for older men.[19] However, were the Japanese so thrifty because they wanted to or because they had to be thrifty? The leading purpose of savings was for protection against illness and injury, the second as a fund for retirement, the third to purchase a house or land, and the fourth to provide for the children's education and marriage. Each one of these items, one way or the other, resulted from a need for security in a society where there was little social security, old age pensions, or the like to fall back on. When asked, in another poll, just how much money they needed for retirement, the average Japanese admitted a need for about four years' wages.[20] Thus, if anything, the Japanese had inadequate savings.

Once upon a time, the Japanese lived quite frugally,

with very low salaries which, after deducting essentials and putting something aside, left little over. Then wages began doubling every half-dozen years, and, even after paying for essentials and savings, there was still a fair amount left over. Frugality was thrown to the winds and would seem to have been more of a necessity than an urge to judge by more recent experiences. Indeed, another of the reasons for saving had been simply that many of the things the Japanese wish to possess cost so much that money has to be accumulated over a long time, to be spent on big occasions. A person's major expenditure is usually for a house and some bit of land, costing many times his annual salary, and often paid off in twenty years or more. The car is another such expense. Marrying off the children in state yet another. On these matters, there is no question of frugality or meanness and money is usually spent quite lavishly.

Although thrift is a well-known virtue, one tends to forget that making sumptuary expenses or engaging in conspicuous consumption have no less noble a tradition. They, too, were very prevalent from ancient times. The rulers and upper class had to live in state, everyone had to make worthy donations to the temples and shrines, gifts were required by customs and, since they often went from inferior to superior, had to be suitably impressive. Modern commerce apparently got started with the need for rich attire and exquisite surroundings for the nobility, especially when forced to attend court. Women also have a very old tradition to uphold. For, the *kimono* —which costs a handsome sum— is a must for every young lady. Fashions and accessories have long been a vital part of her life. So, today, modern shoppers put stress on the "quality" of goods and, alas, have to spend greater sums to acquire such quality goods. They still insist on service, which may entail going to her house for *kimono* fittings, or at any rate providing far more sales personnel and attractive premises than necessary. People still make some purchases to maintain face and, to avoid losing face, often spend more than they should and end up trying to keep up with the neighbors or impress all and sundry. They are also constrained to offer gifts on many occasions, including the twice annual gift giving seasons of *o-chugen* and *o-seibo*.

This may help explain the vast increase in consumer spending in recent years. It is not quite enough to justify what has turned into almost an orgy of spending on expensive, luxury and prestige purchases, status symbols of every sort. The object is no longer even to acquire things of value or beauty but more exactly to command objects that enhance one's position. Scarves must clearly bear the designer's name, dresses must come from such-and-such-a-boutique (at twice the cost of the department store), perfumes and make-up could be nothing but the finest. Japanese men end up buying the most expensive golfing equipment and memberships in overpriced clubs no matter how poorly or rarely they play. Their children want championship skis for their first attempt on the slopes. People go on trips to Paris and Rome not even to see the sights but to buy up and bring back the precious objects found in famous boutiques. The age in which the Mitsuis set the tone by austere living and all for business was replaced by an age in which businessmen gaily spent company money (and some of their own) to dazzle the public. Thus, the Atakas helped ruin their company, one of the major trading companies, by spending as much as ¥300,000 on a single evening in a Ginza bar and collecting classic cars, paintings, and other works of art worth billions of yen.[21]

This spending, or overspending, has had a definite influence on the Japanese individually as well as the nation as a whole. It was particularly bad due to two factors. First of all, the economy had risen steadily for over two decades, and the Japanese not only got used to spending as they earned but also in advance, often calculating future earnings rather optimistically. This was promoted by the practice of receiving huge bonuses twice a year. The other factor was that, just when the Japanese really got into the swing of spending, the economy slowed down and many of them got caught in the pinch. Many Japanese were now finding it hard to make the payments. Yet, apparently, they had not quite accepted the new facts of life and were still making purchases. This was bound to become even more prevalent when buying on credit became widespread, which seemed to be the case. The "new family" crowd in their thirties who bought on credit increased from 1976 to 1977 by 108%, those in their twenties by 105%, and the teenagers (often using their parents' credit cards) by 180% according to the Director of Sales Promotion at Marui Department Stores.[22]

Indeed, living beyond one's means was rapidly becoming an accepted practice. According to a survey of office workers' consumption behavior, the average pocket money did not cover expenses, leaving a deficit of some ¥18,000 a month.[23] Their wives were not much better off. Another survey indicated that only 11% of the housewives were satisfied with the amount they got for housekeeping and few thought much of their miserly personal allowance.[24] The problem was obviously how to make ends meet. One solution, the traditional one, would have been to cut back on expenses and make savings wherever possible. There were doubtlessly a lot of people, especially older ones, who did that. But, spending and conspicuous consumption seem to have become as much a way of life as saving and frugality had once been.

Moreover, it was not so easy to curtail expenses. Cutting back sharply hurt the ego and was also a clear admission of failure. This would have led to a loss of face for someone who still had to adopt an optimistic view of the future. Obviously, many were also "hooked" on luxuries. So, even years after the oil shock and well into the recession, the only trade figures that constantly and rapidly rose were those for all sorts of luxury products ranging from foreign whiskey and wines for the men to Paris fashions and foreign cosmetics for the women. No matter how high the tariffs, and how big the profit margins, these goods could be sold and the number of boutiques and gift shops rose while more normal shops and grocery stores closed down. The 1977 White Paper on the Economy came up with the amazing result that the Japanese consumers were saving money by buying cheaper, lower quality necessities, stinting even on food, while spending more than ever on clothing and luxuries.

If the gap could not be closed by lowering one's demands and expectations, it had to be closed by raising one's income. In earlier days, this had simply meant to do more overtime. However, overtime was drying up. Now that the working hours had been reduced and many had free weekends or evenings, they began "moonlighting." But, there were limits to that. Some endulged in gambling, hoping to make a killing. But, far more got slaughtered somewhere along the line. What else was left but to borrow? The lucky ones could borrow from their parents. But, especially with the recession and old folks living longer, that source might be quite limited. The banks were another possibility. But, no matter how happy they were to make a loan to an up-and-coming salaryman, they had nothing much to offer anyone who was down-and-out. The only alternative was the "salaryman's finance" companies (*sarakin*), loan sharks who preyed on employees and housewives, lending small sums of money at a deceptively small daily interest rate of 0.3% that added up to . . . 110% per annum. The results of this were often tragic. In most cases, the loan was kept a secret from the rest of the family, creating a heavy moral burden. Even a petty sum rapidly grew into a major debt. When it could not be paid back promptly, the loan company did not hesitate to intimidate the debtors. Many of them found no way out, some lost their jobs, others got divorced, and a few committed suicide.

* * *

Herman Kahn and some other commentators have assumed that the swift economic rise of Japan was bound to be accompanied by a flourishing of the arts and sciences as well. The reason for this is uncertain, since periods of economic upswing have been accompanied throughout history as often by cultural revival as by decadence, with perhaps a slight predominance of sheer mediocrity. For some time, indeed, it did look as if the recent outburst of economic activity would, as in the earlier Meiji era, produce great artists, writers, and scientists. There was a period, long since past, when piercing and sensitive Japanese films were shown in art cinemas around the world. In literature, Yasunari Kawabata and Yukio Mishima, then Kobo Abe and Shusaku Endo, gained considerable fame. They have been followed by many other younger authors. But, their fate is rather symbolic of culture in Japan. The first two, like many others, looked backwards to the old virtues, and they committed suicide. The second pair, and many others, looked inward sometimes in despair. The more recent writers have been largely anti-establishment. Few brought a message of hope.

Japan also raised painters, sculptors, musicians, actors, people to express every form of the arts, and some have achieved fame . . . all too often abroad. Neither the pe-

Japan's aesthetic impulse in bygone days: purity of line, simplicity of form and harmony with nature.

Photo credit: Foreign Press Center-Japan.

riod of reconstruction, when people were kept busy at work, nor the boom, as people relaxed or thought of home and family, nor the recent "new affluence" and the spending it generated, have created much support or understanding for culture. There were simply different varieties of Philistines to put it down. When wealthy Japanese bought up big chunks of the world's cultural heritage, it was as often as not just a hedge against inflation or an investment. Those attending gala performances of foreign artists were not all culture-lovers and many regarded their presence as a source of personal prestige. The hordes of tourists taken around to foreign museums rarely absorbed much. This is very unfortunate, for one senses a tremendous receptivity and even hunger in the young, one which wilts and dies as they go through school and become salarymen or housewives. Culture becomes something that is uncommon, exotic for some, dull for others, and not a part of daily life. Patronage of the arts, and the artists, is quite limited. Like the intellectual in general, those involved in art are not regarded as a really integral, or integratable, part of society.

The fine aesthetic sense of the Japanese, the simplicity and beauty of the architecture, the innate good taste of the people, are touted in every tourist guide to Japan. How this can be ingurgitated by those who visit the country, however, is hard to understand. All around them, and all around the magnificent palaces and austere temples they photograph, is the most unattractive maze of buildings, large and small, wide and narrow, of every possible shape and color, all squeezed together in a hodge podge determined by the lay of the land and the roads. This refers not only to the cheap tenements or *danchi* but also the new luxury apartment houses variously called *mansion, palais, chateau* or *heim*. Each has its own peculiarities and frills, forming some Japanese neo-gothic or baroque, a far cry from the simplicity of earlier architectural forms. On the outskirts of the cities, the trees are torn down and the hills

Modern Japanese architecture: complex, confused, and crowded. Typical scene in the big city.

Photo credit: Japan National Tourist Organization

razed to build packed rows of tiny houses with a few small rooms, a miniature garden, and of course a parking spot. Inside the houses, there may be a family shrine, a bit of flower arrangement, a scroll or calligraphy, but this is uncertain. The interior remains a crude jumble, not blend, of traditional and modern: *tatami* mats and TV sets, pickling barrels and automatic rice cookers, kerosene stoves and 4-channel stereo sets. These are Japan's famed "rabbit hutches."

In the field of science, one would expect considerably better results, given the tremendous economic capacity of the country, the fact that it has drawn to the forefront in many industrial sectors, and that so many students are studying and so much personnel is working in science-related activities. Yet, the result has not been a vitalization of science so much as of technology. Japanese technology is fantastic, among the best in the world, and this does not mean mere copying or imitation. Japanese engineers, technicians, and designers carry through considerable amounts of "innovation," taking whatever they have borrowed a few decisive steps further. There is excellent work going on for R&D. However, little of it is disinterested, as it takes place under the auspices of commercial companies or government research institutes looking for practical spinoffs, and little of it reaches into theoretical fields or pure science. That sort of research might be accomplished, as elsewhere, in the universities. But, Japanese universities have not developed into centers for work in pure, or even applied science, as much as elsewhere, and few scholars devote themselves to creative and original research. Thus, the results are lacking. As former Education Minister Nagai wrote:

"If research is given serious attention, outstanding results will be produced; if it is neglected, they will not. The productivity of contemporary Japanese research does not increase because research is not being taken seriously. The number of scholars and universities is the source of a dangerous illusion. The total number of scholars is large, but not many among them can forget themselves and become fully involved in their work."[25]

Instead, the economic boom has been accompanied by a much touted "leisure boom" (*reja bumu*). The statistics show clearly that the amount of time devoted to work has decreased and leisure time risen. There is no doubt that there has been a very visible expansion in leisure activities when measured by the amount of recreational and sports equipment sold, the number of TV sets and radios disseminated, and the purchase of tickets to various events. The depth, however, is very hard to gauge. The polls and surveys show all too obviously that there is a tendency to indulge more in games and appreciative activities than in active sports and cultural ones. Moreover, those actively engaged are only a fraction of those who passively observe. And even those who engage in anything often do so quite rarely.[26]

The Japanese speak of a golf fad or a skiing fad. But this is not exactly what one would call a passion. People tend to engage in such activities perhaps once a month, for the former, and twice a year, for the latter. The only strong commitment to sports arises in college clubs and subsides very rapidly after graduation. Far more typical is the "pachinko" fad, which has been around for decades, with over 10,000 establishments where amateurs or addicts can play Japanese pinball to their hearts' content and perhaps win some little prizes. Or, the lure of petty gains in some 36,000 mahjong parlors. Or, the excitement aroused in Japan when Sadaharu Oh hit his 756th homer, becoming the world's home run champion and winning him a People's Honor Award (*Kokumin Eiyu Sho*) hastily created for the occasion by Prime Minister Fukuda. Those seeking Japanese traditional culture can find it, in small doses, since Kabuki and Noh trail far behind Western records or movies, flower arrangement and tea ceremony are practiced by fewer than golf or bowling, and martial arts cannot keep up with baseball. More Japanese are travelling than ever before, but it hardly looks like leisure to the naked eye, and more time is devoted to shopping than sightseeing.

None of the signs foretell any great cultural resurgence, trend toward creative or dynamic activities or a preservation of the cultural heritage. A breakdown of hobbies by generation shows this quite clearly. Those in their fifties gave precedence to visiting hot springs, reading, home gardening, carpentry and pachinko. All younger categories raised the priority of pachinko and mahjong and added listening to records or seeing foreign films. No category showed much interest in sports or culture, and, if anything, it was the older ones who did anything particularly active or that took them out of the daily routine. In fact, as the leisure boom developed and people had more free time, there was a shift away from sports on Sunday (the only possible day) and toward watching TV even more. In all categories, especially the young, those who spend (or waste) time on games and gambling is impressive.[27]

Japan has often been praised for the intellectual level of its population, due to the high literacy and "excellent" educational system. It is also a widely heralded fact that newspaper circulation in Japan is the highest in the world, the circulation of its national dailies dwarfing those of any other papers in the world. Thus, the *Asahi* and *Yomiuri* newspapers have a circulation of about 8 million each, and *Mainichi*, 4.5 million. Newspapers are delivered daily to 34 million households. The circulation of magazines is also impressive, with a general monthly magazine like *Bungei Shunju* having 850,000 and a weekly like *Shukan Asahi*, 500,000. A women's magazine like *Josei Jishin* has a circulation of 850,000, and one of the top fashion magazines for young ladies, *Non-No* hit 930,000. The quality of these newspapers and magazines is neither high brow nor low brow; as might be expected in Japan they aim mainly for the middle. But these more conventional bearers of the written word are gradually being overcome by comic books, often massive volumes an inch thick, and comics infiltrate many of the more serious magazines as well. The comic magazine *Shonen Manga* has a circulation of 1,900,000, topping any other magazine, and it is only one among dozens. Worse, the readership is constantly growing. The extent of this phenomenon can be readily assessed by observing the large number of adults reading comic books on the subways and commuter trains.

Now, reading itself seems to be on the way out, while television keeps increasing in popularity. An NHK survey showed that housewives spent an average of almost five hours a day viewing TV and another report indicated that even 42% of the senior high school students, those preparing for college entrance exams, spent two to three hours daily on weekdays and more than three hours on holidays watching television.[28] One can only imagine how much time their younger brothers and sisters spend. It may be added that most television channels, aside from the state-run NHK, devote much of their time to low brow comedy, pop singers and dancers, quiz shows, and reruns of old movies. There is also the usual admixture of violence and, at night, even porno shows for the tired working man. Leisure in Japan is thus equated to an amazing extent with television and reading of the most uninspiring kind.

* * *

Few myths about Japan seem to be dying slower than that of a people in intimate communion with nature, loving and worshipping it, somehow always living with it. There is no question but that traditional Japanese religion, like that of every other people on the earth, grew out of a worship of nature. Until urbanization came, most Japanese lived in the countryside or near it and there was ample opportunity to preserve some relationship to nature. The great temples with their splended natural settings, the lovely Japanese gardens, the *bonsai* trees, the bit of shrubbery in many family gardens is a tribute to that. However, most of the people now living in Japan, and even more so for their children, will have been born and grown up in an environment that has left little nature behind. No city in the world has spread as fast as Tokyo, tearing down the forests and hills, rooting out every speck of green, to build homes and factories. Thus, the Tokyo-

As the old Japanese saying goes, "dumplings before flowers."

Photo credit: Japan National Tourist Organization

ites, and Osakaites, and many more now have to spend hours in their cars to reach anything resembling nature, and this filled to the brim with other visitors.

As we saw, in the above statistics, gardening, fishing, and visits to hot springs are for the older categories; the hobbies of the younger generation are often city or home-centered. Moreover, the little bits of nature that remain have yet to become a serious cause for youth, unlike the youth of America and Europe, which is demanding a preservation of whatever untouched nature remains. Japan's youth is screaming for more homes. Thus, the green belt originally planned around Tokyo was ignored and the city permitted to sprawl as far as conveyances could take its commuters, which can run as much as two hours or more. Even when visiting "nature," young Japanese do not seem to appreciate it or take in its grandeur, turning such trips into outings or pleasure junkets, one more excuse to drink together, leaving their trash behind them. Hiking over Japan's trails are mainly older people, the younger ones getting stuck in some inn or picnic facility along the way. The greatest perversion of this love is the cherry blossom viewing season, originally to catch the moment of beauty when the flower blossoms and falls, now turned into a hideous caricature with groups of friends and relatives sitting under every tree, fed by ambulent food stands, drinking themselves silly, and then crawling back home to sleep it off.

How can a people which loves nature so much, many foreigners ask, permit the hideous pollution in Japan? It is quite simple. The love is vastly overdone, and another native tradition, summed up in the saying "one is without shame when away from home," leads to people who are meticulously neat in their own home while leaving an incredible mess anywhere else. Japan was clearly being polluted years before anyone complained, and then the complaints came mainly from those directly affected. There was a series of local causes, which did have a cumulative if not clearly defined impact. One of the first serious cases was an outbreak of mercury poisoning that resulted in the incurable "Minamata disease," named after the place it was found, a result of the chemical company Chisso Corporation's waste discharge. Cadmium poisoning from Mitsui Mining's mine waste, dumped in the Jinzu River, led to another disease called *itai-itai byo* (ouch-ouch disease) because of the pain. But, this was just a start, for environmental pollution was overwhelming the land and seeping into the soil and the food grown there, and flowing down the rivers or directly out into the seas from coastal factories or city garbage dumps.[29]

For an amazingly long time, nothing was done about the spread of pollution, permitting ever more environmental damage and ecological destruction (*kankyo hakai*). First, the polluters tried to cover up, aided and abetted by local elected officials who closed their eyes, government bureaucrats afraid to intervene, and even trade union members worried about a scandal involving their company and threatening their livelihood. Only those directly affected, and some few others, complained or later brought suit. With time, however, the danger became obvious. Many small towns that would once have welcomed factories bringing work had second thoughts and local committees were formed to check any new facilities were safe. In some cases, they even rejected "progress." More often, however, they were ultimately convinced that there was no danger, although it was not always certain whether the most telling arguments were technical or financial. Small groups of "environmentalists" running all the way from victims of some disease demanding compensation, to vigilantes trying to keep industry out, or scientists seeking a more balanced policy, do exist. Yet, they never grew into a nation-wide movement and ecology or just love of nature remains a marginal cause.

At least, as the level of complaints rose, the government found it harder to remain on the sidelines, and an Environmental Agency was established, although it remained relatively tame and less influential than business lobbies. Specific legislation was also adopted forcing factories to adopt effective, and expensive, anti-pollution devices. The rules on handling and deposit of wastes were stiffened. And the toughest legislation on automobile exhaust gases in the world was enacted in an attempt to combat the smog over the cities. Unfortunately, most of the measures grew out of hindsight; rather than impose ecological studies before any new facilities could be built, the concern was still with cleaning up the mess after it was made. Yet, to solve Japan's ills, far more was needed, at least of the scope, if not necessarily along the lines of ex-Prime Minister Tanaka's plan for remodelling the archipelago.[30] It was absurd to group most of the population along a narrow corridor and leave the rest of the country underpopulated and abandoned.

* * *

Once upon a time, Japan was known as a land of sexual freedom, passionate love, and romantic dalliance. Many books on Japan relate the love stories, romances and bawdy tales of olden times. Unfortunately, most people fail to realize just how far back some of the stories go, a few centuries for many, and prewar Japan for the rest. For, one of the Meiji "reforms," in an attempt to show the Japanese as being a highly civilized race, was to restrict the much freer sexual mores of earlier days and impose an increased separation of the sexes which has led to innocence or prudery. For example, many private schools were for boys or girls, and even in a co-educational classroom, they were seated separately. Relations were strictly regulated in proper families, with women expected to enter marriage a virgin. Nowadays, although there is some tendency toward looseness in certain circles, the number of families that regard themselves as proper has also increased sharply. And the pressure these families exert to keep their children on the "straight and narrow" is extraordinary.

If anything, Japan's problems in the sphere of sex result far more from prudishness, innocence, and ignorance than the freedom and eroticism which perhaps once pervaded sexual relationships among the upper classes and with various sorts of "loose" women or the "healthier" attitude of peasants. Some recent polls indicate that more and more young people believe that sex should be permitted even before marriage for those who "love" one another. However, such responses are just as likely to emanate from some who believe that sex should be freer but don't quite have the courage to act on this. Indeed, even in the universities today, men and women are quite likely to be seated in different parts of the lecture hall or cafeteria and do not mix very much. Moreover, most of the young men still expect their wives to be virgins, and the women have to think of their future. Of course, there are exceptions and accidents but the Japanese surgeons have found a solution. They are excellent at redoing a virginity for a goodly price and abortion can be had almost at request . . . although the "pill" is still very difficult to obtain. Thus, for most men and women courtship is a rather wooden affair, consisting of formal meetings at hotel restaurants (the *omiai* couple) or informal ones in noodle shops or coffee houses (the "love" couple). For the latter, there may be some petting, an occasional bit of car sex or a quick stop at a motel or "love hotel." But, even "love" couples scarcely know one another socially, let alone sexually, before marriage. And this has led to no end of traumas and complexes.

Society, in many ways, is far more prudish than the individuals. For the parents strictly police their children, sons as well as daughters, although in a mobile society this is increasingly difficult. They look into the morals of their child's prospective spouse. Even the companies lay down rules to protect morals such as that unmarried female employees must live with their parents or in company dormitories. Although many salarymen daydream about hanky-panky with young OLs in the office, this rarely gets very far since its disclosure could lead to their dismissal under very unpleasant circumstances. Oddly enough, this even extends into "show biz." In most other countries, an affair or divorce is almost a publicity stunt; in Japan, young pop singers and film stars usually behave like silly virgins on stage, and are expected to appear the same in their private lives. Those who do have affairs keep it a secret to protect their reputation and appearing in public with one's mistress can lead to sharp criticism. In the case of divorce, some film stars have seen their job offers dry up and old films or commercials withdrawn from circulation so they may be better forgotten.

But, prudishness does not necessarily lead to well adapted men and women or happy marriages. It is just as likely to do the opposite. There is no Kinsey Report on Japan, but it would make very dull reading. A small survey of middle-management employees in the Tokyo area showed that about one third of them made love to their wife once or twice a month, another third once a week, and only a third twice a week or more. This, according to some Japanese doctors at least, is quite healthy. Dr. Masatoshi Yasumi felt that a good average for a man in his thirties to have sex relations was twice a week, with the frequency dropping to once a week at forty, and once in two weeks for those in their fifties. Perhaps Japanese are physically different from other people. Or, the explanation may be that the Japanese simply separate sex from marriage and seek the sex they crave in other forms. Thus, fully two-thirds of the above sample admitted to having extra-marital relations during the past year, and 4% had mistresses.[31]

This survey would seem to indicate, as anyone who knows Japan a bit will realize, that prudishness on the surface and officially has only made sex go underground or assume other forms of sublimation. One alternative to real sex has been the flood of pornography that has invaded Japan in recent years, first from abroad, now reinforced by local production. The amount of porno is incredible, and it fills not only specialized magazines but takes up a few pages even in straight magazines and gets into proper newspapers. Porno films are shown late in the evening on TV and special theaters have been opened. One can get just about anything: infidelity, sodomy, lesbianism, group sex, X-rated films, hard core, the works. There are also live shows and strip tease joints, often offering the crudest and most vulgar of performances, sometimes with audience participation. What is strange about all this is that pornography is forbidden in Japan. However, the definition of it is the appearance of pubic hair and blotting out certain parts of the anatomy is quite enough to get by the censors. What the authorities do not seem to realize is that it is not pubic hair but ideas that pervert a society. And that some of the ideas are not particularly healthy becomes evident on scanning the more popular porno. Tenderness is totally lacking; brutality (by the men) prominent. There is a sadism toward women that doubtlessly wells up from a deep sexual insecurity, frustration and distorted machismo.

Prostitution, by the way, is also illegal, thanks to an Anti-Prostitution Law pushed through the Diet by the feminist movement in 1956. Yet, Japan's past had laid a very solid tradition for such acts. Before Meiji's day, concubines, mistresses, prostitutes, as well as the more correct *geisha* were very numerous in Japan. To regulate rather than eliminate what could hardly be avoided then, red-light districts were set up as of 1876. By 1924, there were more than 550 such segregated areas, with some 100,000 indentured women. This did not include the large number of amateurs or the mistresses which well-to-do businessmen or members of the elite regarded as a status symbol. In addition to this, a visit to the hot springs was not only for a cure in the waters but the services of women attached to such establishments. This will explain the large number of older respondents of the earlier poll who regarded visits to hot springs as a major "hobby." In addition, trips abroad, then and now, were often a chance to revel in the charms of more exotic (and cheaper) girls. This is the trend that feminists and others had hoped to reverse. Prudishness, naivety and fear may have helped with their children, but a healthier attitude toward sex within the couple might have been a stronger barrier.

For, twenty years later, one could hardly say that prostitution has disappeared. If anything, over recent years, there has been a tremendous upswing in the profession. There are today "pink zones" (*pinku zon*), often on the very same spots where red-light districts used to stand. They have simply changed form. Turkish baths, some 1,500 employing 20,000 women in 1980, manage to provide their clients with considerably more than a bath. The number of bars is even greater, and bar hostesses usually round out their earnings with additional services. How many such hostesses there are is again uncertain, but the estimate of some 10,000 Caucasian and Asian women working in bars can give an indication of the tremendous number of Japanese who must be employed there. Then come the night clubs or more exclusive escort services.

Finally, and it is really sad to shatter this illusion now that foreigners have finally been taught that a *geisha* is not a prostitute but a traditional female entertainer, some of them have been forced by the recession into practices that would once have been frowned upon. Why? The reason is very simple. A pleasure-seeking businessman may only earn about ¥300,000 a month. The Turkish bath attendant, who rubs his back and then moves on to other parts of the body, can earn a minimum of that and as much as ¥2 million a month. A foreign bar hostess can make ¥10,000 a night in salary, her Japanese colleague a bit less, and a golf escort ¥5,000, all more than they could make during the day in a normal job. But . . . the tip for "special services" can run ¥40,000 and more. A bar hostess who becomes the mistress of some wealthy gentleman earns ¥300,000–500,000 a month on the side, without interrupting her regular career. Your poor *geisha*, on the other hand, despite her strict training, only gets about ¥350,000 a month. No wonder she occasionally accepts a one-night affair for ¥100,000.

Once started, this is hard to stop. The professionals are now being joined by amateurs. The number of married women and working girls serving in Turkish baths is growing. To round out their pitifully small pocket money, and perhaps relieve some of their frustrations, housewives have been picking up their own little clientele whom they accompany to a nearby motel. On the other hand, well-healed women can now visit houses and clubs for women, where male attendants meet them in black suits and ties, drink and dance with them before moving on to a private room. (Here, much of the personnel is ex-salarymen and students.) This shocked Japan a bit. But the thing kept on spreading. University coeds, who were expected to get by on a modest allowance during their studies, soon found that one did not have to study at the university and that the best way to pay for the little baubles every girl likes was to peddle their services. Some led a double life until shortly before graduation, returning to correctness, virginity, and marriage just on time. Others ended up in the profession, and a few were found dead. Then came the turn of the senior high school girls, who entered into "sex-for-gift" arrangements in which the gift was cash to buy clothes with. Next were the junior high school girls, some of whom formed their own groups. By 1978, things had gotten so far that in one year 4,384 junior and senior high school girls were taken into custody for "sexual delinquency," and the biggest rise was among those 15 and under.

How this could happen is quite simple. The Anti-Prostitution Law made both partners, and those who arranged it, guilty . . . without providing any penalty. Periodically, the police got tipped off about such-or-such a place, although none too often since the clients, the girls, and the patrons were quite happy with the arrangement. The place would be raided, people arrested, and then let off. There was simply no point to the operation and anti-vice raids were carried out just to show the public something was being done. In the case of Turkish baths, which are regulated by health inspectors, policemen could not even get in without a search warrant. What adults, even college girls, did, was regarded as their own business, as long as they did not offend anyone. Only in the case of minors has any action been taken, and this by provincial authorities who have adopted strict penalties for contributing to sexual delinquency of primary or junior high school students. On the national level, despite insistence by the few women members of the Diet to amend the Public Bath Law and put teeth in the Anti-Prostitution Law, nothing has been done. Indeed, how could it? The patrons and protectors include politicians, top businessmen, entrepreneurs, show biz stars, doctors and dentists, owners of flower arrangement schools, namely Japan's elite.[32]

This phenomenon should not be mistaken for a sexual revolution. What is being done is regarded as outside of normal life, and the goal is certainly not to work out new relationships in general between men and women, husband and wife. Most often it is an escape from boredom or frustration, quite frequently merely an urge for status, and it is always done for a price. Just one more transaction in a materialistic world. Some have spoken of "hedonism" in Japan. This is a very big word. What is happening can hardly be compared with the revels of decadent Rome. Many of the clients are old, some even decrepit, since much of this is too expensive for the young. The establishments often provide a mixture of fun and games plus sex that is not removed from what once happened at cus-

Japan has made great strides in the cultural field.
Photo credit: Japan National Tourist Organization

tomary *geisha* parties (without the sex). Comments from a satisfied customer at a *pinku zon* will give a bit of insight into Japan's sex industry:

"There are so many young and nice girls here. And it is so wonderful that one time out of three they really 'come' for your pleasure. They really make lots of effort, these Turkish baths. Some make their girls dress like nuns, another makes them dress in school girl's uniforms and when we go in they sit on the floor and bow low and say 'welcome, my teacher.' There is another place where the girls wear paper panties and come into the tub with you and make you rip the panties. I use these places very often to entertain business clients. It is a very good way of entertaining. After all, how can you say 'how about another drink' after you have just finished *that*?"[33]

* * *

A far more prevalent behavior is drinking. This is not drinking for the pleasure of it or for escape. Rather, in Japan, drink plays an integrating function. Drinking is almost never done alone but rather in social groups. Over time, it has actually become an essential part of the whole social fabric. And, as long as Japan's society remains as it is, one can hardly imagine the nation without drinkers. The primary reason is that people have built up such tremendous internal pressures due to the complex social structure that forces them to follow patterns and play roles which are so omnipresent and crucial, and where a failure to react quickly and correctly enough can lead to tremendous loss of face or worse, that they must some time throw off these constraints and release any resentment or frustration. Thus, during drinking, most men spend a considerable share of the time speaking about work, and almost as much pointedly criticizing superiors and the like. Even among equals, which is how drinking usually occurs, there are so many inhibitions that the closest of colleagues or friends, let alone more distant persons, cannot find out what one another is thinking or just what sort of a person they are when sober. Drink is necessary to break down the barriers so that people can really relate and often so that a person can get to know himself.

Japanese are not introduced to drink in their families so much or at a particularly young age, but when the pressures of life begin to mount. Drinking is a major activity for many students, showing their manhood and letting them discover their souls. It is carried on throughout a career. First it is only a friendly session among colleagues. However, if one rises to a sufficiently high position, taking customers out on the town or attending high level meetings also implies drinking. In the evening, it is quite normal to see well-dressed salarymen trying to hold one another up as they wend their way to the subway or seek a taxi. One, however, finds amazingly few habitual drinkers or drunkards. The purpose, at least so far, really is one of social release and adaptation or accommodation to a complex and painful social situation and not escape from it.

Given the reasons, debauchery would also be a very big word for what happens. It is rather the traditional "friendly drink" between colleagues or occasionally with superiors or inferiors to break the ice. A person who refuses to drink, in fact, is the one more likely to suffer opprobrium, since he may be regarded as unmanly, or worse, unwilling to reveal his true self to others. Drinking in Japan, tame as it is, is nonetheless assuming absolutely incredible proportions. The range of drinks taken is spreading to include not only traditional drinks like saké, or beer, but anything produced in any part of the world, with an increasing preference for nothing but the best and most costly, especially when this is paid for by the company. Given the situation, there is also little talk of having to limit the extent of this live-giving plague or to censure those involved. To the contrary, it is pretty well understood that to tamper with it would be self-defeating and perhaps dangerous in the long run. As Jack Seward pointed out: "To try to correct this situation by legislating more severe penalities for public inebriation may result in serious trouble in other quarters. As suggested, drunkenness is a major safety valve on the pressure chamber of the society. Clamping it shut could cause the excess pressure to seek release through even less desirable avenues."[34]

* * *

Tokyo, as one of the hand-outs to tourists indicates, is probably the safest large city in the world. There is far less crime, especially violent crime, in Japan than elsewhere. The honesty of the average person is proverbial: the lady who finds a purse on the street and brings it to the police station; the taxi driver who hunts all over Tokyo's hotels for a foreigner who left his camera behind; the simple fact that one can walk around with a wallet in the back pocket or not clutching one's handbag when shopping with no real risk of theft; the idea that your flat or house can be left empty all day without much chance of being broken into. A person in Japan quickly gets out of the habit of counting his change . . . it's always right. Huge sums of money transit from company to bank in the bags of messengers or office girls and almost never get lost. The honesty, decency, and sense of responsibility of most people are admirable.

Japan has every reason to be proud of its low crime rate. This is particularly true of violent crimes, which are incredibly few. For the 1977 White Paper on Crime, a comparison was made with the levels in other countries and showed the extraordinarily good performance of the

Japanese people. For example, in 1975, the number of murder cases per 100,000 persons was 9.6 in the USA, 4.8 in West Germany, 2.3 in Britain, and only 1.9 in Japan. The number of armed robbery cases was 218.2 in the USA, 33.4 in West Germany, 23.0 in Britain, and 2.1 in Japan. The number of cases of rape were 26.3 in the USA, 11.1 in West Germany, 2.1 in Britain, and 3.3 in Japan. The reasons for Japan's low crime rate were given as its "racial and cultural homogeneity," the lack of racial problems and class barriers, the relatively high educational level and happy family life. Finally, it modestly mentioned the effectiveness of the law-enforcement agencies.[35] For, the police authorities certainly deserve great credit for an exceptionally high arrest rate and the courts for seeing to it that suspects are promptly tried and, if necessary, imprisoned.

Part of the excellent record may also have been due to the prevailing situation of relatively full employment, which meant that few were sufficiently needy to commit crimes. However, the key factors were actually the same sociological ones that influence every person's behavior at all times: social pressure, conformity, responsibility to the family or group, the notion that a criminal's or deviant's shame is shared by the whole group and others thus have the right to mix in his personal affairs to see that nothing improper occurs. In an island nation it is harder to escape abroad. Far more important, in a closed society, punishment consists not only of fines or prison sentences but a criminal record that may prevent future employment, loss of the support one can expect from friends and associates, difficulty in forming social relations except in marginal sectors of society, and many more things that would make it hard for a person to live a decent life.

Yet, the opprobrium of society not only helps prevent crimes, it also leads to numerous cases where they are covered up so that the individual or group will not be shamed. There is no doubt that many girls would never report a rape for social reasons. There is an increase in the amount of shoplifting. Much of it is not reported since the sums are so petty and the procedures so time-consuming. But the biggest number of crimes that are never reported are those committed by young people. Often, they cannot be prosecuted anyway. Yet, the indulgence of youth is such that many parents, no matter what they do at home, would never permit society to know, schools cover up to avoid harming their own reputation, and even the police goes easy on them. Youthful offenders are often caught in the act, and yet get away without joining the statistics. Akira Ishii, checking on the crime rate by interviewing people, found levels that were well above the official ones, as much as 11 times for burglary, 24 times for shoplifting, and 54 times for assault and battery. His figures may have been high; the official figures were just as likely to be low.[36]

There are other reasons for suspecting considerable under-reporting of crime. As we saw, pornography charges can be avoided by the simple technique of blotting out the pubic hair. Prostitution is a crime for which there is no punishment. And, who would report it anyway? Another category of crimes, peculiar to Japan, is very prevalent although it rarely ends with an arrest. This consists of shaking down companies by threatening to disturb their annual meetings (*sokai*). By purchasing just a few shares, the *sokaiya* are able to attend, and their threat is often enough to get a bribe from the officers in charge, who might lose face or even their job if something were to happen. With time, however, the game has changed a bit, since some corporate officers are willing to pay the *sokaiya* to shut up potential critics among the genuine sharehold-ers. A further wrinkle has been to publish small bulletins filled with scandals, real or imagined, about the companies that do not kick-back, while refraining from attacking the others. The total bribes and hush-money paid in 1976 was estimated at ¥100 billion. Yet, charges were hardly ever made. Why? Maybe some of the companies have a lot to hide.[37]

In fact, there has been an increase in "white collar" crimes of all sorts, from embezzlement to outright theft. Tax evasion is rife among professionals. And there has been an increase in bribery. Here, too, few charges are made and apparently most of the crimes are never discovered. A further complication is that the dividing line between a gift and a bribe is paper thin in Japan, and as flexible, with almost anything coming under the heading of gift or legitimate expense. Substantial gifts are given to teachers for recommending their pupils to colleges. The colleges get gifts for receiving second-rate students. Gifts are given to get people jobs. There are the *o-chugen* and *o-seibo* seasons, when everyone must give his patrons, benefactors, bosses, and sundry superiors gifts that usually amount to more than just an expression of sentiment. Bureaucrats get gifts from underlings or from friends in the business world. Politicians get them as well, either directly or into their campaign chest, for arranging things. Some would even classify the "peanuts" involved in the Lockheed scandal as gifts or campaign contributions for the politicians and perhaps brokerage fees for the middlemen. In such circumstances, it is not surprising to find that so few people are ever arrested for the crime of bribery.

Apparently, according to the police, only about 10% of the crimes are committed by organized crime and the gangs (*boryokudan*). This is amazing, given the fact that there are apparently some 2,500 gangs with 110,000 members. The biggest, Yamaguchi-gumi has as many as 10,000 members.[38] It is even more amazing given the proven efficiency and professional ability of the *yakuza*, who have become heroes of a sort for an otherwise timid youth. After the war, the number of criminals was far larger, although efforts by the police and perhaps the good employment situation gradually eroded the membership. Now, however, the gangs are making a comeback. They could only be contained by unrelenting efforts to prevent them from getting guns, and at one time some only had knives or clubs. Now sufficient arms have been smuggled in to make them more dangerous than ever. At the same time, they have spread their turf to new areas, sometimes engaging in gang wars over the boundaries. They have also increased the scope of operations, moving from gambling and prostitution into business shakedowns and protection. Finally, as had to be expected, they realized that the biggest money was in drugs.

No matter how well the situation may compare, Japan would be unwise to assume that it can last forever. And the police at any rate is showing less complacancy than the citizenry. The number of criminal offenses has been rising steadily since 1974. Although the amount of violent crime has dropped somewhat, theft and nonviolent crimes like fraud and embezzlement are on the increase. Recently, Japan has also been hit by a wave of bank robberies, kidnappings and crimes against the old and weak. The most ominous trends are the constant growth in juvenile delinquency, runaway children, and the illicit use of stimulant drugs.[39] For they all foreshadow more crime to come.

The worst threat will arise if, as seems likely, there is an increase in drug addiction. Japan, realizing that much of its youth is disaffected and weak, is aware just how dangerous this can be. No country has better sealed off its frontiers, patrolled its coasts, and busted the possessors of drugs. The penalties for use and possession, let alone sale, are among the stiffest in the world. Yet, arrests for crimes under the Stimulant Drug Control Law have been rising, and rising at a terrific pace since about 1970. The number of persons arrested in 1978 was 18,027, twenty-five times the 1969 figure. But the police think this is only the tip of the iceberg, since most of those arrested were drug pushers and the number of actual users is probably ten times higher. According to the White Paper on Narcotics and Stimulant Drug Use, the users are predominantly younger people in their twenties and thirties, although still relatively few in their teens, and include even housewives. More people than ever are also arrested for narcotics-related crimes, including traffic accidents, arson, kidnapping and murder.[40] If youth does become more involved, if the gangs do get into the drug traffic, then the situation could go from bad to worse very rapidly.

*　　*　　*

Japan has been an amazingly vital country over the past centuries. If not always as well or fully as claimed, it has been receptive and capable of absorbing parts of the most extraordinary mixture of philosophies: Buddhism, Confucianism, and Christianity, democracy and totalitarianism, capitalism and communism. It has repeatedly transformed itself to meet new requirements. It has seized upon one cause after another, although not always good ones, ranging from exceptional openness to the world to fierce zenephobia, from rabid militarism to militant pacifism. After the war, it had to drop the second half of the Meiji slogan of "rich country and strong army" and make economic growth and prosperity its prime aim. To prove their own ability, the Japanese might attempt to double GNP in ten years or, to show the world how good they are, catch up with and pass the West. Well, now they have a strong economy and affluent country, they are recognized economic leaders, what more is there to be done? Has Japan reached the end of the road spiritually? What is its goal today?

If there is one thing that all Japanese, and all students of Japan, agree upon, it is that Japan seems to have run out of goals. Frank Gibney, whose writings reflect both admiration and disappointment, concludes: "No generation has ever needed an additional challenge so badly. No generation has ever so badly needed people to inspire it, as well as to direct the traffic. . . The changes that need to be made among the Japanese are drastic. They are drastic not so much in the strain they put on Japan's physical capabilities, which are immense; but they are drastic in the changes they demand in Japanese attitudes."[41] Edwin O. Reischauer, whose pride in Japan cannot be doubted, admits: "Neither religion, nor ethical principles, nor political and social ideals serve as the great unifying forces they do in many other lands. The keystone appears to be missing in the intellectual or spiritual arch, and this lack in turn gives a certain instability to the whole structure of modern Japan."[42] Many Japanese have condemned the spiritual vacuum as Japan's greatest danger. Shintaro Ishihara wrote: "There is a spiritual void at the core of the Japanese nation, a moral degeneration that characterizes everything that goes on in this society."[43] Yukio Mishima expressed his despair in suicide.

In Japan, leader after leader complains of the lack of national goals. Most propose further materialistic ones, a bit more growth, or a bit less pollution, somewhat better housing, or somewhat less crowding, and on and on. Those with more vision, or better speech writers, simply suggest bigger goals: a "remodelling" of the whole archipelago by Tanaka or the creation of "garden cities" by Ohira. Unfortunately, these aims are not even picked up by the population. Only the real estate companies and land speculators invested in Tanaka's program and the spread of dinky *homus* in ticky-tacky suburbia makes it impossible to fashion any finer environment. Worse, the young people aren't even interested in material goals any more, not if this means that they have to work hard for them or show discipline. Youth wishes to receive affluence, not fight for it. Whether its wishes can be fulfilled much longer, however, remains a very open question.

Wagering somewhat awkwardly onto the trickier terrain of moral goals, many a politician or thinker has proposed his vision. Apparently imitating Mao Zedong, the then Prime Minister Tanaka set forth "Five Essentials"—to cherish people, to cherish nature, to cherish time, to cherish things, and to cherish your country and society. He followed this up with "Ten Subjects for Reflection" by school children: Have I been friendly to my playmates? Have I been kind to elderly people? Have I bullied the weak? Have I taken good care of all living things and plants? Have I kept my promises? Have I observed the traffic rules? Have I listened to the advice of others, such as my parents and teachers? Have I been finicky about my food? Have I been a nuisance to others? Have I acted courageously in what I believed to be right? Ryoichi Sasakawa, one of the richest men in Japan, regards moral training of today's youth as his primary task, taking out prime time on television to flash messages such as "take good care of your father and mother," "one good deed a day," or "let's keep Japan clean." Not to be left behind, the usually prosaic Ohira was capable of sheer poetry in presenting his goal of a garden-city state:

"Since ancient times, Japanese society has not erected walls between urban culture and life in the rural expanses, and our lives have featured city and country interrelating and complementing each other. Today, there are strong calls that the city be fitted with the country's comfortable-ness and the country with the city's vigor so as to take even more explicit advantage of this characteristic. The age of culture is at the same time an age of emphasis upon the local. We would like to make the creation of vigorous and richly independent local communities in the big urban centers, in outlying cities, and in rural villages the basis for our nation building and our community building for the twenty-first century. In line with this concept, we hope to create verdant areas linking city and country, to nurture leadership personnel in the local communities, to positively promote policies such as those for developing cultural vigor in the community, and to seek the enrichment and reorganization of existing policies."[44]

There will certainly be no shortage of proposals for other dreams. But, is a new dream and a new goal what Japan really needs? After all, it already has a multitude of ancient virtues that have not entirely lost their validity, the only thing that is gone is the ability to practice them. There is also a vast array of goals that can be adopted from foreign philosophies and ideologies, some of which could be quite helpful. Moreover, everyone already knows the problems, many even know the solutions. What is needed most is a few more people with the courage to admit them and do something about it. Perhaps by rejecting all dreams and goals which can galvanize them magically and make them act again as a mass, by merely facing reality as simple and fallible human beings and doing what little can be done, the Japanese would accomplish more than by waiting for the next "miracle" to come along.

NOTES

1. William H. Forbis, *Japan Today*, p. 107.
2. Dale Saunders, *Buddhism in Japan*, pp. 267–8.
3. "Inside the Weeklies," *Japan Times*, July 15, 1975.
4. Ronald Dore, *City Life in Japan*, p. 329.

5. *Japan Times*, July 27 & August 24, 1979.
6. Forbis, op. cit., p. 95.
7. "Question of the Week," *Japan Times*, September 25, 1977.
8. *Sunday Mainichi*, October 9, 1977, pp. 17–22.
9. *Japan Times*, September 18, 1977.
10. Michiko Inukai, "Agreeing to Differ," *Japan Quarterly*, April/June 1966, p. 182.
11. Richard K. Beardsley and John W. Hall, *Twelve Doors to Japan*, p. 387.
12. Robert J. Lifton, *The Challenge of Youth*, p. 273.
13. Edwin O. Reischauer, *United States and Japan*, London, Oxford University Press, 1950, p. 172.
14. Edward Norbeck, *Changing Japan*, pp. 19–21.
15. Herman Kahn, *The Emerging Japanese Superstate*.
16. Kahn, op. cit., p. 22.
17. *White Paper on Youth 1977*, Youth Bureau, Prime Minister's Office.
18. *Japan Times*, July 27, 1979.
19. *Sankei Living*, October 29, 1977. p. 2.
20. *Sunday Mainichi*, January 8, 1978.
21. "Inside the Weeklies," *Japan Times*, December 20, 1976.
22. "Inside the Weeklies," *Japan Times*, July 6, 1977.
23. *Survey of Office Workers' Consumption Behavior*, Foreign Press Center, June 1977, p. 14 & 2.
24. *Japan Times*, December 5, 1977.
25. Michio Nagai, *Higher Education in Japan*, p. 128.
26. *Leisure and Recreational Activities*, Foreign Press Center, April, 1977.
27. *Survey on the Living Hours and Leisure Activities of the Japanese*, Leisure Development Center (Yoka Kaihatsu Center), in *Shukan Asahi*, November 11, 1977, p. 117, and *Quarterly Bulletin*, Dai-Ichi Kangyo Bank, Mid-Summer 1979.
28. Mariko Bando, *The Women of Japan*, p. 19; *Japan Times*, November 30, 1977, p. 2.
29. See Jon Woronoff, *Japan: The Coming Economic Crisis*, pp. 272–82.
30. See Kakuei Tanaka, *Building a New Japan*, Tokyo, Simul Press, 1972.
31. "Inside the Weeklies," *Japan Times*, August 10, 1976.
32. Gleaned from "Inside the Weeklies," July 8, October 28, November 4, December 9 & 30, 1974, June 9, November 3 & December 15, 1975, June 14, July 5, November 15 & 23, 1976, December 12 & 19, 1977.
33. *Shukan Shincho*, December 8, 1977, p. 96.
34. Jack Seward, *The Japanese*, p. 56.
35. *1977 White Paper on Crime*, National Police Agency, Ministry of Justice.
36. *Japan Times*, October 16, 1978.

37. "Inside the Weeklies," *Japan Times*, July 5, 1976.
38. *1979 Police White Paper*, National Police Agency, July 13, 1979.
39. Ibid.
40. *White Paper on Narcotics and Stimulant Drug Use*, Ministry of Health and Welfare.
41. Frank Gibney, *Japan, The Fragile Superpower*, p. 332.
42. Reischauer, op. cit., pp. 310–311.
43. Shintaro Ishihara, "A Nation Without Morality," *Japan Interpreter*, Winter 1975, p. 276.
44. Prime Minister Ohira's Speech to the Diet, September 3, 1979.

8

Happiness is a Well-Regulated Society!

In every country there is much idealization and rhetoric regarding the goals of society and how it functions. In Japan, these are a mixture of the noble modern goals of democracy, equality, meritocracy, and a reasonably uniform and harmonious society mixed with hangovers from earlier days, group relationships, respect for the aged, nationalism, etc. These phrases and concepts come up repeatedly in speeches and writings. But, repetition can mean many things: genuine attachment and fulfillment; mere lip-service; calls to revive dying virtues; or laments that they no longer exist. There is no shortage of people who proclaim or mouth these goals nowadays, both Japanese and foreigners, although the latter sometimes express them with a fervor and elegance rarely found in Japan. Take this observation by Frank Gibney, for example:

"In many ways, Japan is a true meritocracy. One can move up, if one obeys the rules, and get quite far through sheer competence. The railroad motorman's son from far-off Akita prefecture who excels in the exams and enters Tokyo University will find himself, by that very fact, elevated to a pre-eminence in the Japanese community that his family might not otherwise have achieved for generations. He will be accepted into a government office or large corporation on the basis of his school affiliation (as long as he does well in the corporation's testing process) and handled as a member of the elite. But he is an elitist the way the Chinese mandarins were elitists, by right of scholarship and merit (plus possibly some help from a few acquaintances). But he does not think of himself as part of an elite social class. And, unlike people who climb from humble circumstances in America, he rarely turns his back on his antecedents. Family is family. Akita is still home. And, after all, everybody is Japanese."[1]

Oh, were it only so! Not only in Japan, everywhere! Unfortunately, certain vices have worked their way into the system and somewhat perverted it over the years. There is a tendency to assume that the newer, fresher, perhaps more idealistic goals have been achieved and remnants of the past have died out. There is also a penchant for hoping that noble virtues will always triumph over vices. And thus it is assumed that meritocracy, equality and democracy flourish while classes, nepotism, clanishness, age and sex distinctions wither. That is not so easy and laws are insufficient to reform societies.

* * *

What is generally regarded as the foundation for meritocracy is the school system and especially the stiff entrance examinations as a careful screening process in which the most decisive step is passing through the "narrow gate" to college. Unfortunately, these tests— which are regarded as determining merit—are not subject to any proper evaluation as to their contents, namely whether they are valid measurements of knowledge or ability to learn, or even up-to-date, relevant to the subject, or correct. Moreover, the tests are usually devoted to subjects that can be learnt by rote memory and often marked by methods that leave little room for the student to display ability. There are also any number of extraneous factors that can determine who passes or fails. The amount of hours studied, access to cram courses, use of private tutors, things that cost money, can heavily tip the scales in one's favor. The place a person lives at is important, which explains why many fathers have their children remain in Tokyo or a major city even if they are transferred to the provinces, say Akita. For the tests are given at the school and most are in the cities. Outsiders have to go to considerable trouble, pay great sums, and study under less than ideal conditions during the test weeks since they have to travel and stay in hotels. How many tests one takes, or can afford to take financially, makes a difference, for the more one takes the greater the chance of passing one. Even more random elements are seen by the students themselves as crucial: how many other candidates are taking the same test that year; which faculty one tries out for; whether the questions you prepared particularly well turn up in the test, and so on. That may be why most young people regard luck as so important to success.

Even if there is some basis for meritocracy in this kind of screening, one may well wonder why the race is so largely won at the age of seventeen or eighteen, when a person passes a test to get into college. It would seem more logical to judge a person's education by what he knows on graduating. But, since such general tests on completion do not exist, few students bother to keep up good marks, and it is the name of the school itself, something decided four years earlier, that counts. This is very odd, when just about everywhere else in the world it is the length of the education and its contents that count. First of all, whether one took courses of some relevance to the requirements. Then, how well one did during the years at the university. And, finally, how long one studied. Elsewhere, to prove educational merit (but nothing more than that), a person would stay on to obtain a Masters, a Ph. D., perhaps even a second doctorate. The Japanese system assumes that a school education is the only basis for rising, that a self-taught person who knows just as much cannot even be considered. This is not absolute, and people with enough ability or force of character can rise outside of this channel, but their rise is much harder, and there seem to be fewer and fewer who make it.

Worse, merit has been taken one step further, to simplify the whole "evaluation" process, and been tied to the particular school one attended. First of all, a person who has attended college, any college, even the worst, will have more "merit" than someone who only got through high school. Then, one checks *which* university he or she has attended and not what that person accomplished there. A top student from a second rate school can sometimes rise faster than a mediocre student from a top school, but it is rare that he can ever attain the level of a good student from the top school . . . even if he is clearly and demonstrably more capable. Unfortunately, this ranking of schools is not even based on their relative value or the sort of students they turn out. Many of the factors in deciding which schools are better are perfectly extraneous: whether they are national or prefectural, whether state or private, when they were founded, by whom (government, church, temple, some famous leader), their size, success of their alumini in infiltrating jobs, etc. This rating is hardly kept up to date and it is extremely rare for one school to rise although its academic level improves or for another to drop when its quality does. For such reasons, it is absurd to talk of meritocracy, once this has been institutionalized to a classification by school, and better, as we said, to speak of "schoolocracy."

After school, the next "narrow gate" is to get a good

job. Once again, it is the entry that counts, since one usually stays with the same company throughout a career. And, having become an employee, a person ceases to have his own merit and assumes that of his employer. "I'm a Hitachi man, a Mitsubishi man, a . . . " Whether the person is high or low, brilliant or worthless, president or janitor, his first claim to "merit" is who he works for. The merit rises if one is with an old and respected company. It is also helpful to come from a big company, the number of employees playing a definite role, and certainly from the major ones and not just a subsidiary or subcontractor. People from the head office or Tokyo branch will do better than those from the provinces. The same applies to the bureaucracy, where certain older or larger ministries impart greater prestige, and central government always wins out over local government. Being a politician in the ruling party or the larger factions has a similar aura. Yet, none of this proves that the person concerned is any better than anyone else, that he is even highly appreciated where he comes from, or that he or his company or office are more productive, more socially-minded, or simply more profitable. Reference to his position does not help much, since this is a function of seniority and having a top post can be as much a result of longevity as ability.

So, rather than personal merit in any form or on any basis, be it the Japanese virtues or the Western ones, be it intelligence or loyalty, courtesy or dynamism, hard work or obedience, a person is usually judged by his school, his employer, and his ranking there. None of this has much to do with a pure or even greatly adulterated system of "meritocracy" and it makes such claims seem a bit absurd. Obviously, merit is harder to prove than simply looking at a person's "credentials," but one would have thought that the Japanese might make a somewhat stronger effort.

Nowadays, even that vestige of meritocracy seems to be

fading as various tricks are used to get around the "narrow gates." There has been no end to the scandals about schools accepting donations or outright bribes to let in "back door" students. This has been so strongly resented that some of the schools concerned and the medical and dental professions whose schools were most involved have lost much of their standing. But, the practice has not ceased. There is also a strong feeling among all concerned that personal relations with teachers and administrators in both the high schools and colleges can facilitate entry to a university. This usually does not work for the worst third of the graduates, and the top third will get into university anyway, but the middle third may make it or fail depending on connections. That already is a significant breach of the rule. Connections, either through the school or friends and relatives, are a far more widespread manner of getting into good jobs, all tests notwithstanding. Indeed, some schools have no trouble opening magic doors into certain companies or professions. Sufficiently high executives never have trouble placing a few potential employees, nor do politicians, bureaucrats, and many others.

* * *

An even more essential reason that meritocracy plays a limited role in Japan today is that another attempt at constructing a "modern" Japan went awry, namely the hopes of eliminating age as a qualification. For, where "merit," such as it is, leaves off, age and length of service take over. Respect for the aged and seniority have a long, long tradition, going back to the earlier ancestor worship, reinforced by the Confucian philosophy, and strictly regimented under the Tokugawa Shogunate. But this continued on into the modern period. There was a breach during the upheavals of the Meiji Restoration when the destiny of the empire was entrusted in younger men. These advisors (*genro*), however, managed to stick around for a long time and ended up as elders or elder statesmen. The founders of political parties, companies, schools, newspapers, anything and everything, tended to stay on at the top. Of course, the slate was wiped fairly clean again after the war, or so one thought, but some of the older leaders did come back as the "new" postwar leaders. The position of the parents, the father, and husband were officially downgraded in the legal codes and legislation was adopted to protect women and children. Yet, once again, the parents found ways of getting back some of the power, as did the aged in every form. So, this thread that has run throughout the whole history of Japan has been bent or ravelled at times, but never cut. Indeed, even today, by custom and not by law, seniority has been built into the system as a basic principle.

This principle works in each sector and group, permitting the elders or seniors to restore their joint rule. Take the business world. A person's position is determined not by his ability, drive, intelligence, productivity, or even largely favoritism, but basically by seniority in that company. Each year, in April, a new class of employees is accepted. This age group (rather, seniority group, because age is less important than the Showa year of entry) rises by and large together. As the escalator goes up, these young employees age, and receive better positions, salaries, bonuses, privileges, and treatment. Any attempt to pull someone out of line, up or down, is resisted by the whole group. Even when a person has amply proven his worthlessness, he will continue rising if he does not make a horrible blunder. Even if another person has shown special worth, at best he might rise a bit, a Showa 44 man could bypass a worthless Showa 43 man, but even that is not easy. Being dropped or fired, and going into a new company, where you start near the bottom again, would be nothing short of a disaster. Staying on the escalator, with luck—and connections—you make it to the top.

This same pattern exists in just about every sector. Obviously, grades and promotions in the army, navy, or police force follow this monotonous pattern. One would not expect otherwise in the bureaucracy either. One may assume the same in traditional activities, like tea ceremony or Kabuki, or in religious cults and temples. But it is also there in the newspapers, where one rises from freshman reporter to editor with the years and not the "scoops," and perhaps most strongly in the university, where the older *sensei* are adulated and guide the acts and thoughts of the younger ones. In the hospitals, the directors, head physicians or nurses, are usually old, not necessarily the most qualified. Even in research work it takes more than novel ideas to lead the team. For women, the fresh young housewife hardly knows how to speak to the older ones, who rule over the informal neighborhood groups, and no comments can be expected at the PTA meeting from a mother whose child has just joined the school. Even the kids have to play up to their seniors (by a few years at most) in school.

The situation is as bad, if not worse, at the top as at the bottom. The highest titles and best paying jobs, although removed from day-to-day management, go to people usually well beyond the official retirement age. Keidanren, the key business lobby, consists of vice-presidents in their seventies and President Doko was in his eighties. Bureaucratic vice-ministers are naturally getting on in years and heads of state corporations often start their second career after fifty. The Liberal Democratic Party, which was somewhat more dynamic when its members were younger, has aged considerably since once elected a person tends to stick around. In fact, when party "elders" like Kishi and

Materialists come to visit Buddha.
Photo credit: Foreign Press Center-Japan.

Shiina step down, they are already in their eighties. Even in Fukuda's "rejuvenated cabinet," most ministers were in their sixties and seventies. Thus, it was quite an upset when Kakuei Tanaka, a mere 54 then, edged out senior men to become Prime Minister. But things were set right with Miki, in his sixties, and Fukuda, who was squeezed out at the age of 73 by Ohira, then only 68. Since the average age in the Lower House is 55, it must be assumed that the opposition is not much better. Asukata took over as head of the Japan Socialist Party when he was 62. Kenji Miyamoto, already a prewar leader, was still at the helm of the Communist Party in his late sixties, the Chairman of the Central Committee stayed on into his late seventies, although the Secretary General and "crown prince" Tetsuzo Fuwa was only in his late forties. The only ones who can compare with this are the present Emperor Hirohito, 79 years old in 1980 and chief of state since 1926, and the 46 year-old Crown Prince.

However, the reason that gerontocracy has remained so strong despite the process of modernization is not just that the Japanese venerate old people. It has a far more solid basis than that. Society is very largely governed by personal relations and it takes a long time for one to create and consolidate links with people. Obviously, the older a person is, the more time he has had to work his way into the hierarchy, to pick his friends and protectors, and later on his own backers and protégés. He can make more connections and exert more pull. He can accumulate more human capital. The reason old men are kept on in honorific, but extremely well paying posts, in their sixties, seventies, and eighties, when their contribution to the company is nill, is not only respect but that they have nurtured and still partially control a solid network of allies in the more actively managerial class. The reason old men become prime ministers is not that the Japanese think their wisdom or prestige is superior but because it took a very long time to form a large faction. The reason a venerable *sensei*, who may spout utter nonsense, is still chosen as chairman of meetings or head of committees is that a lot of his younger colleagues got jobs through him. An older person who has lost these connections, this support, and social debts due, will not get overly far on respect alone. An old person with no power is just as likely to disappear into oblivion.

What does this do to the school, company, government or society? On the one hand, this does cut down immensely on the squabbling for promotion and permits those with the most experience (even if much of it is irrelevant) and, far more important, the best or broadest networks of contacts, to lead. However, on the other hand, it further stifles initiative, which is poorly received in society to begin with, for what purpose does imagination or drive serve if a person will rise anyway and primarily with the years? This lays a heavy burden on the young, who have to kowtow to the old, and often have to use the most devious paths to attain their ends (even valid and rational ones) because they are either blocked by or most pass through the seniority chain of people who may be les able, trained, or aware of the situation. It also means that when the "young" have finally reached positions of power or authority, they are already "old" and their novel ideas which might have solved earlier problems in earlier days are a bit outmoded for the crises they will actually encounter so many years later. Thus, the ferment of Meiji days and the new opportunities to start from scratch after the war have been replaced by a situation where seniority again prevails, keeping society much more stable, if less dynamic.

*　　　*　　　*

There is an incipient elitism everywhere in the world. How it can be denied in the case of Japan, where even the external features are so obvious, is hard to comprehend. After all, traditionally there has been a very sharp and rigid class structure with, at the top, an elite. After the elimination of classes during the Meiji Restoration, it was still found necessary to grant titles of nobility and create a House of Peers. Feudalism was perhaps done away with as regards the persons involved, but it was much harder to root out a deep feeling for rank and an apparent need to have rankings and to know one's position. In Japan, one simply cannot live without distinctions for the simple reason that it is impossible to speak Japanese without knowing one's relative position. This is further surrounded with acts and gestures of deference—or superiority—which further condition the action of the Japanese, young and old, and are perfectly noticeable even to the casual observer.

After class and social ranking was relaxed or removed, the Japanese wasted little time in attaching their ranking system to education. Obviously, in the early days, a superior education was a step toward becoming a superior person, in the eyes of the individual and nation. And, surely, those responsible for giving education, the *sensei*, deserved even greater respect. There were very few schools in the beginning, and thus the few graduates very quickly and very naturally rose to high positions and status, often further graced by the Emperor's favor. What sense this grading makes today, with everyone going to elementary school and half the population continuing on to college, is unclear. But, a ranking once started is hard to suppress. Parallel to this, the oldest college, Todai, and the next few, including Kyodai, and then some select private colleges, like Waseda and Keio, achieved a higher ranking that was spread to their graduates. Despite considerable efforts, this ranking could not be wiped out either. Today, the University of Tokyo basks in a prestige that is without parallel throughout the world and its mere diploma bestows a status, a visible and concrete benefit, on its graduates that hoists them into an elite.

There has also been a ranking of professions, partly affected by the older class structure and partly by the element of money. The bureaucracy, due to its close links once to the Emperor and today more nebulously to government, enjoys considerable prestige, which once compensated for lower salaries. Businessmen, often looked down upon for their money-grubbing ways, were nonetheless respected if they could amass enough of it. Teachers lost status simply because they were paid less. Even today, the service industry, especially the smaller stores and shops, restaurants and hotels, but also automobile repair places or translation agencies, have to fawn on their customers and accept their every whim, while the client uses a distinctly superior language in expressing his needs. The farmers and fishermen obtain that much less respect as they are less educated. Then, the companies are ranked by age, size, listing on the Tokyo Stock Exchange, and so on, until one can tell the relationships between them. The bureaucracies receive their own ranking. And so on down the line.

The social gap between city and countryside has narrowed considerably over the years, but it has not been closed by any means. Indeed, many city folks regard the farmers as peasants and yokels and the term "*nokyo-san*" or member of a farm cooperative conveys the meaning of vulgar. As under the *shoguns* and emperors, living in the capital of Tokyo is somewhat more than just a question of domicile, it too brings prestige. The same applies to a lesser extent to Osaka and other large cities or the prefectural capitals as opposed to the hinterland. There is not much likelihood that a boy from Akita who made good would go back to live there, although he might appear occasionally to spread largesse and be praised for his success. His children would appear there more rarely, if ever. There is still some regionalism, due to different customs and accents, and this can cause snobbery. In the countryside, where traditions and customs have held on much better, there are obviously also rankings accepted by and large. Some may be based on hard facts like who owns or runs what; others a remnant of earlier days when such-and-such-a-family held certain powers or were big land-owners and gentry.

On the basis of these rankings, people work out their relations more than such almost random factors would affect relations in many other countries. Within each group, there is considerable competition to pick up anything that connotes rank. Most people have as their ambition to become a something-*cho*, be it section head (*kacho*), division head (*bucho*), committee chairman (*iincho*), or head of anything. To give this craze further scope and so that the craving for title may be more readily satisfied, most hierarchies are chopped up into small enough parts for there to be many titles around, even if some of them bring no enhancement of authority or increase in salary. Still, on the basis of this promotion, one has risen a notch and can talk down to more people than the day before. There are also some supreme honors, most of them bestowed by the Emperor. There are any number of orders to which one can be appointed and medals galore. There are also command performances and receptions whose mere attendance raises one out of the ordinary mass.

That this is an elitism is clear enough, for one would not be making such great efforts for status and prestige otherwise. The hopes of entering Todai, not Kyodai or Keio, will drive a student on to incredible efforts. As will the hopes of getting into the forty top companies. Once in a job, many employees will not rest in peace until they have gotten a title, and then another one. This ranking is clearly shown on the *meishi* or calling card, whose main purpose is most definitely not to make things easier for foreigners, but rather to announce to all other Japanese who one is. Many casual conversations do not progress very far before announcing one's age, what educational background one has, or what company one works for (and the year of entry). Once the pecking order is established, the loser is expected to express all due respect—and anything less would be an insult—to a person he has never met before and thus has no special reason to respect. The new "elite" may not be time-honored, particularly large or brilliant, or decked out in fancy regalia, but it cannot be avoided.

*　　　*　　　*

This elitism may seem a bit nebulous for the moment. But it has been growing in more palpable forms, as elite individuals try to attach that status and its advantages to their families and make it hereditary. This, too, is a very traditional approach in a country where, from time immemorial, family has played such an important role. Parents have always done everything they could to help their offspring rise, be it for noble reasons or more base ones such as expecting to be even better taken care of themselves later on. In a society in which personal relations play such a major role it is that much easier to twist the rules to give their children a head start or help them to success. Indeed, this often seems to be the main goal in the parents' lives.

First, they can help out at the early school level to cross the successive barriers. They can put their children into nursery school and kindergarten and later on send them to special prep schools. They can help them get through the "narrow gate" by providing tutors, cram courses, an extra year's preparation, and so on. Or, putting them in "feeder" schools. They can try to get around the "gate" by cultivating relations with the teachers and principal, using connections, getting recommendations, or offering large donations. They do not even stop at giving bribes. Worse, the sheer cost of university education is putting it out of reach of many. Even for public colleges, the cost of a student's upkeep is not negligible, especially for those living away from home. And tuition in private colleges is rising so fast that some families cannot accept the burden. The most exorbitant rates are charged by medical and dental schools, an average of ¥19 million in tuition fees for the six years, something only doctors can afford.[2]

The next "narrow gate" is entry into a big company or leading bureaucracy. This gate is forbiddingly narrow to someone without "*koné*" but amazingly wide if you have pull. Here it is even easier for parents to open side doors and thus cheat the system at a higher level. As an executive in a big company, a top bureaucrat, a well-known professor or doctor, it is easy to make contacts and use pull to get your son or daughter into a good job or give them a clientele. Where nepotism is frowned upon, one can always work out an exchange of favors with a friend, who will get your offspring into his company if you do the same for his. Mitsubishi and some other leading companies apparently prevent father and son from working in the same head office, but there are still the subsidiaries and suppliers. Thus, someone from a "good" family can always get precedence over someone with a better educational record.

Obviously, the offspring of a "good" family can also be put a few steps ahead of others when it comes to the third "narrow gate," namely marriage. For a girl especially, this matter is taken very seriously. She has to undergo rather stringent training and show many accomplishments. It does not hurt if her family is also a better one. The boy may think this is superfluous but, if the potential in-laws do not agree, he may wind up out in the cold. *Omiai* is a natural instrument for arranging such things as the couple get to know one another not only as persons but also are informed about their respective backgrounds. To make certain there is nothing wrong, one expects information on at least all immediate relatives and some hire private detectives to investigate. Or, it is not uncommon for the future mother-in-law to visit the girl's high school to check her records. Parents can play a further role by arranging contacts or presenting sons of "good" families or potentially "good" matches working under them.

Let us dwell on this point a bit longer. In a family-oriented and even family-based society, marriage is often more than just the union of two young people who will strike out on their own. Marriage traditionally in the world, and not far back in Japan's own history, was the means of forging alliances, building companies, or accumulating wealth and power in its many forms. Judging by present trends and the scrutiny with which potential mates are screened, and often rejected, the movement would seem to be backwards once again. There is an urge to create or enter a "good" family, be it in terms of wealth, position, status, blood or whatever. With luck, the members of each succeeding generation will start from a position that much better and be able to hoist their offspring higher still.

Even where it is not done consciously, society is structured in such a way that it promotes this kind of intermarriage of girls and boys coming from an already preselected group, usually through the school they attend or the company they (or their parents) work at. Japanese life as such is rather closely regulated and there are few enough opportunities to escape from one's circle of school chums, office buddies, or friends of one sort or another.

There is not much promiscuity in the sense of accidentally meeting and getting to know someone let alone "picking up" a girl at a movie, party, or vacation. So, even without parental control, the trend is for a Keio boy to marry a Keio girl, a Mitsubishi executive's daughter to marry a Mitsubishi salarymen, or most of a doctor's children to marry medical practitioners.

In addition to status, families have increasingly been passing along wealth. Despite a growing propensity to spend, families still build up savings and can pass along substantial amounts of money and property. Even if the family house is nearly worthless by the time the children grow up, the land will probably be worth a fortune. When the parents pass away, the children can come into some considerable money and landed property by their standards, and increasingly by any standards, especially since with small families there are few heirs. The inheritance taxes are rather high (70% on sums over ¥150 million). But the Japanese are extremely good at giving gifts, and much of this can be covered up quite nicely. Then, the young people, if they are not profligate, can pass this on to the next generation. Indeed, the rise in inheritances has skyrocketed, more rapidly than economic growth, reaching a figure of ¥1,300,000 million in 1972 up 29% from the previous year. By 1976, 4,695 people left an estate of more than ¥100 million, also up sharply from the year before.[3]

If there were a conjunction of both movements: namely to get the children into good schools and jobs, to marry them off suitably, and also to leave them money and property, there would definitely be the makings for the rise of a new class which would have ever greater possibilities of protecting its position financially and, due to close relations with government, even politically. Classes have arisen in the past, why can't a new class rise again? Already one has the funny feeling of seeing names again and again, but once it's the father and another time the son, or the brother, or the stepson. The president of X company is succeeded by a man of the same name, his son, and another son is the head of Y department for the moment. Doctors leave their clientele to their children, also doctors. Books are written by such-and-such a *sensei*, was it the father or the son? Nothing is more visible than the politicians who leave their constituency behind or create a new one for a son. There's former Prime Minister Sato whose son is also a Dietman. There's also the young Hatoyama, and the young Kono, and on the progressive side the Minobes. Are the narrow gates getting narrower, are entries to school becoming somewhat hereditary, are professions passed on from father to son, is a new class system forming? Perhaps. It will be much easier to tell in the not too distant future.

* * *

A general and widespread "middle-class consciousness" is very deeply rooted and tenacious in Japan. This could hardly be made more obvious than by the repeated public opinion polls asking the Japanese to categorize themselves as compared to the rest of the population. In 1977, no less than 90% of the people regarded themselves as having a "medium" standard of living, a mere 5% as having a "low" standard of living, and not even 1% as being in the "high" category. To be most emphatic about it, fully 60% claimed that they were "middle-middle" class. The results of this particular "Public Opinion Survey on National Life" carried out by the Prime Minister's Office did not come as any surprise since the figures had been moving in that direction for decades. As far back as 1957, when economic growth began accelerating, 72% of the people covered by a similar survey claimed to be middle class and as many as 37% regarded themselves as middle-middle.

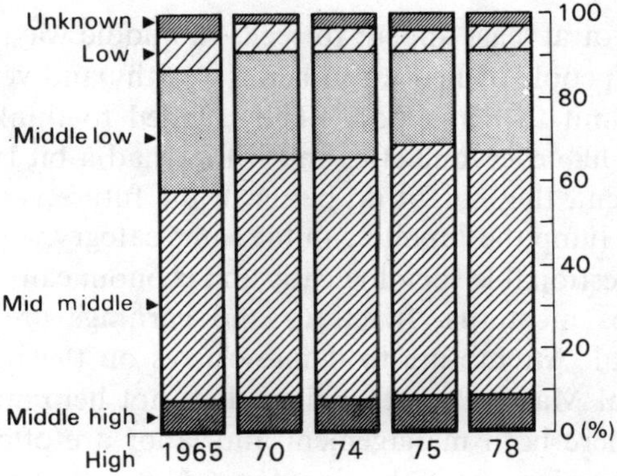

Social stratification in Japan: a rising middle class, a dwindling lower class, and a well-nigh invisible upper class.

Credit: *Japan '79*, Prime Minister's Office, p. 6.

These groups have continued to swell, absorbing the vast majority of the population, while the self-proclaimed upper and lower classes shrank.[4]

There was some dismay among the experts regarding this phenomenon, since according to most of them it did not seem to be constructed on any rational basis. Perhaps, it wasn't. And the feeling of belonging to a broad middle group with common characteristics was probably much more psychological or emotional than real. All concerned had doubtlessly reaped the fruits of economic growth and possessed their rice-cookers, gas ranges, TV sets, and so on. Many had cars. They worked less and enjoyed greater leisure. Their habits and customs were much the same, they watched the same TV programs, read the same newspapers, had similar hopes and aspirations, and felt part of a diffuse group of common Japanese. They probably noticed the similarities more than the differences, especially since they had been taught not to stand out and to seek—or at least appear to seek—a middle way. Thus, very few people owned up to being wealthy and very few would admit to being poor. They tended to think they were just like everyone else, and if they had a bit less for the moment, they might do better in the future.

Yet, to lump the Japanese in the same categry would be rather questionable sociologically and economically as the differences in status, function, and earnings are quite substantial. Attempting to define classes on the basis of traditional Marxist or other lines does not help much in Japan where both management and labor are often just salaried employees of the company. Nor are strict divisions according to income that useful in a society where seniority plays such a role and higher wages are often just a function of longer years' service. Referring to the industrial proletariat as an oppressed class would miss the essential differences between those in major or smaller companies and taking the peasants as underdogs is pointless now that they are heavily subsidized. Such attempts have already been frustrated by the Japanese themselves, since the survey showed that not only 83% of the professionals and managers but also 75% of the farmers and fishermen and 73% of the manual workers opted for inclusion in the middle class.[5]

It may be more helpful to take a look at "Japan, Inc.," widely credited with running the country, and see which of its components have managed to do best. The key figures are basically the politicians in the ruling party, top executives in major companies and high-ranking bureaucrats in certain crucial ministries or departments. True, all the people involved have risen from more obscure positions further down and were once just run-of-the-mill politicians, young salarymen or petty civil servants. However, even then, since they had been carefully recruited from prestigious colleges or through influential connections and were put on the escalators that take people to the top and not those that stop halfway up, they already knew from the outset that they were being groomed for greater things and felt part of a more distinguished circle. This seems to apply most to the bureaucratic elite whose rise is more certain than among the businessmen and politicians who have to face opponents repeatedly and claw their way up. But the fact that they have risen from obscurity and may pass into oblivion after retirement does not make them less than a powerful ruling class as long as they wield power over government and business.

If the elite were too small it would have had trouble maintaining itself in power and there would have been much less middle-class consciousness. Thus, its success and support comes from much larger groups associated with it. One is obviously the second ranking businessmen, not the president or directors but the section and department heads and all the intermediate supervisors on down to the foremen. Due to position and seniority they enjoy both greater status and affluence. Without going as far as their prewar predecessors, the bureaucrats and civil servants, national, prefectural and municipal, continue to function as an elite corps in which they obtain due respect from the general public and moderate but secure wages as well as a more comfortable retirement. And, even less prominent politicians, including those in the opposition, have an enhanced status with their backers (support associations, religion, trade unions) and do get some perks.

The middle class itself consists of some groups that are usually identified with it. First come the professionals, doctors, dentists, lawyers, accountants, teachers, etc. While some do extremely well, especially those in the medical profession and heads of traditional art or crafts schools, others have a prestige that is somewhat diminished by lower remuneration, namely the vast majority of teachers. There are also a large number of self-employed or owners of small shops, stores, industrial or service and distribution firms who earn a nice living. Another group that has succeeded consists of the stars of show business, writers, sports heroes and others. Going a bit further, if one may, those in even more liberal professions such as bar hostesses, escorts and the like have done well. But no category seems to have reaped as generous a harvest as the land speculators.

What surprised many observers and did the most to swell the ranks of the middle class was the adhesion of many farmers and workers. This is not as strange as it may seem. Whereas once the peasants were indeed an exploited class and suffered greatly from the prewar dual economy, as a mainstay of the LDP and with a disproportionately strong vote in elections, the farm community enjoys special attention from the government which includes large subsidies or protection. The workers who have entered the middle class doubtlessly also gained from economic expansion that led to higher wages. But, although all workers gained something, it is perfectly clear that there were some categories that did considerably better than others. Those whose earnings rose fastest and whose status improved most were those in the major companies, the ones most closely associated with the government and benefiting from its assistance and "guidance." Others did not do as well.

It is at this point that traditional class analysis becomes most misleading. The sharpest distinctions are not between management and labor but between the regular employees and part-time or casual labor in all companies as well as between those working for big business and those in smaller enterprises. The first dividing line is drawn within the company. Only a share of the personnel, sometimes as low as half or a third, enters into so-called lifetime employment and enjoys all the wages and security advantages, the perks and the chances of promotion. The others do their jobs for less money, have few fringe benefits, and are simply discarded when no longer needed. Those working for small and medium-scale enterprises, from managers to messengers, earned considerably less than those filling exactly the same posts, working under better conditions and shorter hours in a big company. Those in the smallest firms with 1–3 employees earned about one-eighth, and in companies with 1–9 employees, one-third, as much as those in companies with 1,000 employees and up.[6] In both cases, the main reason some of the workers did so well was that others did less well. Regular employees could never have enjoyed the advantages of a "company family" if there were not others whose wages could be compressed or just dropped in hard times. And big business made much of its profits by imposing on the army of small subcontractors who had to deliver at whatever rates were offered.[7]

But those who were bound to suffer most in the future and perhaps become a genuine lower class were the unemployed. For, it is much less money than security of employment that distinguishes between the Japanese. And this scourge is likely to hit the weakest members of the community first. Among them are the temporary workers in most companies, who are the first to be laid off. This often includes women. It also comprises many uneducated or less educated and skilled personnel. Then, since small companies and subcontractors are more likely to go bankrupt, their staff (and owners) face a second disadvantage. The worst problem, however, is that the biggest contingent of unemployed are not young but especially older workers, those from 55–65 most, with more and more succombing in the 45–54 age group. The unemployment benefits, although increasing, are still limited in amount, time and coverage and would only tide them over until a new job, often less remunerative, could be found.

In speaking of losers, it is probably appropriate to add the women as a whole. There is no doubt that they were discriminated against economically. Either they were the first to be fired if someone had to go or, if they were hired in preference to men, it was only because they were regarded as more docile and could be talked into providing more work for less money. In this society, despite all the talk of modernism, they still had to accept a secondary role except as concerns the household. Politically, they had less representatives than ever. Yet, if so many of the losers not only accepted that condition, but accomodated themselves to it, put on a good face and almost clung to what little privileges they had rather than fight for improvement, it is hard to tell whether they really were worse off or simply living by different standards.

Another distinction is drawn along racial and ethnic lines. There are few minorities in Japan, and in theory they could be assimilated or at least accepted and integrated. Yet, that does not seem to have been the case. The tiny minority of Ainus, the original inhabitants of part of the country, are a dwindling group, marginal economically and socially, and almost a mere tourist attraction in Hokkaido. The Okinawans, earlier urging reversion to get out of the clutches of the American occupation forces, seem to be somewhat less than eager to have their island overrun by "Japanese" businessmen. The perhaps 700,000 Koreans and 100,000 Chinese living in Japan, many of them actually born in Japan, still encounter a certain amount of racism in school, business, and social circles. At least, many of them had business acumen, or engaged in less reputable trades, and made considerable money—which is one symbol of success respected regardless of race. The same cannot be said for the largest social minority, the old outcastes (called *eta* or *burakumin*), who were originally defined by their "unclean" trades and can still be identified by the area they live in. Emancipated a century ago, they have not really escaped their isolation and they have not become socially acceptable. There are rather few of them in big business, the bureaucracy or the professions. Nor are their children really permitted to mix with, and certainly not to marry into, better families. Some have managed to pass into the general population despite careful screening, but that does not solve the problem of the masses.

A look at the income statistics will show that, no matter what the Japanese may think, the population is far from homogeneous. The trend towards greater equality of earnings which characterized the high growth period has shifted and the gap between the top quarter and the bottom quarter of all households is growing rapidly. The

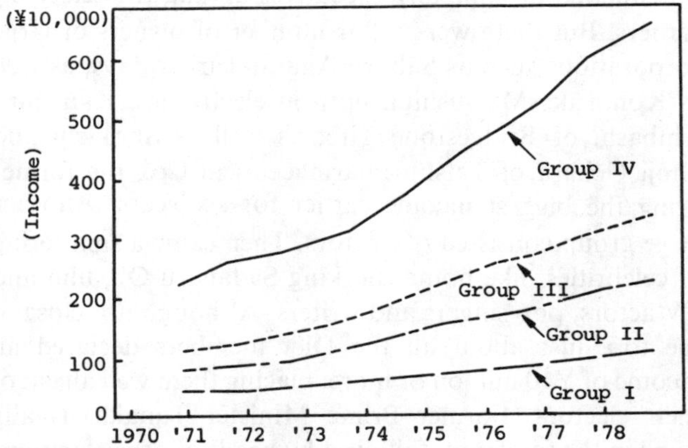

Source: *Summary of Survey on the Living Conditions of the People in 1978,* Ministry of Health and Welfare, May 1979.

The growing income gap between households

income difference rose from ¥3,809,000 in 1975 to ¥5,550,000 in 1978. By then the average income in the highest quarter was ¥6,650,000 while that in the lowest quarter was ¥1,100,000, a differential of 6: 1.[8] Moreover, given the cost of living in Japan, it is hard to conceive how a household could get by on as little as ¥1 million a year and a big chunk of the population, certainly more than the 5% that admitted to being lower class, was probably living under any reasonably defined "poverty line."

At the same time, the annual tax office list of people declaring (and goodness knows what they actually earned) more than ¥10 million a year has not stopped growing. Those declaring ¥10 million or more reached about 380,000 in 1979, some 80,000 more than the year before, and those earning more than ¥100 million rose by 845 to a total of 2,021. Since many of the names appeared year after year, it can only be assumed that some major fortunes were being amassed. There were relatively few bureaucrats or company executives among the really big earners. But there were a fair number of owners of large corporations such as Saburo Akai in earlier days, as well as Konosuke Matsushita, both in electronics, Kanichiro Ishibashi of Bridgestone Tire, as well as Shokichi and Shoji Uehara of Taisho Pharmaceutical Co., the former being the biggest income earner for six years. Another large group consisted of doctors. Then came a smattering of celebrities, like home run king Sadaharu Oh, film and TV actors, pop singers and writers. Although not close to the top, just about all the Diet members declared an income of ¥10 million or more, placing them well ahead of their electors. Former Prime Minister Tanaka usually came in the forefront, followed by heads of other factions, ministers and ex-ministers, and the leaders and members of opposition parties as well, centrist and leftist. However, those who were systematically at the head of the list were speculators who made a killing on land deals with as many as 99 out of the top 100 in 1973 and still 59 out of the top 100 in 1979.[9]

* * *

If there are winners and losers and many of the ideals or principles are flaunted, why has there been so little resistance? In the early postwar days there was tremendous conflict and use of violence to defend principles or merely interests, there were strikes, marches, quarrelling and fighting in the Diet, culminating in the massive demonstration against the Japan-U.S. Security Treaty. During the late 1960s, there was a revival of the *demo* and unrest on many campuses. Then things calmed down again aside from protest campaigns about Narita and like causes. This meets with rather little approval from the general public and the more extreme the efforts to change things the greater the public antipathy. Presently, most of the population not only accepts but seems to be quite contented with the system. Despite any defects, some of which are clearly seen by the Japanese, the major concern has become much less to change than to avoid rocking the boat.

First of all, Japanese upbringing has created a mentality well adapted to the system. The American occupation authorities could impose a Constitution and dictate laws, they could purge thousands of old guard nationalists, but they could not purge the ideas of the old men and women who were in charge of rearing the children after the war while the mothers and fathers were out working to reconstruct Japan. It was not so much that they secretly instilled the old Japanese spirit, and it would seem that the biggest failing in society has been not to instill any spirit, but that they taught the child his primary duty was respect to the aged, the girls that their respect was also due to all men and that one had to fit in to get along in the world. They produced a first generation of obedient and hard working Japanese to carry on the task of reconstruction and economic growth. The girls they brought up, although their outlook was quite different and their approach to child rearing most lax, produced quite a different generation with little discipline or love for work, but too weak to reject society more than fitfully or furtively.

The social "system" took care of the rest. Children were given complete freedom to behave as they would, including misbehaving, until they entered school. Then they were put under tremendous pressure to perform, until they passed—or failed—the university entrance exam. Those who passed, then had four years of rather complete license to do what they wanted, including skipping classes and ignoring studies, until they ultimately graduate. Then, like those who had failed, they also entered the lifetime grind of a job. This process was paralleled by one for girls, who had reasonable freedom and luxury until marriage, followed by household drudgery. This alternation of freedom and pressure could produce many things, but certainly not people who thought for themselves, planned their own lives, and would stand up for their rights. And, to make certain that no such thing happened, the new job, whether in factory, office, administration, or kitchen, whether under a foreman, a manager, a top bureaucrat, or the mother-in-law, was a strict and overwhelming apprenticeship in how one should act in order to get along in life. It also included nothing that would encourage the slightest independence of thought or action.

However, should one seek to revolt, and the ideal time has been the few moments of liberty, especially during the spell at the university, or on entry in a job while one is still young enough to seek another, one obviously could not do it alone. Hence, anyone seeking change was faced with the relative weakness of horizontal links as compared with the established strength of the vertical ones. For, even the most radical movements, where theoretically dedication might overcome or suppress other concerns, have been undermined by the pervasive divisions between sex, age, and social or educational class. In any group, even the most banal of university clubs or housewives' sewing circles, the young had to kowtow to the older, those from good families put on airs, students from Todai might not mix well with those from Keio or Waseda, and the radical students often alienated their female supporters by male chauvinist practices. If one adds to this the jockeying for leadership among strikingly different personalities, such as is likely to occur at the beginning of a new group, one will end up with factions that compete. When ideology is poured into the mixture, especially in a society where ideas do not seem to be traditional rallying points and are often poorly presented and at times incomprehensible to outsiders, then the factions can crumble into groups and combinations which, given the enhanced urgency or sacredness of the cause, are more likely to quarrel with one another than attack the "enemy."

It takes consummate ability or extreme pressure to overcome all these divisions and form a lasting broader front. Many attempts have failed miserably. The radical groups, which were too often synonymous with student groups, lost many of their elements when older members graduated or campus fashions changed. Women's groups were hard to form as long as the women were atomized in their own households with few possibilities of meeting personally and little experience at working through ideas. Even causes like consumerism or ecology, which theoretically should have interested everyone, were too vague or flimsy in many cases to unite people, although there was much greater success with specific groups or people who had concrete interests, like the sufferers of SMON disease or opponents of constructing a factory or nuclear power plant in their hometown. The few groups clearly defined by race or class and often distinguished from the rest of society, such as the *burakumin* or Koreans, had a clear basis for solidarity, but had to decide whether to act as a group or infiltrate the mass by hiding their identity. Moreover, no minority was sufficiently large in numbers to make a dent. More successful have been modern pressure groups, usually members of a given profession, and with clear and limited interests, such as the farmers cooperatives or medical and dental associations. And they were not trying to transform society but rather protect their interests or obtain special favors by manipulating the existing power structure. The political parties, which have become well established and self-perpetuating, have also kept on watering down their personal and ideological differences in order to survive and, where they have not, they proceeded to split.

Of course, where the social system and behavioral patterns have not provided sufficient stumbling blocks to keep people apart rather than bring them together in the support of some cause, especially a "subversive" one, the "establishment" also has means of repression. There is the Self-Defense Force, once berated by the leftists as a threat for use in internal disturbances. But it was never needed since the unrest subsided so rapidly and no clear crisis has arisen. There is also the large and well-disciplined police force and its crack anti-riot squads. But, the amazing thing is that it has to be resorted to so rarely. There are few enough critics of any sort and not many who break the rules. And they are often identified and neutralized before anything can happen. The populace is extremely helpful in this. Parents will warn children, wife will warn husband, *oyabun* will warn *kobun*. Neighbor spies on neighbor, not out of meanness, but rather due to curiosity or as a matter of course in crowded communities and houses with paper-thin walls. Should an individual have evil thoughts or intentions, his friends and intimates can usually be counted upon to dissuade him. If one does misbehave, this news is likely to reach his employer, and dismissal would be as serious a punishment almost as prison, for the next employer would ask for explanations, and many doors would be shut. Radicals in college were amazed to discover how much the potential employers knew about their past, and how hard it was to land a job. This knowledge filtered down to the scond generation of potential radicals. Of course, there are the laws, the fines, and the punishments. Yet, in a tightly knit society like Japan, there is hardly any measure more effective than ostracism. And this punishment can be applied well before anyone could misbehave seriously or commit a crime . . . simply for looking, dressing, talking, acting, or thinking differently from the rest.

Only through a like-minded group might something occur. For, a person tends to adapt his behavior more to the pattern in the group he deals with regularly than the rather nebulous mores of society at large. Thus, political action often took place among radical students—as a group—not as so many individuals. The approach was worked out together and anyone who didn't conform with the group was as likely to suffer punishment. The few counter-cultures that exist are also rather strictly regulated even in their dress and language. You can tell someone from "show biz" by looking at him. The only real and long standing rebels against society in general are the *yakuza.* However, breaking the national laws with impunity does not mean that one can impair the least of the rules in the gangsters' code of honor. Thus, for the individual, it is hardly a question of rebelling as much as being part of a group with different standards. During the student unrest, it was often easier to be a radical than not; now few rebel, and those who do stand out clearly. Society's function is thus to identify them and either convince them to comply or suppress them.

Some authors have written about a recrudescence of fascism in Japan and how the government apparently rides roughshod over its opponents. This is a little hard to bear out. In fact, it would be odd in a party whose leaders have risen through patience and ability at compromise, and are rather old men by the time they wield power. The government, despite its considerable authority, has been rather lax and slow in using it. Since the war, much of the population has been very nervous about such methods and all too often it has turned out to be politically disadvantageous to take a strong position on anything. The means of repression are thus usually held in reserve. Meanwhile, the government does what it can to convince or wheedle, to bribe or buy off, simply sometimes to wait until the fashions in radicalism change. When a crisis arises, as in certain riots or the blocking of Narita, the orders given the police have usually been to wait until the mob becomes so unruly and poses such a clear danger that it is forced, in the higher interest of the nation, to intervene. With Narita, the hope was that the radicals would make themselves so obnoxious to the general public that it would urge the government to do something about it. These tactics have usually been successful. Indeed, one of the most extraordinary sights one can observe in Tokyo is the domestication of the *demo*. There are still demonstrations almost every week somewhere around the ministry area and the demonstrators are given their terms of reference, what they can and can't do, broken up into neat columns so as not to block traffic and to stop when cars have to get through, then flanked by almost as many riot squad men as there are demonstrators, with special vehicles hiding in case of danger, while many of the demonstrators show limited ardor, forget their slogans, and drop out after some distance.

Japan has a stick, a very powerful one, but most of it is social and the harsher methods are rarely necessary. The carrot is often quite sufficient to get people successfully integrated in the "system." For, despite any distortions and cheating, it is still reasonably wide open. A student, by dint of long hours study, can still get into some university if he is really that serious. A graduate can always get some job if he is that good. By showing greater ability, by working harder, by making sacrifices, one can still get ahead and rise, if not to the top, at least well beyond the starting point. There is also enough wealth so that the workers, and the managers, and the owners can get raises and dividends. The husband can still buy his new golf clubs, the wife her Paris fashions, and the kids whatever junk they crave. Obviously, in a recession, things have become somewhat harder and the rise in position and growth of rewards may not be so great. However, as the benefits decrease, the danger of losing one's job makes up for any lack of zeal. The only ones who are on the outside are still a small minority.

However, one of Japan's most striking institutions—seniority—is perhaps the most effective instrument in drawing people into the established order. First of all, everyone rises to a certain degree through seniority, and, as they rise, they have an increasing interest in keeping things going. Slowly but surely, patiently and gently, new generations are coopted into the same "system" they may once have hated. It is certainly rough to be a freshman in college, but only a year later and new students are bowing to you. There is not much fun in the dull work of the first years at a job, but the salary goes up regularly each year, more seniority brings higher status and new rewards. The mother soon forgets her illusions and lays down the law to her children, and then one day she will have a daughter-in-law as her own maid. The old vested interest in change is gradually turned into a vested interest in stability. From fighting the company management, one turns to keeping the company going. From hating capitalism, one starts wondering what would happen if the system changed.

At the same time, everyone gets to put his fingers in the cookie jar. If the factory worker gets little perks like a free trip to Taiwan, how can he complain if someone higher up gets a free trip to Europe? How can one sell a crummy plot of farmland for ten times its value and complain about big real estate companies making a killing? If some politician has gotten your son into college, or quite simply built a school or new road in your town, wouldn't it be most unfair to accuse him of corruption? When your company gets a lot of its contracts through the good services of some guy in the ministry, or its products are protected by tariffs, or MITI is putting in some special administrative guidance to keep it alive, wouldn't it be a bit risky to criticize the "system?" If your whole life is based on how well you get along with people, if your son's job, your daughter's marriage, or your promotion, depend on personal relations, how can one demand that ideals or principles triumph? If you are seriously worried about a change in your own life, how can you become a force for change in society?

Only some sixty years after the Meiji "revolution," the old men were in charge again, the *zaibatsus* and bureaucracy ran the country, the politicians were regarded as rotten, and the population was ready to entrust its fate in the military and emperor. Now, thirty years after the MacArthur "revolution," Japan is again treading its way backwards in many social respects. But, the situation is certainly not all that bad. And, anyway, there is no one else to turn to who looks halfways competent or clean. No group is offering distinct alternatives or policies for change that meet with the approval of many people. The parties are increasingly alike and sometimes act in collusion. So, what can one do to express disapproval or seek change? Not much. Still, if open revolt is impossible, the possibility remains of trying to ignore society or create one's own little niche in it, alone or with others.

In Japan today, there are very few rebels, or even critics, but there are a tremendous number of drop-outs. This consists firstly of those in the few permissible counter-cultures like entertainment or art. But the mass of the drop-outs are just average people who have found they cannot approve of, or simply keep up with, the demands made by society. They are salarymen who decide that it isn't worth the effort to try to make it to *bucho*; they are graduates who accept a job with no title, no status, and little salary, sometimes not because they like it but just to avoid being in a big company; they are the few who go back to their hometowns rather than stay in Tokyo. Some people, including highly educated ones, go abroad and never come back. More broadly, the major generational movements have been a sign of disapproval of the currently and officially reigning social principles and ideology, the *mai homu* and *nyu famirii* generations. After the radical students, the new, tamer variety, are also expressing their rejection with a life style that is hardly compatible with the consecrated values. Most sharply, among the young people, there are many real drop-outs, some who just quit school, others who get into trouble, and a number of glue sniffers and perhaps later drug addicts.

Society does not really know how to contend with this kind of rebellion, which is not only kept underground and often made so intimate that no one else knows, but which does not really flaunt the rules of society although it

Pachinko, a pastime for some, a passion for others.

Photo credit: Foreign Press Center-Japan.

undermines many of them. The lack of striving for success, the desire to live at one's own pace and in one's own way, the growing unwillingness to do anything for society or nation, this can all be as "subversive" and dangerous to the status quo as any protest movement with helmets and clubs. It can also, as new generations replace the old ones, swallow up the whole social code and create a new one. Although based on the principle of individualism, as the majority take on the new ways, they will probably not fail to force the others into their mold, by social pressure or simply because there is no point in being the only one who works or cares. For, conformity, the wish to know what others are doing and saying, and then to behave like them, and finally to make others behave like you, is perhaps the most tenacious of Japan's social customs.

* * *

One other reason that there may be less change in Japan

nowadays is that very often in the past the source of change or ferment has come from the outside. Relatively insular Japan was suddenly opened to new ideas and cultures, which it blindly embraced or were simply forced upon it, but which at any rate brought about far-reaching and deep changes. This occurred when it was overawed by the Koreans and the T'ang Dynasty in China, both of whom the Japanese accepted as offering superior models to be copied. This almost occurred again with the early arrival of Europeans, had not Christianity appeared so subversive and colonialism so threatening. It did come about when the door to Japan was torn open by Perry, and the Japanese themselves seized upon many Western ideas and material objects as essential, copied them, and evaluated their own civilization by the extent to which it could catch up with and surpass the West. The effort may have been too great culturally, for the nationalist movement managed to close the door once again and demand authentically Japanese models. Finally, after World War II, Japan was re-opened to the outside world and some of its institutions were quite simply remodeled for it by the occupation forces while the people picked up anything they thought useful.

As we saw, the periods of curiosity, of copying, of willingness to learn, were followed by periods of suspicion, of rejection of new values and return to old ones, and a feeling that Japan had little to learn from others. This was not surprising when, in the earlier period, Chinese civilization seemed to dip just as Japanese culture reached its peak with Nara and Kyoto. Fear of the Mongol invasions, dissipated by an almost miraculous victory, caused them to look down on the Chinese later. For centuries the West was banned when it became clear how divided the European nations were, and defeat of the Russians followed by early successes over the colonial powers may have convinced the Japanese that there was little to learn from such people. Now, after another few decades of openness to the world, the Japanese may have grown tired of importing new ideas, swallowing new ideologies, and copying new fads. In addition, the Western countries are showing clear signs of decadence, some are faced with anarchy, others have a dissolute younger generation, and hardly any have an economy that can match Japan's. Japan has a polite and well-dressed youth, it apparently follows the sanctified rules and avoids extremes, there is little crime, and people seem to know their place and be satisfied with it. At the same time, abroad, people have begun copying and admiring Japanalia, from arts to Zen, from food to flower arrangement, from court music to martial arts. Whatever Japan produces it manages to sell abroad and these products are highly evaluated.

It is true that Japan is part of the world, participates in major meetings, and sends its diplomats and businessmen to every corner of the globe. But, it is a follower more than a leader, and its interests are narrow and specific. True, there is a craze for travel and Japanese tourists show up en masse in the most unexpected places. However, they go through their whirlwind tours with little deeper understanding of the places they visit and often merely collect souvenirs and gifts to bring back home. Left on their own for a considerable time, most Japanese do not fit in or assimilate, but rather form small groups with other Japanese. Where any sufficiently large number congregate, they end up in a "ghetto," albeit a comfortable one, with Japanese clubs, schools, and commercial centers, where they can find Japanese restaurants, shop for Japanese food, and read Japanese magazines. Moreover, should a Japanese adapt too well and in so doing lose contact with his brethren, he would be rather suspect and might well become so alienated from the mainstream that he would end up a non-Japanese Japanese. Learning from the foreigners is fine, but acting like them or getting too contaminated with foreignness (*gaijin kusai*) is unforgivable.

Even when the Japanese borrow from others, they do it with some discernment, in an attempt to take nothing but the best. Whether or not they get that is uncertain, since it takes a lot of expertise to choose the best and many chance elements actually influence the choice. However, it is obvious that it is far easier to adopt material objects or external appearances than it is to assimilate philosophies or ideologies. Today, Japan has not ceased importing new technologies and machinery, its factories develop every conceivable sort of material gadget, the children are clad in the latest fashions . . . but social customs and manners change much less. Democracy, equality, meritocracy, capitalism, communism, socialism, all have been introduced and tried out (as once Buddhism, Confucianism, and Christianity), and yet the differences with the original are tremendous. Even when importing a whole factory, the workers, wearing similar garb to those elsewhere, will be organized according to Japanese models. In his neat suit the salaryman will be following the social cues of personal relations and not working things out the way he was taught in Harvard Business School. In the latest Yves Saint Laurent fashions, or in sloppy blue jeans, the daughter of the family may well be waiting for her parents to choose or help her find a husband. In a modern apartment, with all the modern paraphernalia, a wife may still be restricted to the kitchen and do nothing more than serve her husband's friends, should he ever invite them to his home.

The introduction of outside ideas seems to have slowed down in recent years and there are a large number that do not exist in Japan, or only in very small doses, and thus the ferment is less. Of the vast sexual revolution in the West, porno and sex films have made their entry. But the heightened equality, comradship, and cooperation among the sexes, the need to understand and bear with one another, and the desire for warmth or sexual fulfillment have not. Democratic experiments like enhanced equality of the races and sexes; educational experiments like the university without walls or merely evening classes or graduate school; social movements like back to nature or the commune are lacking. Concern with the environment, ecology, consumers' protection both as regards price and safety, are weak. Voluntary associations and charitable groups are not formed to help the minorities, the poor, the sick, or people in developing countries except in very rare cases. Even many of the trends in the arts, music, theater, and other cultural fields find but faint reflections, and most of the best proponents end up abroad if they wish to gain recognition or simply have a chance to work in a more congenial atmosphere. Gone are the days when the Japanese avidly sought ideas from all sources, gone perhaps because so many of the ideas nowadays are not particularly good or downright frightening, gone also because the Japanese have lost their earlier curiosity and vigor.

* * *

There is nothing inevitable in the progression of any society, a nation can move backwards as easily as forwards, and sometimes actually with more ease. This will depend on many factors, some of them material, others human, and just about all of them unpredictable. Japan, in particular, has shown a repeated tendency to slide back after having lunged forward. Its society is partially at fault for that. A society can be kept more or less stable by a strong leader for a while, but never as well as when the balance is so arranged that the people also support the attempt at making time stand still. When the Tokugawas tried to perpetuate their rule in Japan, they seized upon Confucianism as one of their tools, making the head of the family the ruler over his small unit and the elders a loose council to see things continued along well-trodden paths. This attempt was so successful, and the routines so well learnt, that despite the two turnabouts of the Meiji Restoration and the postwar reforms, despite over a century of progress in many ways, conservatism is still strong. Perhaps the key to it today is not anything ideological but quite simply that the parents, the grandparents, the elders and seniors in every sense, have an exceptional amount of power and are all joined in the vested interest of slowing down social change. What is an elite or a new class, what are conservative leaders, what even would be a dictatorial regime compared to this system where every person with a few years more than the next is clinging to the petty power this bestows!

Japan is still deeply conservative, and its periods of progress are still followed by relapses. This phenomenon was particularly clear and much commented on just after the war, when the "roll back" began. The earlier liberal laws were sometimes toughened, the trade unions were put in their place (not crushed, but worked into the system), the socialists after the briefest of periods in power lost to the conservatives, the bureaucracy recovered its force and its hierarchization, Todai became the center of the whole educational system again. It has continued, sometimes much less perceptibly, since. The role of women has been downgraded, not only in that they have fewer representatives in the political bodies, but that they themselves accept to be relegated to the household. The role of youth has been downgraded in that one can only rise through age and not ability. Those with radical ideas are even further out and less effective. The political parties have all become more conservative, and the range between left and right has narrowed, while the leadership all around has aged. Society has become stiffer and more rigid and probably an elite is forming.

But, there is little complaint from the Japanese, aside from those who quite simply can't fit in and those who are young or at the bottom of the hierarchy and thus have grievances. The rest seem contented. This may be because a conservative society, no less than a more dynamic one, has definite benefits. It is comforting to know that one will by and large live one's life with little trouble and misfortune, that one can by and large count on tomorrow being much like today, as today is like yesterday. One would love to be at the top of the heap, and rise high through one's efforts. Then again, it is nice to know that one will not suddenly find oneself on the bottom of the heap because some upstart has jumped ranks. Mobility may be fun, flitting from place to place, company to company, one group of friends to the next. But it is a relief to know that by sticking to the same place, people, job, one will never be out in the cold. What it may lack in challenge, opportunity, titillation, Japanese society more than makes up for in solidity and continuity. This may not appeal to all. It's a question of taste. But, taste is largely formed by one's environment.

If there is a revolt against this well-regulated, comfortable, protective, cotton-coated society, it comes from the younger generations. However, to the extent that the challenge has gone underground and is not really voiced or sometimes even sensed by society at large, society does not really know whether there is a threat to it, whether it faces any perils, and especially what they may be. That is why the present situation can be potentially as dangerous to continuity as the earlier days of unrest and revolt.

Societies are not only changed by people who attack their institutions or impose reforms but also by those who simply stop following the accepted rules. Civilizations do not only cease functioning or, in more serious cases, collapse, because they are overthrown by some determined and ruthless group or sapped by a pernicious philosophy or ideology. They can simply fall apart because people stop doing what they were supposed to do or they can crumble because no one bothers to hold them up any more.

NOTES

1. Frank Gibney, *Japan: The Fragile Superpower*, p. 79.
2. *Japan Times*, January 20, 1979.
3. *Japan Times*, November 25, 1977 & June 11, 1978.
4. *Public Opinion Survey on National Life*, Prime Minister's Office, October 1977, and *The Japan Interpreter*, Winter 1978, p. 2.
5. Ibid.
6. *White Paper on Small and Medium Enterprises 1977*, Ministry of International Trade and Industry, p. 76.
7. Jon Woronoff, *Japan: The Coming Economic Crisis*, pp. 171–197.
8. *Survey of Living Conditions of the People 1978*, Ministry of Health and Welfare, May 1979.
9. *Japan Times*, May 2, 1979 & May 2, 1979.

9

Can There be a Crisis in Japan?

Looking at things from the surface, Japan is indeed a prosperous and happy society. The economy improved radically over the past decades, rising like a phoenix from the ashes of the war. Even today, Japan manages to maintain a tolerable rate of growth that still permits a gradual spread of affluence which, since all classes do share in it to some extent, gives the population as a whole a relatively high standard of living. More people than ever have rice cookers, televisions, cars, homes. They take vacations and go on trips. Women walking around the streets of Tokyo look as if they stepped out of a fashion magazine. Education is given more youngsters than ever. Youth, after the earlier campus unrest, has calmed down and become outwardly compliant. The present goals are all tame and reasonable, my home, new family, or a life at my pace. The masses are not disruptive and they seem willing to let the wheels of state turn in the same old ruts. The LDP, for all its failings, has offered an incredibly long period of political stability and a rule that falls lightly on the shoulders of most.

When they look at other countries, the Japanese, who increasingly tend to be pleased with their own record, become positively smug. If they consider their former models and masters in the West, they find that this time

Japan really has caught up as far as the economy is concerned. As to political power, that seems to create more headaches than anything. More shocking is the utter decadence and depravity seen in so many once proud nations: collapse of the empire and economy in Britain, something approaching anarchy in Northern Ireland, Italy, and Spain, social and racial problems in the United States and elsewhere. Throughout the West, youth seems to be more dissolute than ever, unwilling to work hard yet demanding, "into" everything under the sun, from drugs to sexual experiments, from hippie life to subversive groups and religious sects. Those whose economies have lagged behind get an even lower evaluation from the Japanese. Communism has not worked out well in the Soviet bloc and the excesses of the Cultural Revolution quenched the appeal of China. The developing countries, still stuck in the muck of poverty, ignorance, and disease could at best learn from Japan . . . if only they would make the effort.

Of course, in dealing with the Japanese (and most Orientals), one should never look at anything from the surface, any more than one should believe the more extreme rantings of the approach of doomsday in the West. Rather than trumpeting calls of alarm, issuing warnings of impending danger, or shrieking that disaster will follow if action is not taken immediately, the Japanese become more silent than ever. There is reason to fear, or so they believe, that action taken under such circumstances will be precipitate and poorly conceived, that there could well be an over-reaction, or that panic may break out. Moreover, aside from being trained as optimists and having had more than thirty years to develop a solid confidence in Japan's ability to surmount every crisis, they find it hard to believe that anything serious really could be rising on the horizon. But, the surface calm can probably be traced back most to the strong tradition that, even in the worst of situations, a person does his very best not to "lose face."

Companies and banks always put on a prosperous facade and exaggerate their business successes, while playing down—or covering up—any failures, since a sign of weakness would only undermine confidence in them. The government repeatedly claims that things are going quite well, or at least not as bad as the opposition says, recites all its past victories and, if there is trouble, insists that a solution is around the corner or that it sees the light at the end of the tunnel. The bureaucrats, fortunate people that they are, are not too concerned by the problems of others. And the average Japanese walks around with the broadest smile that can be mustered and admits any qualms only to close friends, and only in private, or keeps it in until anxiety starts gnawing a hole in his stomach. In the midst of recession, one dips into savings to keep up the same lifestyle and, if necessary, one will scrimp on essentials but not a little luxury now and then to build up the morale and some conspicuous consumption so that no one else can guess how bad things are. Only the elderly complain, that things aren't like they used to be, that youth is weak and lazy, that the state accomplishes nothing, that elders don't get any respect, and more of the same. But no one takes this griping too seriously. After all, old people are supposed to act like that.

True, Japan still cuts an amazingly good figure when compared with the other countries in the world. But, their failure cannot be interpreted so simply as Japan's success. And, as time passes, the fiction of a happy and prosperous nation is becoming more threadbare. Despite the sacrosanct institution of lifetime employment, some people are out of work nowadays. Despite the might of "Japan, Inc.," the number of bankruptcies climbed above the

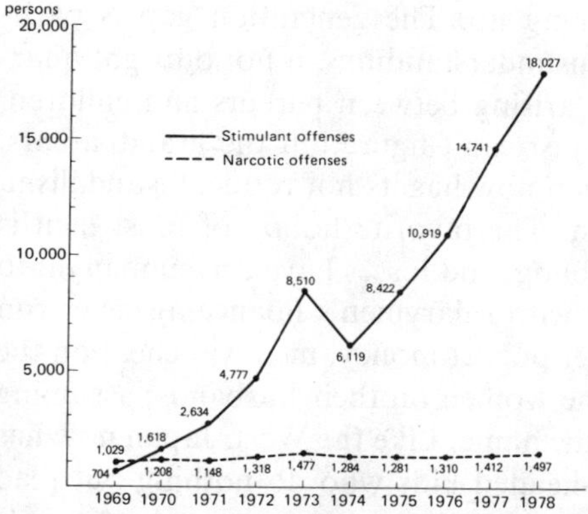

Source: *Mayaku, kakuseizai torishimari gyosei no gaikyo* (Review of Narcotic and Stimulant Drug Control Administration), Pharmaceutical Affairs Bureau, Ministry of Health and Welfare, 1978.

Some trends are more than just alarming.

Credit: *Facts and Figures of Japan 1980*, Foreign Press Center-Japan, p. 108.

danger level, and even some big companies collapsed. Lots of people are rich, many more are moderately affluent, but some still remain who cannot be regarded as anything but poor. Their plight has been aggravated by the mentality that "it can't happen here." Because it couldn't happen, Japan failed to build up its stock of housing and social security system. The lack of unemployment insurance, and the minute size of retirement benefits and pensions, has put many old people in very tight straits. And this comes at a time when it is increasingly risky to assume that the younger generation will look after its elders.

Burrowing a bit deeper into things that the Japanese do their best to conceal from others (and often from themselves), there is the beginnings of what can be regarded as "decadence," earlier restricted to the West. In this sector, too, Japan is catching up. The generation gap is particularly large and misunderstandings, if not outright quarrels and splits, are arising between parents and children, while the children just can't figure out the grandparents, and vice versa. Japan now has its hot rodders, vandalism, and drug addiction. The favorite hobby of most men is some form of gambling, and losses have driven many into hock, occasionally with salarymen's finance agencies run by gangsters. To get pocket money, men will cheat on the company, and some women on their husbands, assuming they even deserve the name. Like the West, Japan now has millions of empty-headed kids who do nothing but read comic books and watch TV, teeny boppers who trample one another at rock festivals, runaway children and teenage prostitutes. Some parts of Tokyo look no better than New York, with the red (excuse me, pink) light districts bursting out of their boundaries and porno shops in formerly good neighborhoods. You can see an X-rated film on the late show and buy a porno magazine in a nearby dispenser. There are "bums" who sleep in the subway stations and others begging on the streets . . . while millions of citizens pass by and try hard not to see them. As for anarchy, just wait until the radical student factions stop killing one another and the Red Army becomes active in Japan.

Here, the frustration and anger have broken out and invaded society. In far more cases, they have been kept in and rotted away the person's insides. It really isn't easy to live up to being a Japanese, especially if you take all the rules seriously and want to be a success. You have to work hard to earn your parents' love, your colleagues' friendship, your company's trust. Sometimes, what you have to do for one cannot avoid conflicting with what you do for the other. Being a good father to one's son and a good son to one's father is hardly compatible. Being a good salaryman, a good colleague, and a good husband takes more days than exist in the week. To be a success you must keep your nose to the grindstone from the age of four or five and then accept an iron discipline in the company or administration for another twenty or thirty years. Not everyone can do that. Those who try, and fail, and are sometimes shattered, can be pitied only less than those who try and succeed, and then spend the rest of their lives living up to society's expectations. No wonder people drink so much. No wonder so many commit suicide. It is a hard life, and many opt out one way or another. But, as long as they melt into the crowd, they pass unnoticed.

* * *

The ripples on the surface are admittedly the doings of what is still, for the moment at least, a small minority. But, to even look in this direction for signs of trouble is a bit misleading. Decadence in Japan does not have to rise out of aggressive individualism and a desire to break rules or experience passions, as in the West. This is a different society; its problems will be different. They are more likely to spring out of its own virtues than someone else's vices. The real trouble with Japan is that the old virtues it clings to are not necessarily suitable any more and in some cases have been overdone. Too much of a virtue, especially a virtue that has ceased to be one, or is not one in a new situation, can be very dangerous. Among other things, Japan is suffering from an excess of conformity, stability turned into rigidity, hierarchy that imposes a fixed ranking, conservatism that stifles initiatives, and discipline for discipline's sake and not because the goals sought merit it. Even when customs and traditions have not become pointless, as long as they are rejected by many people, attempts to preserve them must encounter resistance, hidden or open.

Nothing has been more harmful in its way than an abuse of some of the leading Japanese "virtues," such as the stress on hierarchy and knowing one's position, the flexibility and accommodation implicit in human relations, the use of personal relations to solve problems, and the need for harmony to prevail at all times.

In many ways, the strict hierarchical structure and the need to follow precedents have forced the Japanese into a mold that leaves little leeway for differences of approach, attitude or needs. As long as all the rules were obeyed, without necessarily appearing wise but simply because they were customary, there was little trouble. However, with each generation rejecting more of them, the rules have become a straight-jacket. They have forced the young people to follow antiquated patterns, on the surface at least, while adopting their own methods, within their own groups. It would have been far wiser to permit them more freely to question, accept, or reject rules, and develop new life styles without a feeling that they were tampering with something holy. After all, the few "experiments" that have gained a major following, the my home and new family movements, were not particularly virulent and had many positive elements. Within business, government and administration, it is also fine to follow precedents . . . as long as the circumstances do not change. Alas, they always do.

The existence of almost incestuous groups and social codes in constant flux have together created unnecessary barriers between social categories, educational levels, sexes and age groups. There is a pervasive pattern of insiders versus outsiders and too few meeting points. This has made each group establish its own standards. In such a situation, a person will consider the group's values first, and if need be flaunt the values of all other groups and society as a whole as long as he has group backing. This permits politicians to work for themselves and their constituencies with little regard to the nation's needs, bureaucrats to think of their own retirement provisions while forgetting those of the citizens, or gangsters to steal and radicals to lay bombs. Such situational ethics may indeed be very flexible, take ample consideration of the members' interests, and in their own way appear eminently "human" and "Nihonistic." But with no solid pole, no certain code, such reactions can be very perilous and one never knows whether the person doing the adapting is doing it wisely, for the good of all, or merely manipulating the rules for his own or his group's convenience.

The deepest essence of all, according to many authorities, is the priority given to the network of personal relations. This can be the ties that bind parents and children, husband and wife, employees and company, bureaucrats and administration, or the allegiences worked out between politicians and their clientele, protectors and their protégés. It includes the older *oyabun-kobun* relationship or the more recent *koné*, as well as many lesser and some clearly disreputable variations on the same theme. Just as it is dangerous to adapt the rules to the circumstances, it is risky to bend the rules for personal friends, clients, relatives, and so on. This can corrupt society and be the source of favoritism and nepotism, the destruction of equality, meritocracy, democracy and any higher, absolute order. Yet, the sanctity of human relations almost justifies otherwise impermissible actions. The politician was only taking graft for the party's campaign chest, the company gave a bribe so its workers would not starve, the bureaucrat had to help out an old school chum. It is the rare Japanese who does not seek out someone to help him rise, it is the rare Japanese who insists on standing on his own two feet rather than calling on connections. Thus, widespread as it is, who can cast the first stone? When people at all levels are involved, no one can point a finger at the others and there are no longer any bounds on how far one can go aside from propriety and following the forms.

Harmony is an excellent thing when it grows out of broad agreement or willingness to put the general good or some higher interest first. But it seems increasingly to arise out of very different situations. In the political arena, either between factions or parties, the amount of genuine agreement may be quite limited and arrangements are made by trading benefits, sharing advantages, or incorporating otherwise unreconcilable wishes expressed by each side. The harmony maintained between cliques in business, administration, even religions, is often quite similar. Harmony can prevail where the strong are in a position to impose their will, as was done earlier through the LDP's "tyranny of the majority" and the use of riot police. But it arises no less when children follow rules because they are brought up to be weak or minorities cannot get a hearing because they are too small or disorganized. Finally, the easiest way to avoid unpleasantness and complications if one feels weaker is to simply do what one wishes surreptitiously. Thus, harmony is frequently more an appearance than a reality.

* * *

These old "virtues" have long been pitted against a number of modern "virtues," equality, meritocracy, justice and intangible rules. Where they did not blend, as often happened given the tremendous differences, they tended to compete or conflict. This clash has not always had the desired outcome. And many changes have been occurring that were unawaited and unpredictable. Rather than consolidate society, they have probably undermined it. For, by being secretive, hidden, timid, they escaped control and sometimes even notice. Their effects have not resulted in a head-on clash which might have at least warned society but varying degrees of erosion, slippage, decay. Some of this occurred at the highest level, implying almost a confiscation of power by a limited elite. More disruptive seeds were sown in the major social institutions which could sap their strength and distort their functions. Yet other trends occur in the most personal and intimate level affecting time-honored customs and supposedly immutable principles and replacing them with faintly subversive ideas and actions. Taken together, they may add up to a sweeping revolution, one that will make tomorrow's Japan entirely different from today's.

For over three decades the conservatives have been ruling Japan. There had once been some expectation that a shift in voting would eventually bring the socialists to power. Now a coalition with various centrist parties seems more likely. The problem is not so much that conservative views prevailed (progressive ones may be no better), but that the same views have won out so long. Far healthier would have been an alternance, so that those ruling and their policies would occasionally be challenged and others tried out. Now it is all too often the same people, year after year, and the same ideas, decade after decade, that prevail. When it comes about that a fifth of the representatives are already "inheriting" their position, then obviously there is a danger of a ruling class arising. That the relations with the business leaders and bureaucrats are so close, and not always above board, strengthens this. Yet, the opposition is not too very different either.

In a more general manner, the hope for equality and meritocracy has been gradually frustrated. First of all, much of this process is concentrated in the school system. The fact that tests are given is not a sufficient guarantee if success results from the special training some can afford and others cannot. It means even less when entry results from connections, status or even bribes. And it is very much contrived when the whole operation consists of a single test at a rather young age. Entry into better schools or families is also affected by such things as luck or contacts. Meanwhile, relatively less leeway is left for those who might rise in other ways or at other times. It is very hard to make up for the initial handicap of an unsuitable education, but there have been many self-made businessmen, politicians and other leaders in the past. Making educational background the main criteria thus constricts individual opportunity and cuts off society's access to a broader range of talent.

Running a nation through an elite, rather than on a more democratic and freer basis, can work. However, this assumes that the elite is a genuine one and that it accepts its responsibilities as such. There is already some doubt as to the rationality of entrance into the elite. Tests can only prove so much. But the use of personal connections is a more serious flaw which seems to enhance the rest of one's career as well. At the same time, there is reason for concern regarding why one enters the elite. It was once felt that business was a pursuit for dynamic youths with ambition who wished to get ahead. Increasingly, we have seen that many candidates are simply seeking a secure job. This has flowed over to the bureaucracy, apparently the safest job of them all. As long as students become civil servants because they are assured of a long and comfortable career, there is little reason to hope they will have the nation's welfare most at heart. Although sometimes overlooked, the most important field, especially in Japan, is education. As long as teaching is seen as a job of last resort, there is cause for fear that any anger or frustration will be passed on to further generations.

Connected with this is the trend toward preferring an

easy life. There is no doubt that earlier generations went too far in their loyalty or service to the company and neglected other aspects of life. In their favor, it may be said that the economy was badly in need of such dedication at the time. However, despite the tremendous strides made, the Japanese economy will probably always require a higher degree of sacrifice than most others. The country is simply not blessed with enough natural resources and it is too crowded. Rejection of hard work, shirking of responsibility, unwillingness to seek executive posts, wish to leave work on time and return home or desire to chat and drink with friends, all this is very comprehensible. But there is serious doubt that the economy can afford such practices to the degree the younger generations think they deserve them. Of course, renewed zeal is even less likely as long as the seniority system and career escalator discourage ambition and initiative and reward the time-servers.

The institution that has been shattered most by these trends is the family. The generation gaps have been so great that the young, having lost much hope of converting their elders, or even explaining things to them, increasingly behave much as they will. They develop their own life styles and either hide them or ignore the wishes of their parents. The first generations of such youth now have children of their own and, in some ways, may be patching the family together again. Husband and wife try to be on closer terms, they are more concerned about how to get along with (not only how to direct) their children, the home is replacing the office, the family the company, as a major focus. This has not always been successful, but at least it is promising. Yet, despite this, younger generations are seeking still greater dispensation from constraints. It is not even a question of freedom, breaking away from the established order, but of just being left alone to do as one will, perhaps to drift pointlessly and aimlessly. This can erode the new family as surely as earlier events undermined the traditional one.

Individualism, supposedly non-existent and supposedly un-Japanese, is running strong. But it rarely takes the form of outward revolt. In fact, it can even be compatible with an acceptance of conformity. For, it does not imply going against society as much as simply ignoring it, retreating into small groups and calling that society, and conforming with the very particularistic codes of these groups even when this means flaunting the broader codes of conduct and especially thought. Opting out is the new reaction. By being ignored, or stifled, individualism has developed in any number of devious ways, most of them apparently tame. A pleasant, hassle-free, easy-going life at my own pace and fitting my own tastes is the goal. Tame or not, this is still a negation of the traditional virtues of hard work, sacrifice and loyalty. It rejects broader units like the family, school, workplace, nation. In their place, it fails to offer much of a positive alternative.

*　　　*　　　*

So, Japan has its problems, too. The question is: how well will it meet this challenge? Some claim that once the Japanese have come to a decision they can move ahead rapidly. It is admitted that a consensus is not easy to reach, since all the various parties concerned must be consulted. In addition, a policy cannot really be imposed on anyone unwillingly and a certain degree of acceptance, or at least accomodation, is necessary. But everyone assumes that once these hurdles have been passed there should be no further hitch. The idea that the Japanese are ruthlessly efficient once they reach a joint decision has become almost axiomatic. Just to be certain everyone understood, Professor Jun Eto stressed: "I do hope this point is appreciated abroad: how slow we are in making up our mind, but how swift we are once we have made up our mind."[2]

This may be true, in a fair number of cases at least, as concerns the business world. It was probably also true, with some exceptions, of the military. Already, with regard to political issues, it seems less than certain. It has been extremely difficult for any consensus to be reached between the conservatives and the socialists over the past few decades, even when their own policies were diluted and softened with age. The limited coalitions with centrist parties have not gone much further toward a national consensus. The more violent confrontations, the "tyranny of the majority" versus obstructionism, have simply been replaced by a degree of horse trading. But one could hardly speak of consensus building among the parties (and sometimes even within the LDP) and thus of serious implementation of any plans to solve national political problems.

With regard to social matters, the situation is far more difficult. Firstly, there is no forum in which representatives of all groups meet. The Diet is very unrepresentative in that sense. Although it allows differing ideologies, it stops short of accepting many women, younger members, or those representing non-establishment bodies. Even the trade unions are seen more through regular officials than workers. The attempt at making up for this with consultative bodies has not helped much. But the schisms often go much further, for one could hardly claim that youth, women, labor, intellectuals, or any group has really fashioned its own consensus. There is an incredible fragmentation within all movements due to the preponderance of small groups which have trouble relating with other groups even of the same category.

Of course, the process could take place on a much lower

level, rather than a national scale. This could be at the "grass roots" in village or neighborhood committees. More simply, it could grow out of personal contacts, husband speaking openly to wife, parents to children, teachers to students, ruling party to opposition politicians. This is quite normal elsewhere, but the barriers are so numerous and the lines of communication so tenuous that it is not really that feasible in Japan. Even within the groups, there are many divisions. The links between workers are severed by company allegiences, those between teachers by school affiliations, those between women by extraneous factors like age and status. Until the small groups merge into larger groups and the larger groups enter into relations with one another the atomization will continue. And a consensus would be very hard to find.

The next step is to admit that there are problems. Economic and political issues are usually quite clear and unescapable. Social problems are usually more subtle. In addition, they arise in fields which are particularly touchy for the Japanese. Due to the constraints of harmony and the usual customs, it is rather hard to admit that there is any trouble within one's family or other intimate groupings. It is not seemly for one to criticize youth openly, and youth would be transgressing by attacking the elders. Friction in companies, bureaucracies, parties and so on are hushed up. Some have spoken out, but each time this created more embarrassment and fuss than improvement. Thus, many of the problems have been conveniently tucked behind a veil of harmony. Rather than nip them in the bud, differences grow into disagreements and then into conflicts which are allowed to fester and rot.

One almost wonders sometimes whether the Japanese are aware of the problems. Yet, they could not possibly ignore their existence. The factional infighting among politicians, the various scandals, the lack of action in the

Diet, all this is broadly covered by the press. The social malaise has been uncovered, and confirmed, by poll after poll. Trends are followed by an unending stream of surveys by the press, research institutes, private and government bodies. The results are then commented on widely in the media and taken up in private conversations. The increasing unwillingness to work or the desire to seek one's own life style are played up widely in popular magazines. Television is full of round-tables on such themes. Although these polls and surveys must lead to an awareness of the problems, do any of them lead to action?

Many of them obviously do not, for some problems have been with Japan for ages. They arose where old and new met . . . and did not merge. The flaws of the democratic process and political parties have a long history. Close links between business, politics, and bureaucracy got started after the Restoration (and grew out of feudal practices). Now flatteringly referred to as "Japan, Inc.," before the war this nexus was sharply criticized by right and left alike. Concentrations of economic power, which are again reaching substantial levels, once gave birth to the *zaibatsu*, now the looser *zaikai*. The evils of "examination hell" and elitism in the educational system have been criticized since prewar times. Complaints were raised about ecological damage decades ago and Tanaka's plan is years old now. The awkward relations between the classes, races and religions, between men and women, young and old, can be traced back to traditional patterns which no longer serve modern needs. Japan has recognized these and other problems and periodically pledged to solve them. But they are are still here!

If a consensus is not in sight, then the solutions might come from dynamic action by the leadership. This, of course, is less likely in a conservative society, which Japan increasingly is. The country is ruled by a conservative party, which is backed by an increasingly conservative electorate, and this has made even the opposition parties moderate their aims and blunt their criticism. The economy is no longer one of free enterprise with openings and opportunities for newcomers. Social institutions are even less receptive to new ideas. The follower-leaders in the universities, bureaucracies, companies and unions show little ambition to break new ground, but refuse to be eased out of their positions by others who might. By now, the word "leader" almost implies by definition a man in his fifties, sixties or seventies. Gerontocracy has rarely been heavier or more widespread. And old age joined with conservatism hardly equip leaders for dealing with new problems in new ways.

Worse, rather than at least tackle the old, well-known problems, the standard mode seems to be to escape them or ignore them by rushing ahead to new but remote goals. Leaders are constantly searching for attractive dreams, compelling yet vague aims, anything from a world's fair to high GNP. As fashions change, they pick up all the popular slogans, from affluence to welfare, from anti-pollution to amenities, from rapid growth to no growth. In dealing with foreign countries, they are full of hopes for cooperation, one world, harmony. But most of these dreams never get anywhere. They peter out. And in the meanwhile the old problems are still there.

Will this change? Professor Eto, who is a member of the Prime Minister's Committee on Seeking National Goals for the Twenty-First Century wound up his remarks by stating: "What we need now is a dream for the Japanese people. Unless we have a dream, we will continue to embarrass the rest of the world...What kind of a dream? I think it has to be housing and urban renewal. I imagine there are ways of promoting this as a cooperative international venture."[3] But he was easily outdone by Prime

Minister Ohira's dream:

"We stand on the threshold of a new age transcending the age of modernization; we have moved from an economic-centered age to a new age with its emphasis on culture. The new society which is our goal is one in which distrust and confrontation are overcome and understanding and trust are cultivated in pursuit of the truly worthwhile life in all its aspects, home, community, state, and global society. It is a society in which the individual's creativity is welcomed, his labor is justly rewarded, there is respect for law and order, each is true to his own responsibilities and restraints and there is ample understanding and consideration for others."[4]

If the leaders are too busy with dreams for the next century, perhaps the rest of the population has some time to cope with the problems of this century. If the more successful members of society are satisfied with their lot, perhaps those who have lost out would be willing to press for some changes. This does not seem much more likely. The "masses," whoever they may be, are inward looking with regard to group relations or retire into home and family life. Those who are more dissatisfied more fully opt out. Although few people seem to be truly pleased with the prevailing situation, fewer would risk the danger of standing up and criticizing anything. Resignation seems to be the standard mode: what can we do about corrupt politicians? what can we do about inflation and pollution? what can we do if our parents or children are beyond our reach? what can we even do to make our personal lives richer?

And this is what much of the crisis stems from. It is these attitudes that have driven people away from society rather than toward attempts to modify society. Displeasure with politics now leads not to action but abstention. Displeasure with the company leads to a retreat to the family. Displeasure with the family leads to dropping out. Obviously, in this way there is little hope that the public will rouse the leaders from their immobilism or that individuals will do their part by improving or reforming those limited aspects within their own control let alone overhaul society. And there is more reason to fear that the changes will come through a collapse of presently constituted society due to a lack of support. That, too, is change, although not really the best kind.

There seems to be a tradition that in dealing with the land of the rising sun one must be positive and optimistic. The final words are supposed to be uplifting and full of promise. I have to break with that tradition. For, the sun also sets, as Japan has repeatedly shown, although it may rise some time later. Not enough is being done to come to grips with the problems appearing on the horizon (or already here) and the social trends do not augure well for the future. Crises can occur in any country. Why not Japan?

NOTES

1. See Isiah Ben-Dasan, *The Japanese and the Jews.*
2. *Look Japan*, December 10, 1977.
3. Ibid.
4. Policy Speech by Prime Minister Ohira at 87th Session of the National Diet, January 25, 1979.

BIBLIOGRAPHY

Abegglen, James C., *Management and Worker, The Japanese Solution*, Tokyo, Kodansha International, 1973.

Azumi, Koya, *Higher Education and Business Recruitment in Japan*, New York, Teachers' College Press-Columbia University, 1969

Ballon, Robert J., editor, *Doing Business in Japan*, Tokyo, Sophia University/Kodansha International, 1971.

———, *The Japanese Employee*, Tokyo, Sophia University/Kodansha International, 1969.

Bando, Mariko, *The Women of Japan*, Tokyo, Foreign Press Center, 1977.

Beardsley, Richard K. & Hall, John W., *Twelve Doors to Japan*, New York, McGraw-Hill, 1965.

Beasley, W. G., editor, *Modern Japan*, Tokyo, Charles E. Tuttle, 1976.

Ben-Dasan, Isaiah, *The Japanese and the Jews*, Tokyo, Weatherhill, 1972.

Benedict, Ruth, *The Chrysanthemum and the Sword*, Tokyo, Charles E. Tuttle, 1954.

Curtis, Gerald L., *Election Campaigning Japanese Style*, New York, Columbia University Press, 1971.

De Vos, George & Wagatsuma, Hiroshi, *Japan's Invisible Race: Caste in Culture and Personality*, Berkeley, University of California Press, 1971.

Doi, Takeo, *Amae no Kozo* [The Anatomy of Dependence], Tokyo, Kobundo, 1971.

Dore, Ronald P., editor, *Aspects of Social Change in Modern Japan*, Princeton, Princeton University Press, 1967.

———, *British Factory, Japanese Factory*, Berkeley, University of California Press, 1973.

———,*City Life in Japan: A Study of a Tokyo Ward*, Berkeley, University of California Press, 1958.

Facts and Figures of Japan, Tokyo, Foreign Press Center, 1977, 1978, 1979 & 1980.
Forbis, William H., *Japan Today*, Tokyo, Charles E. Tuttle, 1976.
Gibney, Frank, *Japan: The Fragile Superpower*, Tokyo, Charles E. Tuttle, 1975.
Halloran, Richard, *Japan: Images and Realities*, New York, Alfred E. Knopf, 1969.
Japan Center for International Exchange, *The Silent Power, Japan's Identity and World Role*, Tokyo, Simul Harmondsworth, Penguin Books, 1970.
Kahn, Herman, *The Emerging Japanese Superstate*, Harmondsworth, Penguin Books, 1970.
Kawasaki, Ichiro, *Japan Unmasked*, Tokyo, Charles E. Tuttle, 1969.
Kishimoto, Koichi, *Politics in Modern Japan: Development and Organization,* Tokyo, Japan Echo, 1977.
Kosaka, Masataka, *100 Million Japanese,* Tokyo, Kodansha International, 1972.
Kraus, Ellis S., *Japanese Radicals Revisited*, Berkeley, University of California Press, 1977.
Kubota, Akira, *Higher Civil Servants in Postwar Japan: Their Social Origins, Educational Background and Career Patterns,* Princeton, Princeton University Press, 1969.
Leisure and Recreational Activities, Tokyo, Foreign Press Center, April 1977.
Mannari, Hiroshi, *The Japanese Business Leaders*, Tokyo, University of Tokyo Press, 1974.
Matsumura, Gentaro, *The Emperor's Islands,* Tokyo, Lotus Press, 1977.
Nagai, Michio, *Higher Education in Japan: Its Take-off and Crash,* Tokyo, University of Tokyo Press, 1971.
Nakane, Chie, *Japanese Society*, Berkeley. University of California Press, 1970.
———, *Kinship and Economic Organization in Rural Japan*, New York, Humanities Press, 1967.
Norbeck, Edward, *Changing Japan, Case Study in Cultural Anthropology*, New York, Holt, Rinehard & Winston, 1966.
Ozaki, Robert S., *The Japanese: A Cultural Portrait*, Tokyo, Charles E. Tuttle, 1978.
Palmore, Erdman, *The Honorable Elders: A Cross-Cultural Analysis of Aging in Japan*, Durham, Duke University Press,

1975.
Public Opinion Survey on National Life, Tokyo, Prime Minister's Office, Public Relations Office, October 1977.
Reischauer, Edwin O., *Japan: The Story of a Nation*, Tokyo, Charles E. Tuttle, 1970.
———, *The Japanese*, Tokyo, Charles E. Tuttle, 1978.
Richardson, Bradley M., *The Political Culture of Japan*, Berkeley, University of California Press, 1975.
Rohlen, Thomas P., *For Harmony and Strength*, Berkeley,University of California Press, 1974.
Saunders, Dale, *Buddhism in Japan*, Tokyo, Charles E. Tuttle, 1972.
Scalapino, Robert A. & Masumi, Junnosuke, *Parties and Politics in Contemporary Japan*, Berkeley, University of California Press, 1970.
Seward, Jack, *More About the Japanese*, Tokyo, Lotus Press, 1971.
———, *The Japanese*, Tokyo, Lotus Press, 1971.
Thayer, Nathaniel B., *How the Conservatives Rule Japan*, Princeton, Princeton University Press, 1969.
Thomsen, Harry, *The New Religions in Japan*, Englewood Cliffs, Prentice-Hall, 1963.
Vogel, Ezra F., *Japan's New Middle Class*, Los Angles, University of California Press, 1967.
———, *Japan as Number One, Lessons for America*, Cambridge, Harvard University Press, 1979.
Ward, Robert E., editor, *Political Development in Modern Japan*, Princeton, Princeton University Press, 1968.
Woronoff, Jon, *Japan: The Coming Economic Crisis*, Tokyo, Lotus Press, 1979.
Yanaga, Chitoshi, *Big Business in Japanese Politics*, New Haven, Yale University Press, 1969.

INDEX

Yohan Lotus Books Series

NON-FICTION

AMERICA AND JAPAN	J. Seward
JAPAN: THE HUNGRY GUEST	J. Seward & H. Van Zandt
THE JAPANESE	J. Seward
MORE ABOUT THE JAPANESE	J. Seward
ASIA'S MIRACLE ECONOMIES	J. Woronoff
INSIDE JAPAN, INC.	J. Woronoff
JAPAN: The Coming Economic Crisis	J. Woronoff
JAPAN: The Coming Social Crisis	J. Woronoff
JAPAN'S COMMERCIAL EMPIRE	J. Woronoff
JAPAN'S WASTED WORKERS	J. Woronoff
THE JAPAN SYNDROME	J. Woronoff
WORLD TRADE WAR	J. Woronoff
IMAGES OF JAPAN —A Photographic Souvenir—	A. Tsuchiya & B. DeMente
PIONEER AMERICAN MERCHANTS IN JAPAN	H. Van Zandt
SHOPPING YOUR WAY AROUND JAPAN	B. DeMente
THE EMPEROR'S ISLANDS	G. Matsumura
NINJUTSU	D. Draeger
THE SHOGUN'S RELUCTANT AMBASSADORS	K. Plummer

FICTION

THE DARNED NUISANCES	J. Seward & C. Beardsley
THE DIPLOMAT	J. Seward
SAMURAI SIX	J. Stanley